THE SOOTHSAYER
Copyright © Jennifer Pearce 19 – 08 – 2018

Thinking of Jack and May, and all the happy memories.

Thanks to my amazing husband, David for his healing and love.

Thanks to my friend Nikki for all her hard work, help and encouragement.

Thanks also to my son Matt for his help with technology and patience.

Also my wonderful daughter Edwina my muse for the front cover.

This book is a map of my own life and only intended as an introduction to the history and use of ancient leaves of the Tarot. It is my belief that lessons may be learned from a study of each of the Major Arcana leaves, to help us navigate the sometimes rocky path of the material world.

Half of all profits from the sale of this book will help research for Arthritis and Scleroderma, also sufferers of these debilitating ailments.

Contents

Introduction	The Awakening	3
Chapter 1	1949	11
Lesson 1	The Fool	17
Chapter 2	December 1951	19
Lesson 2	The Magician	37
Chapter 3	December 1956	39
Lesson 3	The High Priestess	44
Chapter 4	1956 – 1957	46
Lesson 4	The Empress	51
Chapter 5	1957 – 1958	53
Lesson 5	The Emperor	59
Chapter 6	1958 – 1960	61
Lesson 6	The Hierophant / Pope	67
Chapter 7	Early 1960's	70
Lesson 7	The Lover or Lovers	78
Chapter 8	1962 – 1964	80
Lesson 8	The Chariot	89
Chapter 9	1960's continued	91
Lesson 9	Justice	95
Chapter 10	1963 – 65	97
Lesson 10	The Hermit	103
Chapter 11	1964 – 1965	105
Lesson 11	The Wheel of Fortune	110
Chapter 12	1960's continued	112
Lesson 12	Strength	121
Part 2	Looking for Enlightenment	123
Chapter 13	1956 – 1966	126
Lesson 13	The Hanging Man	134
Chapter 14	1960's continued	136

Lesson 14	Transition	142
Chapter 15	1960's continued	144
Lesson 15	Temperance	154
Chapter 16	World Cup Year 1966 onwards	156
Lesson 16	The Devil / Adversary	162
Chapter 17	1967 – 1968	164
Lesson 17	The Falling Tower	172
Chapter 18	The First Summer of Love	174
Lesson 18	The Star	182
Chapter 19	1967 – 1968	184
Lesson 19	The Moon	198
Chapter 20	August 10th 1969 – Christmas	200
Lesson 20	The Sun	205
Chapter 21	1970 – 1976	207
Lesson 21	Judgement	224
Chapter 22	1970's onwards	226
Lesson 22	The World / The Sphere	240
Chapter 23	Into the 1980's and beyond	242
Lesson 23	The Comet	256
Chapter 24	1980's onward	258
Lesson 24	The Suit of Swords – The Air Element	274
Chapter 25	1980's – 1990's	277
Lesson 25	The Suit of Rods/Batons – Fire Elements	294
Chapter 26	1980's – 2000 onward	296
Lesson 26	The Suit of Cups – The Water Elements	304
Chapter 27	1990's onwards	307
Lesson 27	Suit of Coins – The Eart Elements	318

THE SOOTHSAYER
Part One: The Awakening.

INTRODUCTION

It was one of those extra warm nights we sometimes get in spring. The red, orange sunset was just visible through the branches of the big oak tree at the end of the garden as I got into bed. Little did I expect to have any kind of supernatural experience as I reached for the book I was reading for my mock exams due in a couple of weeks. My brother John and I were sharing the Queen size bed at grandma's for the night. John was in a deep sleep, being five he had gone to bed an hour or two earlier. Mum and dad had gone out with grandma to try and cheer her up. Gran had been very sad after my auntie Joan had passed away in February. Mum said they would only be gone for an hour and I was not worried about being left to baby sit as they were only going to the pub at the end of the road, in fact I was so carried away with 'Pride and Prejudice' that I couldn't wait to get to bed to have a read.

After reading a chapter or two I started to notice the room had become very cold. It was a lovely clear moonlit night and I could still just about read without the light on. The room seemed to be getting colder, beginning to shiver I decided to snuggle down rather than putting on the bed side lamp. At first pulling the covers up over my head to try and get warm. After a moment or two I put my hand up to get more of a breath. As my hand reached up to the top of the eiderdown I froze with shock. My hand had been lightly clasped by the ice cold hand of someone else! It felt like the cold hand was wrapped in cloth or a muslin glove. I quickly pulled my hand back under the covers without looking. My thoughts were all of a jumble, to whom could the hand belong. Trying to be rational and looking for explanation I felt around to see if John had his hands under the covers. His hands were there and were smaller and very warm in comparison with the ghostly hand!

A notion came to me that whatever had occurred I must peek out just a little. This strange atmosphere permeated the room and the chill was even more apparent. My heart was pounding when I heard the sound of someone on the stairs; surely it was mum back home! Hearing footsteps coming down the landing I expected to see mum, dad or grandma enter the room.

The door already ajar, slowly opened. There stood the familiar figure of Granddad Ted, head and shoulders visible as he leaned part way into the room. For just a moment, relief flooded through me as he smiled. Then I felt a wave of heart gripping fear! My next thought was that this was not possible, this could not be happening. I remembered granddad was dead, he had died almost two years ago; I could not be seeing him! On recollection I realised his lips never moved and yet he asked me if I would like a cup of tea. As I gawped in dismay, still smiling he stepped back out of sight and the door closed to just stand ajar again. The footsteps seemed to walk away down the landing but I did not hear them go down the stairs.

Though gripped by fear I sprang out of bed in a kind of knee jerk reaction and quickly switched on the bed side lamp and then the main light. Looking back, I cannot say if curiosity got the better of fear or if I moved on some kind of automatic instinct. I slowly opened the bedroom door and went along to the next bedroom, opening that door, I looked inside...nothing there! On to the third bedroom, opened the door, looked inside...nothing there! I ran down the stairs feeling as if the Devil himself were after me! Standing on the front doorstep looking down the road I could see mum, dad and grandma a few yards away. Trying to control my thoughts I realised grandma must not be told of what had just happened, after all she had to live there on her own when we went home. I ran back up to bed and got under the covers but not before mum had spotted me at the front door.

This strange event, though not the first ghost encounter for me, would lead me on my search for some kind of understanding of life and what happens after death. Have you ever questioned who you are, why you exist, what is life and what, if anything lies beyond the veil of death? The many unusual events in my childhood and adolescence prompted me to think hard on these things and start to look for answers.

You will find the dictionary definition of the word soothsayer is 'teller of truths' but from medieval times the word has also been used as a name for a psychic person or fortune teller. During the time of the Spanish Inquisition those persons who had any kind of psychic experience would no doubt try to keep it hidden in fear of their life.

Despite those harsh times there were many people in all different parts of the world that were known as Shaman or Wise Women that could not always hide their 'gift'. Thankfully the more open minded and enlightened of our forefathers kept some of the ancient wisdom and preserved the hidden knowledge of the Tarot, known in olden times as 'Taroc'.

The Gypsy people have a superstition that only those that find or are freely given a pack of Tarot should read them for others. They believe the reading will bring luck to both when a piece of silver or some sort of reward should pass from the sitter to the reader. It is also the custom to do some small ritual that shows respect to the divinity of 'The Father, God, The Son, Jesus and the Holy Ghost. This is often done by cutting the pack into three piles before the reading begins.

I intend to live up to the title of soothsayer in this, my life story, my own book as I intend to tell the truth to the letter and as far as memory serves me. To this I now swear on all I hold dear.

*Below some sections of my story you will find a RUNE and brief description and interpretation. The first one is shown at the foot of this page. Reader...

This is the RUNE 'Thurisaz'

This symbol I place here as to me it represents the gateway between the self in the material world and the realm of the Divine, Heaven.

FOREWARD

All books take us on a journey, be it fact or fiction. Reading lets us in part see into the mind of the writer, if only what they want us to know! We can learn facts but we can also taste a little of the emotion, feel what the characters feel and glean perceptions of what life is like through the eyes of another person. My story charts my journey through life, from early years growing up in post war Britain through to my personal experience of haunted houses and poltergeist activity.

Thinking back through the individual stories my many hundreds of sitters have brought to my attention over the past thirty years, plus my own weird and wonderful experiences, I felt the need to write this book, in part to explain my interest in all things 'esoteric' and in the hope it may help those whom have gone through similar issues in their lives.

From the perspective of a seventy something, through eyes that have looked at many sides of religious belief, and many of the problems in life that can shake our faith, I shall be happy if this book may point even one person into the hope that there is some kind of power above and beyond us all. Sometimes we can glimpse the evidence of this and it can make us strive to reach our own personal potential.

Whilst recounting my early years, for this book, it made me think that perhaps, as an only child until the age of nine years eight months I was extremely lucky. My mother was at home with me up to the age of four apart from an hour or two here and there. When I started school she got a job working five hours a day during the school week but was always at home on weekends. Times were hard for many families after the war, perhaps not as bad as the 1930's but much like today the 1950's held austerity, also things we take for granted now were either not invented yet or so expensive that ordinary working families could not afford them. We, the children of the 1950's were still of the 'make do and mend' generation! I look back and realise now how lucky we were and how amazing my life turned out to be!

Before the age of ten I experienced what is now called a paranormal experience. Later I was to learn that many people with a 'gift' of second sight often see the aura colours around living persons and animals. For as long as I can remember I had been able to see auras and because this was normal for me it would be some years before I remarked on it to another person. Just as we do not remark on hair or eye colour of someone because it is normal to see, I assumed this aura of light was normal and there for all to see. Also I was taught that it was rude to comment on someone's appearance.

During my teenage years in the 1960's I started to gain some mystic knowledge through people and books that just seemed to come my way. As the world entered the era of sex, drugs and Rock and Roll, not forgetting peace and love, for me it was more ghosts and poltergeist's, but there was quite a lot of Rock and Roll! From child to woman in the year 1964-65 my dreams literally started to come true! During these years I started a search for enlightenment. It would eventually take me through many philosophies and world religions. I fought my 'down to earth' background, the 'doubting Thomas' side of my nature to come to terms with my so called 'gift'. My psychic ability became more apparent through the years and in the discovery that I could see facts or events from holding an everyday object (the wedding ring of a friend) to my forehead.

Several chance meetings and experiences seem to act as pointers that eventually would set my future path! The first one came in childhood as I saw my first spirit friend. Many other strange events would occur before I became the professional soothsayer! At the age of fourteen, myself and two members of my family started to experience a lot of poltergeist activity! A short time later, after starting work came a strange connection with people involved with spiritual matters. It happened one lunch break eating with a five ladies, all members of the same family, a conversation took place that would have an effect on the rest of my life!

You will note that each section of my story is preceded by the name of a Tarot Card. This is because it is my belief that sacred knowledge has been passed down to us within the images on the cards. The Tarot card has been vilified over the centuries as being a tool of evil. In medieval times anyone looking into the mysteries of the universe and even found to be reading about the sacred knowledge would risk an early and gruesome death, many branded a Witch. It is however my theory that men of early Christianity must have been

Involved, designed, or had an input on some of the Tarot images as they show 'The Pope', 'The Temperance Angel', 'The Judgment day', 'The Lovers' depicted in the Garden of Eden, 'The Star' that we are told in the Bible the wise men followed! 'The Hermit' (cloaked figure of a medieval Monk), and also 'The Devil', which is a figure that was only introduced into the consciousness of man by the advent of Christianity! These cards are not only early works of art but also a fountain of knowledge if we look at them and understand the imagery. If life has it's learning curves, then surely we must all look to whatever helpful knowledge can be gleaned from past experiences. These cards are a gift to us from our ancient forefathers and so there is much to be pondered over in the imagery of the designs. Tarot is not just a tool for predicting future events, but a way we may tap into guidance from our forefathers. The Tarot can be seen as a kind of map of our life with the lessons we can all learn!

To my mind a pack of cards cannot be evil though I will concede that a person using them could be. If we are guided to a certain occupation and find an aptitude for it then we will likely want to pursue it and hone our talent, and that is eventually just what I did! I like to think I have used my 'gift' in a positive way to try and help those who came to me. If one believes the adage 'as you give so shall you receive' then my gain was certainly not riches, though through necessity I had to make a small charge for my time. My real gain has been finding satisfaction and contentment in life and for this I am truly grateful.

You will note that below each chapter title there is a title of a song. Most people have several songs that bring back treasured memories. These are some of the songs of my life! All I ask now kind reader is that you suspend any preconceived notions, any prejudices you may have about the topic of poltergeists, fortune telling or of the Tarot cards and read on with a truly open mind.

This book is a true account of my life, the stories of some of my clients and of my own quest for what God is and if or where we go after death. Preceding each Chapter, you will see I have given a name and my own interpretation of a Tarot card from what is known as The Major Arcana. There are 22 Major cards in most packs and 56 minor.

One pack of Tarot in my possession has an extra card, The Comet. Common to all packs of Tarot cards are all the four elements, EARTH, (represented by Coins or Pentacles) WATER, (represented by Cups or Chalice) AIR, (represented by Swords) and FIRE, (represented by Rods or Batons) these are the numbered cards of what are known as the minor Arcana. Each of the four suits are numbered one up to ten. The meaning of these minor cards are not gone into in great detail as it is not required for the purpose of my story. Many books are readily available from book shops and on line.

For those wishing to study the Tarot it could be helpful to begin by a little research into numerology and Astrology. Remember the Gypsy peoples believe that the Tarot pack **must find you** before you read it for others. If you want to begin 'reading' the signs for others but have not had a pack 'find you', then you might consider trying to 'read' from other methods such as normal playing cards, or from symbols in a pattern formed by tea leaves left in the base of the cup after a brew of (loose leaved) tea or coffee grounds.

If you have a feel for working with natural wood or stone, you might try etching a set of traditional Nordic RUNES or get in touch with me if you would like to make your own hand etched natural wooden 'PREDICION' cubes. The original are a set of (seven of my own devised modern RUNE symbols) and come together with an information leaflet containing my easy to understand interpretations.

For some it will not be a surprise to know that even patterns of sand, clouds and froth on the top of a beer can be read by those who use their 'Third eye'.

Before we get to the peculiar and spooky events that shaped my life and led me to psychic work and use of the Tarot, I must start from the beginning, like all births it starts with the parents. Looking back now I realise that mine had a deep and life long love affair. Sometimes, like all love affairs there were arguments because passions would often run high, but in our home there were many sunny happy days that made up my almost perfect childhood.

Reader...This is the RUNE Inguz

The RUNE Inguz is said to be linked to the Moon and thus to fertility, preparation and intuitions.

Chapter 1

Events leading up to January 7th 1949

My parents, John Arnold Smith (Jack) and Edwina May Laverty (May) were second cousins but had only met once or twice at their mutual grandma's house. So in the winter of 1942, whilst on leave from the Merchant Navy, when Jack had been sent to tune the piano for the Laverty cousins they were virtual strangers.

When Jack arrived at the house young May answered the door wearing a turban over her long black hair. She had a been painting a flower pattern onto some plain drinking glasses ready for the New Years Eve party her parents always gave. May opened the door and was greeted by this tall, dark and rather handsome figure of a man in naval uniform. Embarrassed at her dishevelled appearance and smudges of paint on her denim dungarees May quickly dragged off her turban and made an excuse to dash off to smarten up. Jack was smitten at first glance and if truth were told May too was quite taken with her now grown up handsome cousin. It was love at first sight according to dad's telling of their story.

As the war was on all the young men would come home on leave at various times and then back they would go to the Army, Navy or whatever war work they were involved in. May, like most young women of the time had been writing to a soldier when she and Jack became reacquainted. May always had several ardent admirers all trying to woo her whilst they were on leave. May's mother (also May) invited Jack to the New Year celebrations and that, as they say was that! All May's other admirers were swiftly shunted out of the picture by Jack, although May did lead him a merry dance by all accounts during their courtship.

During the war Jack had three very narrow escapes from death, twice being on ships that were blown up by German U boats. Five days out on the sea in a lifeboat the first time his ship sank. Three days in a lifeboat the second time on a ship that sank. His third escape was due to a burst appendix, in itself a trauma, but this actually saved his life as he was taken to hospital and missed the boat he should have sailed on. The boat was again sunk by a German U boat and all hands were lost at sea!

When dad recounted his experiences to me as I was growing up I thought of these events as adventures, like my Famous Five books. Later when thinking back I began to realise that if he had lost his life in the war would I not have been born, or would I have had another dad? These questions made me start to think more deeply than perhaps most children would about fate and mortality.

In 1946 just after Jack had left the Merchant service on May's request they were married. The two love birds rented a room in a boarding house for a short time close to Jack's work on the railway police. The room was fine for the two of them but after a couple of years with a baby on the way they moved back into May's parental home.

Before a posting for Jack's new job would come through, on January 7th 1949 at 2.30 pm little Jennifer would add to the picture! I was born at grandma's house in what was one of the worst winters on record, in a wild and windy heavy snow storm. A blizzard warning had just been announced on the radio as Jack set out to cycle five miles to fetch the midwife! Snow ploughs had cleared a track along the main road but the snow was already at least a foot deep and heavy clouds seemed bursting with much more snow yet to fall.

The slippery icy conditions made for slow progress! As Jack struggled along the road he must have pondered on how much his life had changed from his wartime days at sea in the Merchant Navy. Many crew members that had drowned after their ship was torpedoed and he must have felt lucky to be alive and thankful for his chance of a life and family when so many had been denied that chance! At last the home of the midwife came in sight. Large flakes of snow swirled around as Jack struggled to her door. Back at grandma's house the tense wait seemed to stretch on as the clock ticked and the cuckoo called each hour! At exactly half past two in the afternoon as Gemini was rising in Capricorn I entered the world!

Although young May was tired after eight hours in Labour, Jack was allowed into the room and May was sat up with her hair in a neat pageboy and with a touch of lipstick on as she cradled me, her baby girl. She handed Jack his daughter, 'What shall we call her?' he asked? They had gone through names in the baby book before the arrival and had not been able to settle on one. 'I think we should call her Jennifer. In the name book it says the meaning is Little White Wave!' May said. This seemed to fit because of the white snowy day and the fact her father loved the sea. May smiled as she watched Jack cradle their new baby. And so life had now started for me!

That night as they settled down I was told that Jack had switched off the light and a few seconds later I started to cry. The light was switched on again and the crying stopped! This was repeated many times and each time the light went off the cry started. After a while Jack decided to leave a bedside light on to get some rest. Throughout my childhood I had great fear of the dark! Later as an adult I would discover through study of Astrology that I was born during an unusual 'Trine' in the heavens between the Sun, Moon and Saturn, perhaps a sign of the person I would become, always drawn to the mystical and the magical and always knowing and respectful of the light and dark powers of the universe that would shape my destiny.

Jack had been posted to Blackpool, and with a new baby my parents had to quickly find a place to live. Short on cash they rented the upstairs of a large old semi. May wasn't too keen as the old man's house seemed spooky! At first old Joe seemed a good landlord. Little did they know events would soon to take a rather sinister turn!

Jack was asked to work all hours, doing overtime, patrolling the main platform on Blackpool station. May was content to be at home looking after me though she missed her family back in Manchester. With Jack out of the house a lot May began to feel uncomfortable around Joe, their landlord downstairs. At first May kept these feelings to herself, after all what was there to tell Jack? This feeling persisted even though Joe smiled whenever she saw him on her way out.

Wanting to get out of the house, May would push me in my baby carriage all over Blackpool and often down to the sea. One day she sat and watched the waves lap against the sea wall and thought of her past stay in Blackpool when she and her brother were evacuated there in the war. She wished for a home of their own if only Jack were to be accepted into the Lancashire police force they might be housed on a nice police estate hopefully near Manchester.

On returning from the walk, mum opened the front door to find Joe marching up and down the hall. He was wearing a tin helmet and carried a rusty looking old rifle over his shoulder. May thought these must be from the First World War by the look of it. Joe sang a marching song and seemed oblivious to her as she quickly picked me up and went upstairs. Later that night when dad was told about it he laughed it off saying it was probably nothing to worry about. He pointed out that on the rent they were paying, they could hardly start telling Joe not to sing.

The next day after her walk with me to the local shop May could hear Joe marching and singing even before she put the key in the lock. She knocked to see if he would stop the marching when he heard her enter. Again he seemed to be in a world of his own as he marched and sang. May saw he again had a rifle over his shoulder and it had a bayonet attached. Mum hurried upstairs, I was screaming loudly but this didn't seem to bother Joe. Locking the door, she crossed her fingers that dad would soon be home! By the time dad had arrived home the marching had stopped but dad agreed to have a word with Joe. May said he must do so after tea or she would be going home to Manchester.

The next day mum heard the front door slam and when she looked out of the front window she saw Joe go out along the road. Thinking it safe May popped into the garden to hang the washing. I was sleeping upstairs in my cot. After pegging the wash out mum went to open the door, she pushed it. It did not open, May, was locked out! Panic set in as mum rushed round to the front door. That too had been locked! Mum cried as she hammered on the door realising that Joe had come back the front way whilst she was in the back garden. Deep fear was setting into her as she stood, frantic as to know what to do. Heart pounding, May could hear Joe marching and singing inside. May was pushing at the door just as Jack was turning into the road, home early for once.

'Thank God your home. The old blighter locked the door on me and is inside with Jennifer, and don't forget he has a riffle with a Bayonet!' Dad tried the door and this time it opened! Joe gave them a toothless grin as they hurried past him up the stairs. At the railway station the next day dad waved me and mum off as we were going back to Manchester. Once dad got word about his application into the Lancashire Constabulary he would follow.

Grandfather and Grandma's house was near Platt Fields, an area of Manchester where there had been an Army Barracks with enemy look out and gun stations during the war. Strangely I would, later in life find out that during the war my father-in-law, Roy was stationed here on searchlight for enemy lookout. The area had been quite heavily bombed and some of the destruction was still evident during the 1950's. On her return from evacuation Mum and her sister Joan had been out on a double date on the night of the Blitz. They had a narrow escape as they made their way home that night. The experience in Blackpool had brought it all back to her. The experience with Joan had brought back memories of that night. As Ted drove her home from the station in his Taxi, she felt safe at last!

There was a mound of earth at the end of the garden in Withington where the Air Raid shelter had been covered over and an oak tree mum had planted as a child stood next to it. In later summers I would spend happy hours of play under its shelter but it did always remind us of the troubled wartime years.

Mum and I spent the next few months at grandma and granddad's house. At Mauldeth Road. Withington.
By all accounts mum and I enjoyed a happy time there for several months and I was a contented baby, only crying if left in the dark.
Working on the Railway Police had been dad's way to gain experience so that he could soon gain entry to the Lancashire Constabulary Police Force.

After a few months at Blackpool dad was accepted and was just waiting for a posting.

Whilst living at Withington mum had another scare when she had put me in my baby carriage outside the back door to get some fresh air. After chatting to a friend at the gate she came to check on me to find a big black cat sitting on my face. The cat was shooed off and mum saw that I was still breathing. I wonder now if this was an omen of mysteries yet to affect the path of my life?

Reader... This is the RUNE Perth

The RUNE Perth is said to have links with the phoenix, the mystical bird that rises from the ashes of fire and so depicts mystical transformation.

1/ Tarot lesson, THE FOOL

Card No 0 (or not numbered). The first Lesson of the TAROT...
Musical inspiration... 'Don't laugh at me'... Singer...Version... Norman Wisdom.

Tradition of the Tarot tells us the Fool card is the beginning of the journey and also the ending. It is the only card in most Tarot packs that has no number or is numbered '0' thus it is the start and the ending. In some ancient packs this card may have number 22 as it can portray both the first or last lesson of life. It can also sometimes be numbered 21 as some view the Fool as coming before the World Card. It is the Jester, the Idiot, the Novice, the Baby, the forgetful Old person, the Clown, the Tramp, the comical and the freedom of being unaware! The card depicts a man with a staff and cloth bag tied to a stick over his shoulder. He is about to leap from one rock on a mountain to another as a small dog runs along beside him nipping him with their teeth! The happy wanderer with his torn clothes and his careless leaping towards danger! (In some packs towards the mouth of a Crocodile.) The bag or sack he carries was thought, in bygone times by many readers to contain his sins.

Wisdom to be gained from this card...At the start of our life on Earth we will all have the choice of two paths, the safe or impetuous, cautious or foolhardy, good or evil. Will we take the path of darkness or light? How are we to know the difference? Perhaps we must keep the joy of life that we have as an infant but remember our actions have repercussions. The little dog may represent our fellow travellers in this life, our friend or partner or our guide. The rocks on the mountain path the fool treads are haphazard, so are perhaps symbolic of the stumbling blocks or obstacles that we may face along the way. As a baby, life stretches out before us and we must learn to be aware of danger. We can find stability if we tread the right path, perhaps seeking or perhaps stumbling at times in our efforts to find out what earthly life is about. From the very start life presents us with a choice of the path of goodness as opposed to evil!

In the moment we are born we know nothing of the world, our minds are a blank, thus in a way we are the fool at the open gate to life. We slowly become aware of all our senses, all is new and we are curious! Many situations we encounter require us to hone our senses, sight, sound, taste, touch, smell, and possibly the most important one, the sixth sense, intuition, (a kind of inner knowing of right from wrong)!

Perhaps by use and development of the sixth sense we can be safer and can learn to make wise choices. Then in old age we may find contentment even if we have forgotten the lessons of our life. Then we can be the fool at our birth (the gate) to the next world!
Will we, as the Fool, be led by our passions, or be content with whatever comes our way?

Reader... As you go through the journey of the Tarot in each chapter see if the lesson has been relevant in your life so far, bearing in mind, whilst here we are still learning. If you feel you have been the fool in some aspect of your life, then remember you can choose the right path in what you do onward from this moment!

Reader... This is the RUNE Raido

The RUNE Raido is thought to represent Journey and so I place it here as I start to tell you of my life journey.

Chapter 2

December 1951 onwards.

As winter approached once again, the next few weeks went by quickly for my parents as they prepared for a new life in a police house. The posting came through for Ashton-in-Makerfield. A small village community close to Wigan. There dad was to be the one and only Bobby on the estate. He would patrol the beat on foot around the area and be expected to keep an eye on the estate where we lived.

Heavy snow had started on the day of the move when a small van came to take our possessions to the home we would occupy for the next three years. The van was packed tight with furniture with no room for mum and I. At the last minute grandma insisted on going with us by bus. She would accompany us to Wigan and then see us onto the next bus for Ashton-in-Makerfield. It was a freezing cold evening when we arrived at the Wigan bus station.

Mum was crying as she and granny parted. Not having seen her new home yet and never having been to the town before, she was filled with apprehension.

In their haste to catch the bus from Manchester grandma had come out in only house slippers, they were now soaked. Mum was even more upset when she realised that her mother was to go home without even a cup of tea. Because of snow, the last bus of the night was just about to leave. Mum climbed, struggling with me and push chair onto the bus going the opposite way to gran.

Our new home was well built from Accrington brick and had an arched entrance. The estate was built for miners and their families, ours was the only police house on the whole estate. This then was to be my home for three happy years of infancy. Soon after our move mum and dad would be preparing for Christmas. Once again the snow was falling as mum and I climbed onto the buss for Manchester to spend Christmas Eve with Ted,

May and my uncle Frank. Dad was working but would follow on Christmas day. As sugar was still on rations' we were lucky to be able to pool our rations' with Grandma and have a cake. A great fuss was made over the cake as it was cut into three sections. One was set aside for Christmas, one placed in a cake tin for New Year and a small piece in another tin for my 1st birthday.

After Christmas we went home but we would be back with Ted and May for my birthday. There was now a tiny doll on top of the cake in place of the Santa one we had kept from Christmas. I later found the little figures were made out of chalk. The little doll looked like a baby in a pink snow suit. She was made in sitting position and sat in place on a small iced chocolate log on top of the remaining piece of cake. My very first, though somewhat hazy memory, is laughing and laughing and the adults looking rather puzzled. It was as Ted picked me up and held me to look at a wall plate which hung over the side-board; the plate had a plaster house near a bridge over a babbling brook. Ted placed the little sitting down doll on the wall of the bridge and it immediately fell off. I started to laugh, all the adults laughed at me laughing.

The doll falling was repeated several times. I thought the doll had jumped into the water below the bridge. At this age I was unable to speak and it was only later when my parents would often recall the 'doll' event that I was able to tell them why I laughed. This leads me to think that children as young as one year of age, do think in a language long before talking, and understand much of what is said in front of them!

Known in the area we now lived as 'Bobby Smiths daughter' many neighbours were eager to look after me if my mother needed help. In those days the local bobby was to be cultivated in case of emergency as most households did not have a telephone. Bobby Smith was first port of call on many occasions as we were later to find out.

Some events in my life in the years before the age of three are a little hazy but there are some etched as sharply in my mind now as if the events were only yesterday. For the most part these, for me, were wonderful times!

Like all children I was eager to explore the world around me. In our village there were many new friends for me to play with, though by mum's account I was just as happy to play by myself. By the time I was two years old I would be enrolled in the Sunday school attached to the local church. The church was situated just across a couple of meadows behind our house but was about a mile if following the country lanes. By age three an older girl, Joyce, from the house across the road, came to take me each week. Often we took a short cut across the field. I remember Joyce taking me to the Rectory where a class of about six or seven children would gather for stories from the Old Testament.

On some occasions I went into the Church and it was of great interest to me as the aura colours of the congregation in front of me were mesmerizing. Some individuals had large auras and others small bright ones. At home my wax crayons were of great entertainment as my way of trying to capture these colours. A book that was given to me by the Vicar for good attendance is still in my possession. Looking at the book now, entitled 'The Little Captive Maid and other Old Testament Stories' it seems quite too much fire and brimstone to interest a young child but it fascinated me.

Mum loved to read poetry to me and before school age I had managed to memorise several lines of verse from the poem 'The daffodils' and 'Winter' by mum's favourite poet, Wordsworth.

Another book I had was the Ladybird book of trees. Seeing aura colours, being given these books started my interest in art, also the ancient world and myths. My parents told me that as a child I could keep myself occupied for great lengths of time just drawing and talking to myself. Though my imaginary friends were not visible to me in a solid form I could hear them and always felt they were there around me. I felt they could hear and see me and would speak into my ear as we played together. To me they were as real as the children at school!

My next clear memory is at Grandma's house when I almost fell out of an upstairs window. Mum was chatting to a neighbour in the front garden and did not notice me go inside. Next minute the lady she was chatting to said 'don't look now and do not shout but your little girl is hanging out of the upstairs window. The adults had no idea until then that I could climb onto the high window ledge. Mum crept upstairs, heart pounding and pulled me away from the window. My Angel had saved me again!

By the time of the coronation of Queen Elizabeth II a television had been acquired on rental, paid for as gift from my grandparents. It was about twelve inches square and had a thick curved screen. I confess I cannot remember the actual coronation ceremony as I was in the garden to hold a little tea party for four friends. We had jelly and orange juice on little plates. The table had been covered with red, white and blue crape paper in the shape of the union jack. The memory probably stuck in my mind because just as we were eating it started to rain and the droplets made the blue and red dye of the crape paper run into the white. This treat was to be repeated again each year on 'Jelly Sunday' a party day that seems now to have been completely forgotten but in the 1950's was some kind of festival in the Wigan area. Perhaps this yearly event was to mark the anniversary of the coronation, or the Queen's birthday. There always seemed to be street parties for summer events in those days. Another such party was held on 'walking day' each Whit week. All the churches of the area had a procession around the towns and villages and almost everyone took part. I can remember the summer of 1953, it was a baking hot day and my mother had whitened my canvas sandals to a brilliant white. I had a white frilly dress and wore a coronet of white daisies on my head.

My black hair had been made curly by sleeping in rags. These were strips of rag where a section of hair was wound round whilst still damp after washing to 'set' the ringlets. All the girls had them if their hair was long enough. The day went as planned and photographs were taken of the troupe from our Sunday school. We all looked splendid but sad to say the tar on the road had melted due to the hot weather. All our sandals were ruined and covered in black tar!

Jack was always in demand from one or other of our neighbours. One day an old lady came knocking because her cat was stuck up a tree. He went to fetch a ladder and the puss was duly rescued. The next week the old lady came back to say once again the cat was stuck up a tree. Again, bobby Smith to the rescue. This was repeated week after week until someone told my mother that the old lady was seen leaning out of her upstairs window, placing the cat onto the tree! The word was the old girl was lonely and had developed a crush on bobby Smith! Another strange call for dad was when a little boy had a pan stuck on his head. He had put it on whilst playing soldiers and it was stuck firm! This time it was a case for bobby Smith to find a large jar of Vaseline.

One emergency was due to me and my thirst for adventure. My mother had thought I was playing in the garden but when she went to call me in for tea the garden was empty. Mother was frantic because the only time I was allowed out was with and adult or Joyce from across the road. Joyce was in her garden and said she had not seen me all day. The whole road was alerted and several neighbours were out looking for me as day turned into evening.

Dad eventually found me asleep in the meadow near the church. I had gone along the short cut, across the field that Joyce had sometimes taken me on our way to Sunday school. My aim was to pick flowers for my mother after seeing them on our way to Sunday school the weekend before. Once again my Angel had protected me! This may seem strange but I always felt I was not on my own, an invisible friend whom would speak into my ear was with me! By age seven, I would 'mind chat' to three imaginary friends. There are many other memories from our time in that first 'police house' and now I realise how poor some of the families were on that council estate.

At that time a bobby on the beat got just over £5.00 a week. Even though we were poor by today's standards others had hardly any furniture and larger families struggled to feed and clothe their children. The community spirit was to share and help each other, but pride often got in the way. Sometimes pride must be swallowed!

Once the Lady next door came round to borrow a bar of soap so that her husband could clean the coal dust off when he got home. As we only had one bar my Mother cut it in half. As I write this memory a favourite saying of both my Grandma May and my Mother May comes back to me, 'If you only have a cherry you can cut it in half to share!' My parents had a little furniture given by relatives but could not afford curtains for the whole house so necessity being the mother of invention they pinned two thin strips of material at ether side of the front window. Eventually they managed to curtain all round the house.

With money being so tight my father made most of my toys. One Christmas he made me a lovely dolls house that I later found out was made from an orange box. The other item I remember, also made from an orange box was my bedside table. This was covered with pink paint and they managed to get me a small lamp that could be left on until they came to bed.

Now and again my mother would invite the youngest of the family next door in to have tea with me. Little Daisy was about three years old like myself, and was the youngest of ten children. We would have cheese on toast or stew followed by jelly or honey sandwiches. Then, one day, Daisy asked me round for tea. This sticks in my mind clearly as it was a novelty for me to stand in line with ten other children waiting my turn for food.

Daisy was holding my hand as we waited our turn. In my other hand was a jam jar I had been given. The eldest child of their family was a teenager and therefore first in the queue. The queue stepped down in age. Eventually it was our turn to be fed! A large crust of bread spread with jam (no butter) was put in my hand and the jam jar I carried was filled with weak milky tea! I thought this was wonderful and couldn't wait to tell my mother about the treat I perceived this to be.

On another occasion my tea with Daisy was a piece of newspaper with about a dozen chips placed in it and covered with salt and a shake of vinegar. In the other hand again a jam jar of weak tea. Poor Daisy never had socks on and looking back it seems she had little by way of possessions but she always seemed as happy as a lark.

One morning I woke up to a funny noise. The noise was coming from a box in the spare room. As Jack opened the box lid, inside there were about twenty tiny fluffy yellow chicks all cheeping madly. I squealed with delight! My dad had been given the chicks to rear by a farmer friend of his in order to supplement his meagre earnings. It was about this time that my mother got a job, just five hours a week looking after a shop, whilst the lady owner went for lunch.
In order for mother to start the little job, child help was needed for me as I was not yet old enough to start school. The help came in the shape of seventeen years old Peggy, from round the corner. I had seen Peggy before as my dad had been called on twice when two of her brothers had been in the wars. One had an eye injury from a boy shooting him with a sling shot. Another brother had a fish hook stuck in his leg, dad's first aid training helped yet again.

At that time Peggy was everything I wanted to be when I grew up apart from the fact she had badly bitten nails and the ends of her fingers were brown from chain smoking Senior Service cigarettes. Peggy had a job in the evenings as something called an usherette. I had no idea what that was but it sounded like something to do with cigarettes. Peggy always wore a black pencil slim skirt and shiny black stiletto shoes but no stockings. She had a leopard patterned swagger coat that was all the rage in that era. Looking back I remember Peggy had quite shaky hands and when I told my mother this she said it was no wonder as there was no peace in that house for the poor girl with those eight brothers larking about all the time.

Peggy eventually took me to her house. I was surprised to see just one chair at the table. She told me it was reserved for her dad; none of the children must use it. 'Where do you sit to eat?' I asked. 'We stand up.' Was her reply, I thought it was probably what made her shake!

One of the last memories from my years in Wigan was my first day at school. Miss Jolly was the name of my teacher and I had been allowed into the first class at just three and a half years old because of the small number of children in the village. I asked to go to school as Daisy next door was starting and my older friend Joyce was in the big class there. The building was very old, slightly Gothic, probably Victorian. Jolly by name and jolly by nature is how I would describe my first teacher. Miss Jolly had a lovely pink aura, and I loved her so much that when it was announced dad was to be transferred to Bolton I felt very sad. Looking back now it seems to me that there are some people that truly have a vocation to teach, but little did I know then that not all teachers would be as kind as Miss Jolly. It would not be too long before I would find this out and my days of trusting in an innocent way were soon to be over! Had I then not quite finished the first lesson of the Tarot?

Moving day came just before Christmas when I was almost four. Our next house was on a tree lined cul-de-sac near Bolton. Mum was thrilled to be moving as we would be closer to grandma and granddad in Manchester. Not now needing to travel on three buses as we did from Wigan. Mum dad and I all went together in a large 'Police' moving van to our new home. Snow was once again falling on the day of the move and my excitement was great as we climbed out of the van and the removal men started to bring our furniture into number 4. The house was of similar style to the one we had left but was the first on the road. To the left there were ten houses on our side that were all occupied with police families. On the right was a main road.

Ron and Dot had the first house round the corner on Tongmoor Road and seemed to me to be very posh. They were in their early fifties and they loved the music of the 1940's, Eddie Calvert's band was their favourite. They had no children but had a rather clever police Alsatian named Brandy. He would do amazing tricks.

My mum and dad played cards with Dot and Ron in the evening every now and then and I would be allowed to go with them. Mr Ron as I called him would show me how to make Brandy do some of the tricks. This was magic in my eyes but I knew he had been trained well. Brandy could fetch a cigarette or newspaper without spoiling it!

Peggy was still a feature in my young life and would sometimes come to look after me, and would stay for a night or two in our spare room. She had now got a job in Woolworths behind the counter, but she still had her Senior Service cigarettes so I thought perhaps she had not entirely stopped being an usherette! One day I asked her what an usherette was. 'I will show you if your mum and dad will let me.' She said. The next week I was dressed in my best winter coat and on the Saturday afternoon Peggy walked me to the corner of Crompton Way to the Cinema. A new and wonderful world of magic opened for me from that day. During our time in Bolton I would see many of the epic films of the 1950s!

When Peggy arrived mum would give her a cup of tea and then go upstairs leaving me to chat to Peggy. When mum came down she would tell Peggy she had run her a nice hot bath so that she could enjoy a good soak. With all her brothers and her dad being miners, coming home full of coal dust, the bathroom at their house was never free. I'm not too sure of Mums motive in preparing this treat, but Peggy loved it and would often come to stay for the night.

It was time to start at my new school, a large newly built complex that housed infant, junior and seniors up to age sixteen. Different sections of the school were built around a quadrangle that was open in the centre. The lessons I would learn at Castle Hill primary would not just be the ones on the timetable, I would learn that some people are always kind and there are others that will go out of their way to do mischief or to upset others.

It was the January just after my fourth birthday. My new teacher was Miss Farah whom was small and slim and had grey hair pulled back into a small bun. To me she seemed very old, much older than my granny, she had a lovely kind pink aura and a sunny smile. On my first day Miss Farah asked me to sit next to another Jennifer and look after her. It would be my job to take the other Jennifer to the toilet if and when she asked me. Jennifer had a lovely blue aura, and though she had 'Down's syndrome' she was always happy. She didn't talk much but I liked her.

For a while life went along well for me, until Mum found a new job. Because Mum was working she could not take me home for lunch. I would have to stay at school for 'dinners'. In the dinner hall there was a teacher in charge by the name of Miss Hunter. To say Miss Hunter ruled with a rod of iron would seem like the understatement of the century. She had a cloudy grey aura and wore brown drab clothes that went perfectly with her stern face.

Lunchtime became a nightmare for me as I confess I had become a fussy eater partly due to the fact I had had several bouts of tonsillitis. Each day when we sat down to lunch there would be a cooked dinner of lumpy grey mash potato with cabbage or sprouts and mushy carrots together with some kind of indescribable meaty stew. This was a far cry from the nice little lunches at my house. To top it all the plate was piled high, I felt sick! No way could I swallow any of it! Miss Hunter would tower over me and tell me I must sit there until the plate was clean.

It became a stand off! The other children had all left the dinner hall and gone out to play whilst I sat there looking at the plate of congealing food. Eventually Miss Hunter would allow me to go to afternoon class but I knew she would be there again tomorrow, standing over me. Other children had all been playing out and I had missed the whole playtime. This went on for some time. The same scenario was repeated each lunch hour. Soon my morning protests got louder, I did not want to go to school! Even though I loved my teacher, Miss Farah, the mere thought of school dinners made me fight against going to school each morning.

Winter was upon us once again and the snow was heavy as one morning mum pulled me along. All the way to school trying to reason with me. 'I thought you liked your new school, don't you?' Mum questioned. Unable to find the words to say what the problem was I would just cry. My misery was compounded as the snow seeped over the top of my Wellington boots. By Spring I was still fighting against school each day. One day I was physically sick and mum had to rush back home to get a bucket of water to clean up the pavement in front of our next door neighbour's house.

Miss Hunter was fond of telling me I was a very naughty girl. I did not want mum to find out that I was so bad. She did not realise why I had the sudden aversion to school, when before I had loved it.

Eventually mum was sent for by the head master and told that I would not eat anything. It was decided that I would go home to have lunch with Ann and her mother, Mrs. Allen, our next door neighbours.

Because of the level of austerity in the fifties it would not be expected to be given a proper meal at someone's house unless they were related. Mum would put some dinner from the night before on a plate and cover it with a pan lid. (Cling film was still a long way in the future.) Mrs. Allen was then to warm it on top of a pan of hot water, but I was not told of this arrangement. For several days to follow I went home from school with Ann. 'Would you like some of what our Ann is having?' Mrs. Allen asked. This seemed like heaven as Ann was having chips in newspaper and tinned tomato soup to dip them in, what a treat!

It was some time before mum was to find out that Mr. Allen was having my dinner of meat and two veg for his main meal when he got home from work. From then on I had sandwiches made by mum but continued to eat with Ann as no alternative was found. It was a big relief to me that I would not face Miss Hunter or school dinners ever again. Little did I know then, Miss Hunter would be the form teacher I would face after the summer holidays.

School was a nightmare for me once again as the next term began. It was the September between my fifth and sixth birthday. The class were to line up outside the new classroom waiting to start form 2. Horror of horrors! the door opened and there stood Miss Hunter with her usual scowl on her face. 'Stand up straight!' she barked at us all. 'Hold out your hands' was the second command. All the children held out their hands and she went down the line examining each one. A couple of boys were told to stand to one side and the rest of us were told to go inside and find a seat. As I was near the end of the line going in I heard her tell the two boys to go to the cloakroom and scrub their hands clean. I saw one of the boys had lost a shoelace, it was on the ground in front of me. Thinking to be helpful I picked up the lace and as I got to Miss Hunter I held it out to her. 'What are you giving this dirty thing to me for?' she sneered as she fixed me with her cold eyes. From that moment on she would talk to me as if I were beneath contempt. This was my first, though, sadly would not be my last real taste of the dark side of human nature! It would be a long and lonely year for me as I struggled with what I now know to be dyslexia, along with awful treatment I would receive from Miss Hunter.

At group reading time there were five groups with five or six children in each group. My group were the first called out and were told to open our books and stand up round Miss Hunter's desk. The first boy had to read the first few lines. He stuttered out the words Miss Hunter held a ruler in her hand and began slowly slapping it onto her other hand in a menacing way. The boy managed to finish the section chosen for him then Miss Hunter pointed to the next boy. He managed to get the words out despite being berated a couple of times, as he had to be prompted. Rosemary, the girl next to me managed to read well for her section, now my turn came. By then my mouth was dry and my tummy felt as if it were tied in a knot. No words would come!

'Go into the corner with your face to the wall.' Miss Hunter barked 'And do not turn round until I say so!' It would be the end of the lesson before I was allowed to move.

At home I could read and write quite well but had trouble with spellings. In class it was as if I had been struck mute. The same thing would happen over and over and I began to believe I was the stupid girl, because I was told that was the case. Too embarrassed to tell my parents I would struggle on, all the time trying not to do anything to draw attention to myself whilst in class. Though she knew nothing about it, mum would read with me each evening and I would try to memorise the words to be able to get through them the next day.

It would be not one but two years of Miss Hunter as the teacher for the following year had been taken poorly. I had had just as much of the reading torture session and of Miss Hunter that I could stand. At home I had not been eating and Mum kept carting me off to see the doctor as I kept getting colds and ear problems. During my second year in Miss Hunter's class my father became very ill. There was a Polio epidemic and he was one of the lucky ones to be diagnosed early. He was in the hospital isolation ward when my next problem arose from something that happened on the way home from school.

Miss Hunter had a different persona towards two girls, who seemed to be her favourite pupils, Rosemary and Jean from the 'top reading group'. One afternoon on the way home from school walking behind Jean and Rosemary I overheard two boys 'Miss Hunter is a grunter.' they chanted. I was delighted and so joined in with the chant. After all it was true or so I believed! Next day nothing was said but at end of class Miss Hunter gave me an envelope addressed to my parents and told me to give it to my mother. It did not occur to me that the letter was about my chanting. In my mind it was probably to complain about my bad reading skills. Mum opened the letter but did not comment. Next day during sport lesson, in the hall (this lesson was taken by a younger male teacher, Mr Porter) I spotted my mother at the door. Mum went over to Mr Porter and spoke quietly. She came and took my hand then we left for home together. It turned out the letter was a complaint about my chanting. Rosemary and Jean had snitched to Miss Hunter. In the letter Miss Hunter asked what mother would do about my bad behaviour.

As we walked home mum told me she had been into the teacher's rest room and spoken to Miss Hunter. I held my breath and waited for the fall out, none came, and in fact mum took me to the corner shop and bought me a bag of sweets. Later at home mum said she had given Miss Hunter a piece of her mind. 'What did you say?' I wanted to know as my stomach twisted into a knot. 'I told her that she had a cheek to send me such a letter with my husband being in hospital and did she not think I had more important things to think about than a childish prank.' I had the feeling Mum knew the chant was true.

Dad was soon out of hospital but would go away to the police convalescent home in Harrogate for three months to recover. Thankfully Miss Hunter never told me off ever again, she just ignored me and never sent me into the corner again after that. As with most bully's she backed off when stood up to but another lesson in life came for me swiftly after the 'chant' episode.

Mum had made me a beautiful rag doll with blond hair made of yellow wool and a pretty dress with sequin shoes. I begged to take the doll to school to show my friend. By now I was taking extra reading lessons at the end of the school day just for ten minutes or so. It was a rainy afternoon and because of the reading I was last out at home time. When I got to the cloakroom there was a boy of about nine and a little girl standing by the door.

The two children were from a large family that I knew lived round the corner from the police houses where we lived. The boy said to me that he and his sister were playing a game of jump over a large puddle in the school yard. He asked if I would like to play with them. I had an inkling of mischief about the boy. He told me to put my book and my doll down whilst we played. There were no other children about and I left the book and doll on a ledge by my cloak peg. While the three of us took turns jumping over the puddle and I did not notice but the boy must have sneaked into the cloakroom. After a while the boy suddenly said they had to go home. I went to get my things, the book was there, but not my doll.

Crying on the way home I met Peter, an older boy from my road, his dad was a policeman too. 'What ever is the matter?' he asked. Still sobbing I told him what had happened. 'Well don't cry, go on home and I will go and see if I can find your doll.' he said. Later in tears, I was telling mum all about it when there was a knock on the door. Peter had my doll in his hand but it was ruined, full of mud. He had gone to the house where the other boy lived and made him confess as to taking it.

Why he would want to throw it down a grid was a mystery. Perhaps to them was I the little rich girl? Perhaps it was my dad being in the police.

On this, as other occasions my feeling of foreboding would prove true and I began to realise that the little voice in my head should be listened to.

Looking back today, it seems that those first two years in Bolton were a sharp learning curve and though I was still afraid of the dark my confidence in other ways had been boosted. Peter had become my Knight in shining armour and so I had found not all boys were horrid. My happy home life more than compensated for any negativity experienced at school, plus I had made a few nice friends including a girl named Sandra who sat next to me and also had some reading difficulty. Sandra and I loved to draw Crinoline Ladies. During the 1950's the popular image of 'Scarlett O'Hara' the 'Crinoline' Lady was everywhere.

On one of my birthdays I was given a very large, very 'lifelike' doll. It had been procured from the shopkeeper my mum had worked for before our move. Mum said the name of the doll was 'Rose Marie'. She told me the doll was a shop mannequin! Peggy had brought it all the way from Wigan on the bus. This was no mean feat as the doll was about the size of an average two years old child. The eyes of the doll were extremely life like and it had real hair. Even at that age I was aware that one should not look a gift horse in the mouth as it would be rude and ungrateful. My parents, though now better off than when we lived in Wigan had not had time to feel the benefit of mum's wage and they had probably paid good money for the doll.

For me the doll was a bit too life like for comfort and after thanking mum and dad I took it into the wash house in the garden telling them I was going to play house. When mum asked why the doll was left in the wash house I couldn't explain it was the real looking (dead) glass eyes that I hated to look at. One year my lovely Auntie Joan took me to see a real show at Blackpool the show was 'Rose Marie' but the doll 'Rose Marie' with her spooky glass eyes remained for ever after in the wash house!

Whilst dad was away convalescing from Polio, mum and I went to the Cinema or the Picture House as it was called then. When dad came home he would sometimes take me. Many a Saturday the early matinee was a big treat and we would always have a packet of chocolates called Miss Shapes. These were just like chocolates from a box but much cheaper.

It was around this time when I started to 'see' and hear things more and more often when alone after being put to bed. These were mostly faces and voices and not really frightening to me, though I still liked the light on. I thought of these images as just a kind of magic from the place where fairies lived but I still hated the dark nights. My 'visions' and dreams were quite strong by the age of seven.

There was one time I was reading and a funny feeling came over me. A rustling noise made me look at the wall and before my eyes there appeared, walking through the wall a tiny lady. She was perhaps about four feet eight inches tall. She came and stood at the end of my bed. As she appeared in solid form and looked kindly at me I was more surprised than afraid.

The Ladies clothes were poor and drab and not a bit like our lovely 'Scarlett' Crinoline drawings. Her brown skirt looked like wool and her grey looking pinafore looked like hessian. She had a crocheted shawl round her shoulders that crossed over her chest. She carried a basket with a cloth over the contents. Only the front of her grey hair was visible as she wore a kind of bonnet with a scarf over it that tied under her chin. Later I would learn this was called a poke bonnet that was a style from the 16/17 hundreds era. The lady had quite a wizened face, not unlike my nice teacher, Miss Farah but a lot older looking. The old lady would appear again to my mother in another home, after two moves, about 20 years later.

Another strange experience I had at bed time one evening was a vision of what I thought was a fairy king. My mother always said I must have been dreaming when this happened. I am sure I was fully awake though perhaps may have been sickening for some childhood illness at the time that could have caused delirium. Still the vision and its clarity remain with me to this day! It started with a type of fly known as a 'Daddy long legs' coming in through the open window.

As the movement of the fly caught my eye I watched it flutter onto the eiderdown at the bottom end of the bed. Being next to fields from an early age I was not afraid of the fly in the least, though I never liked spiders. He fluttered up towards me and as he came nearer it seemed as if when I blinked he changed from a fly into a tiny man on a small piebald horse. He wore black pants and had on an old fashioned white shirt open at the neck with a frill at the cuff. On his head was a tiny crown. In fascination I watched him and his horse kind of galloping towards me on top of the counterpane. Yelling mum at the top of my voice to come and see this wonderful spectacle I sat bolt upright but the little man and his horse disappeared as she hurried into the room! To this day I wonder if the other dimensions could house these small magical creatures as there are stories from all around the world that have a similarity to mine.

By the time of my seventh birthday the magic of words had been shown to me and despite my problems with spelling I loved to write little notes and pretend letters to my invisible friends. One birthday my parents bought me a toy post office with mini note paper, stamps and envelopes. This was great as I could pretend to send letters to these 'friends' of my secret world.

Many grown-ups in my life were my 'Magicians' but the lesson from the Tarot Magician continues all through life as life is a constant voyage of discovery.

For me the magic of music has also brought a constant beam of energy throughout my life. From my early years in the 1950's I loved to collect cards that pictured Ballet dancers and came 'free' with a comic. My friend Sandra and I loved to copy the poses of the dancers. Later, grown too tall to continue Ballet lessons I loved to dance listening to tunes on the radio and later on a record player and then at the youth club or 1960's disco. To me the music and dance were and still are another magical vibration of pure joy that can be found in this world of ours. These wonderful things that have been created from humans tuning their soul into the unseen 'God energy' perhaps from another dimension or from the centre of the universe.

Reader... What, or who has brought a magical energising vibration into your life? Think of a piece of music or art, or a book that resonates within you. Something that may have a feeling of harmony to your soul. Revisit that experience. Listen to that piece of music or read again that book and with 'new eyes' or ears, you may find there is a message within it that you missed the first time you saw or heard it. Sometimes it will be a person that can unwittingly project their 'light' towards you. It may just be that their vibrations exude an inner healing light to everyone, or that their 'light', their 'aura colour' is the same as yours because you are from the same 'soul' group, you are on the same rung of spiritual ladder.

Reader... This is the RUNE Ehwaz

The RUNE Ethwaz is said to represent the horse and movement and links to progress in life. Growth through changes, new places and development.

2/ Tarot Lesson, THE MAGICIAN

Card No 1. The second lesson of the TAROT...
Inspirational music...'My Old Man said follow the Van.'...singer... Marie Lloyd.

The four elements are represented by the artefacts on the table in front of the Magician (sometimes called the Juggler). A wand/baton represents the fire element, a sword represents the air element, a coin/pentacle represents the earth element and a goblet/cup represents the water element. In most packs this card is numbered 1. He is the questioner. His hand holding a wand is raised to the sky (to connect to God or his higher self) in his quest for spiritual knowledge and inspiration. On his head is a cap or halo in the shape of a sideways on, figure 8, the number of infinity. The Magician is also the scientist.

In a young child there begins an awakening to awareness of life in all its diversity. If lucky this second lesson should come with help and stimulation from adults around us. The person who cares for us will read us a story or teach us a rhyme or song to help us see the magic around us. In childhood we have a fall and learn to pick ourselves up and carry on. Childhood is the time when we start to open our inner eye and children seem able to find a real magic in the universe. We then find skills to help us gain self confidence.

We start learning about the four main elements of the world around us. We are taught the danger of fire and deep water. We learn a little of nature of the earth as we explore the garden. Mother will say 'Go and get some fresh air.' As we play outside we feel the wind and look at clouds. These are our early science lessons. The world is full of magic to a young child!

A stage Magician may waft his wand to cover slight of the hand. Trickery, prank playing or theft is the negative side of this card. The wand represents a spiritual energy available to us all if we can tap into it. We may use this energy to do good or improve our intuition. Much is said these days about Angel ordering. We could see the wand as a tool that can strengthen the wish. Is wand of the Magician connection to the father/mother god or just to creation? This will depend on our individual belief system; the faith we grow up with. A person dowsing uses a forked branch as a magic wand to detect water or treasure underground. A healer uses hands as the wand/conductor of the 'God energy' Even if we grow up without a religion we can still feel and see the magic as we learn and explore the world we find ourselves in. The abundant gifts the universe gave us all should be respected as we could not exist if it were not for the elements.
Like most children my early years were filled with the wonder of discovery.

Reader... Have you felt the magic of the universe working at some point in your life? It's never too late to tune into higher vibrations as we do as a child!

Chapter 3

December 1956

There was very little evening television watching as after the news, apart from the quiz show 'What's my Line', television was mostly documentary films. Between one programme and the next we would watch an 'Interlude' of fish swimming around under water, then the screen would go all zig-zag as our first television was on the blink. Dad would thump the top to try and get a picture rather than fizzy lines.

Mum and I would do a lot of arts and craft, making our own Christmas decorations. We made little bells out of silver milk bottle tops and strung them together on red cotton to hang on the Christmas tree as garlands. Mum would buy coloured paper and we would cut them into strips and festoon the house with our Rainbow chains. I don't recall hanging tinsel until my teen years, but we had a few little glass tree ornaments which were brought out every year. There was always a special buzz in our home from the beginning of December as we sat making tree ornaments and wrapping gifts.

Just a week or two before Christmas when dad was on an afternoon shift and due in just after six o'clock mum drew my attention to the snow outside. Just before six we put down our coloured garlands and donned our coats, scarves and gloves to go outside. Mum and I made a pile of snowballs and as twilight came, we waited in hiding behind the wash house. Soon, dad came down the path mum and I threw snowballs at him. We all had such fun and after we laughed as we enjoyed our Ovaltine by the fire. It felt like there was a little 'Moon Magic' that evening and in the memory we made.

As a family we only went to church on special occasions but mum did take me to Sunday school and later I joined the Girls Life Brigade which was like girl guides but closer to home. There was much emphasis on feminine activity in dance and stretching exercise in the confines of the Church hall. Though never a sporty girl my physique being more like a string bean at that time, I did love the music and songs that went with the Girls Brigade events. A 'Moon Goddess' phase of learning had begun! At school I had now escaped the watchful eye of 'The grunter' and had a much younger teacher.

The 'new' teacher had a sunny, warm personality and was full of fun. She had shiny blond hair in a bob and she reminded me of a picture of Goldilocks from a book. As her name escapes me, for the purpose of writing I shall refer to her as 'Mrs Gold'. The class was set the task of learning not just joined up writing, but also italic script. My artistic ability had begun to shine a little by this time. Though my spelling still left much to be improved on, finding the scrolls and artistry in the style of italics suited me. After the near torture of the last class, lessons with Mrs Gold were like a breath of spring. A year seemed to fly past.

With my father working three shifts in rotation Mum and I spent some of our time together listening to the radio. 'Family Favourites" was often our choice and 'Forces Favourites' on a Sunday morning. When Dad was in and the song they loved came on, 'Volare', they would dance round together, seeing me watching, dad would pick me up at the end and we three would have a three corner Kiss. These are special memories I shall always treasure. My parents would often kiss each other and Jack would sing 'Volare' as he twirled May around the room.

Those evenings were sparkling with moonlight romance as we listened to the love songs of the day. Moonlight Serenade, and Unchained Melody were tunes they would dance to. Music is an enhancement to life and love, especially the melodic tunes of yesteryear. These tunes take me back to those precious times in a blink of an eye whenever I hear them. At other times there would be some tension as Dad would come in from work with a grim look on his face after perhaps attending a road accident. He never told Mum in front of me as the gory details may have been too much for me to cope with at that age. Arguments sometimes started if Dad was late in and Mum had a meal going to ruin. My tummy would tie in knots then I would beg Mum to say sorry and she invariably did! Mum had a few admirers amongst Dads friends and he always said he got the best looking woman in Manchester.

Ron, the police man round the corner had retired and we were to welcome new neighbours, Mr and Mrs Mainwright, and their daughter Barbara. As she was just a year younger that me I was asked to go round to play with her. Barbara had very fair hair and was an only child.

At first Barbara seemed happy to have me as her new friend. We would have to play in their garden as it was safer for Barbara on a lawn because she had a disability that might make her fall. My parents soon became good friends with Barbara's parents and whenever Mum went round for a cuppa, I would go to play. Unbeknown to my mum and dad, Barbara started to be rather nasty, talking to me about her own parents, she would often say she wished they were dead and would be glad if they were. It was beyond my understanding why she would so often talk of death and be so unkind about her parents. She once asked me to choose which parent of mine I liked best and which one I wanted to die.

There were times when Barbara would swear then snatch a toy from me. On one occasion whilst our parents went to a police dance, I was told I must stay for a sleep over so that my Peggy could look after us both. Barbara had her own double bed and my bed was a single, and so it was decided.

Mum looked beautiful with a rose pinned to the shoulder of a full length dark purple dance dress, borrowed from gran Smith. Dad was immaculate in a dinner suit, also on loan, from his dad.

Because I had had a taste of some of Barbara's antics I was loath to go. Later each time I got into bed Barbara would start to pinch or kick me. When I got out of bed saying I would fetch Peggy, Barbara would beg me not to tell. After three or four times and several bruises I eventually shouted for help. Peggy took Barbara to the landing and I could hear her soothing but chiding Barbara quietly. Things were calmer after that.

Luckily Mum and Dad never went to many more dances at Bolton and the Mainwrights would soon be moved to Preston as Tom had been promoted to Sergeant. There would only be one more time for Barbara to torment me but that would come later that year, after their move. Now we Smiths were to embark on a new adventure too! By now I had experienced two faces of the Moon Goddess. Her darkness but also her feminine aspect too! Like the Moon itself we see light and shadow in the vibrations from the Moon. Is our own 'High Priestess', the 'Moon Goddess' within us to be used for seduction into joy / light or will we use it for gains, or to boost our ego?

A more feminine seductive aspect of the Moon Goddess was gained for me by the romance portrayed in the films I was lucky enough to be taken to see. Films such as 'Little Women'. The artistic, feminine and fruitful side of the 'High Priestess' had been gained from my mother, also Miss Gold, teaching me art and crafts and Peggy, the art of humouring someone. I had also begun to feel a mystic side of the 'Moon Goddess energy' through the vision of the little old Lady whom I would later find was one of my guides in spirit.

Poor Barbara taught me that sometimes the darker 'Moon' energy can take over and make us say and do mean things. Seduction for our own ego. When older, Barbara would show a great generosity, though she found life quite hard. There was nothing in those days to help her come to terms with her type of disability and even today there is little understanding of how a physical impairment might affect mental health. When we can see that a person has an obvious disadvantage with movement most of us will try to be kind and helpful. Many suffer with physical ailments that we cannot see by looking at them and that is why we need to be tolerant if in a supermarket queue if the person in front is rather slow packing, or if a child is throwing a tantrum we must not judge. They may have an ailment that one cannot see. These 'special' souls could have been brought into the material world in a state of bodily impairment in order to give their 'light' to others or to help us appreciate what we have been given.

Readers... Enjoy being a flamboyant moonbeam, sometimes choosing to wear wonderful colours or sparkling clothes, letting your aura colours shine. Make allowances for those around you that may be finding life a struggle under a dark moon shadow. If you have a disability try to throw yourself into something creative, or immerse yourself into colour or beautiful sound to help your mind cope with the pain of restrictions.

Reader... This is the RUNE Algiz

The RUNE Algiz is thought to represent Protection, mindfulness and knowing. It makes me think of the person with arms held up to the sky asking protection of God.

3/ Tarot Lesson...THE HIGH PRIESTESS

Card No 2. The third lesson of the TAROT...High Priestess/ Popess/ Moon Goddess
Song...'Cara Mia'...Singer...Version...David Whitfield

The High priestess (on some older designs named The Popess) is shown as a beautiful young woman. In ancient times thought of as the Moon Goddess! This is very much how I prefer to think of her from the design on many Tarot packs of today.

On this card we see the moon shape at the feet of the woman. This card links to the Zodiac sign Cancer. This represents the secretive aspect of human nature. Mystery, passion, femininity, intuition and artistic ability link to this card. Beauty and seduction are part of the mystery of the moon goddess image. On some Tarot packs there are two pillars representing boundaries of the human mind. As the Priestess, she holds attributes of both science and spirituality. We can link this image to all creative aspects of life including psychic ability as all creativity stems from the inner mind. Listen to our intuitions, and we avoid danger and develop any talents we may possess. In divination the card can indicate the seductive one, the lady of moonlight. A deeper understanding of our own mind and character is perhaps what she tells us to explore.

Influence of the Moon energy is strongly linked to this card. Symbolically the image is showing us there is a natural flow to life, a rhythm. There will be people and things that will seduce us away from our intended goals but in going with the flow there will be pleasure to be had. There is also an air of romance attached to the moon influence as well as fertility and mystery. Just as the Moon has an influence on the ebb and flow of the

Ocean tide it also links to the ebb and flow the female cycle. We might see this cycle in many aspects of life, reminding us there is a time for everything. We cannot always go against the tide of life. By my seventh birthday I had begun to see a magical 'Moon' influence in my bedtime stories from the Anderson and Grim fairy-tale book and throughout my life have kept a love of literature that brings the two aspects of the Moon, light and shadow!

Reader... Has a full moon ever put you into a dark mood? Lift your spirit with creativity. Use the silvery 'Moon' magic to fine tune your inner God or Goddess and you also will become more creative. If love has given you problems, then think of the 'Moon' and the nearest bright star as the mystical bringers of romance, then watch for other portents to guide you. Once you start to believe you can revive your own magic tuning you will start to attract things and people that will enhance your own vibrations. Love breeds love!

Chapter 4

1956 -1957

By the time I had settled into my third year at Castle Hill School my parents had managed to purchase a new television and this was to bring us news and views of the wider world. Most of the programmes on television at that time did not interest me and as dad watched, mum and I would play games by the fire. We would look at the flames and say what we could see. Here a dragon, there a fish and often a face. My dad loved to watch the news at tea time and to me this was a bit of a blessing as it would ensure that he would not be at the table too long. My poor appetite was a constant source of worry to my Mother and my Dad would say things like 'If you had been five days at sea in an open boat you would eat anything!' Mum would make wonderful meals and I would play with the food, making the mash potato into little hills and putting the peas around as people then the broccoli would be the trees and the gravy the river or lake. The meat would represent a giant rock. If we had fish it would be made into little flakes and to my mind it became little Angels or Fairies.

Mum would plead with me; Dad would put on his stern face and lift one eyebrow. Whatever they said or did, no more than a mouthful of food would go down. 'You will be ill if you don't eat!' was the angle Mum took, but to no avail.

Sometimes I would store food in my cheeks to pretend I was eating some of it. Once at Grandma's house I waited until the adults had left the room and scraped the food from my plate into a large vase that stood in the hearth. I often wonder that nothing was ever said about this, but can only surmise that it was a secret grandma kept for me. I cannot imagine she would never look inside the vase or that my leftovers were never found. At home when dad went into the sitting room to watch the news, mum would scrape half the food from the plate into a dish and with a finger to her lips and a shushing sound she would signal that I must let Dad think I had eaten some. I often wonder if my fasting, like the Eastern practise of fasting before a meditation, helped my intuition.

Each summer my parents would take me to stay with granny May and grandad Ted. This was a great treat as I would be allowed to go to work with my gran to the sewing factory. All the women were on piece work which meant the more garments they could make each day, then the more pay would be in their pay packets at the end of the week. The boss of the firm did not mind my being there as I would thread the needles for all the women and so they could work all the faster. There was a big table and the women would chatter away as they worked. At lunch time in summer they would send out for a jug of beer to drink whilst eating the sandwiches they had brought from home. The radio was on most of the day and despite their working week being 48 hours, all the women would be happy, singing along to the popular tunes of the day. Now whenever I hear those tunes of the 50s I can see May, so happy in her work and the companionship, singing along.

At my grandparents, being the only grandchild until the age of almost ten, I was rather spoiled. On Friday evening we would watch their television which had a good picture and was a little larger than ours. We loved the Skiffle bands that were emerging at the time but they could not compete with the Billy Cotton band show. We sang along to all the tunes. Alma Cogan with her fancy full skirted dresses was a favourite singer of Ted, but grandma May, loved Ann Shelton. It was at their house that I first saw and fell in love with Elvis. He was shown on the news as the new sensation from America.

Ted and grandma May, once took me on holiday with them to Blackpool. We stayed in a caravan owned by uncle Len. This was to get me out of the way as my mum got over a miscarriage. At the time I was not told the reason.

The world of sand and sea, fish and chips and of course the house of fun on the pleasure beach had me enthralled. On the beach I made patterns in the sand. My appetite began to improve with the sea air and when we got back mum seemed fully fit and life returned to normal. The next time I would see Blackpool was on a short holiday with my Aunty Joan, wife of Len, when she bought tickets to see a new singer of the day, Shirley Bassey.

Our next family holiday, was at a big holiday camp close to Scarborough. There was a coffee bar, a theatre and a place to rent bicycles or a contraption for two or three to ride on together. We met up with a family staying in another caravan; their two boys Melvin and Jason, became my friends. They were from Harrogate, close to where my dad had been in the convalescent home. Their son Melvin was just a little older than me. When it came to the fancy dress competition I was dressed in my new nurse outfit and Melvin was wrapped from head to toe in bandage. Dad put a partially blown up balloon on his foot to look like a swelling, smeared with lipstick to look like blood and a crutch was procured from somewhere for him. We won the competition and from then on the three of us became inseparable. This was kind of my first innocent Holliday romance, not with Melvin, but with his thirteen-year-old brother Jason. On the beach, I remember writing Jason in the sand with a big heart. The admiration grew from the fact he taught me to ride a two wheeler bike for the first time. Melvin, from Harrogate you have my gratitude for the kind way you and your brother treated me.

During the holiday our family went on a treasure hunt competition. Part of the treasure we had to collect was a live crab. Down on the beach mum and I drew words on the sand and I collected shells and pebbles. We looked into all the rock pools we had no luck, so had to buy a crab from the local fishmongers. We did not win the competition but Dad, said we must not waste the crab.

He prepared and cooked the crab but had no knowledge of the 'dead mans finger' part of the crab, this should be removed! Mum ended up quite poorly in bed for a couple of days! A culinary experience never to be repeated!

Later Melvin and Jason took me to the coffee bar. It made me feel very grown up being allowed to go out with friends rather than my parents. Dad considered it safe as the coffee bar was in the secure walls of the campsite. We put our coins in the juke box and sat drinking milk shakes and listening to 'Last Train to San Fernando' and also 'Story of My Life'. I remember the top of the hit parade was 'Putting on the Style' but my favourite on the juke box was 'Love Letters in the Sand'.

My Mother quickly recovered from the upset tummy, but Dad was never to live it down. From then on the only time dad ever cooked was a year or so later when Mum went into hospital to have my little brother. John Edward was born on the 5th of August in the year I had turned nine in the January, so I was Nine years and seven months the elder, almost ten. It was my turn to become a young version of the Empress as I treated poor little John as my personal baby doll!

Our parents always tried to make our holiday an adventure and even though we were not well off for money, we had a lot of fun. When dad got a weekend off work we would have a day out, going up Winter hill, Rivington Pike or to Tockholes Wood. Now and again we went to Darwin to visit dad's sister Brenda, her hubby David and my darling little cousin Lynn. Lynn had gorgeous curly hair and was as cute as my favourite doll. Darwin and the other places we went to had a special feel to them for me. After reading The Hobbit I see them now as places of inspirational magic. Places where a fairy or elf might jump out in front of you at any moment. In many quaint country places there is an Earth energy. People are drawn to these places and sadly often spoil them with litter. There is a kind of magnetism linked to the many Ley lines around our Islands. Perhaps that is why there are so many legends in country places.

Our home was not quite as modern as the flat my auntie Brenda and uncle David lived in. They were waiting to be allocated a police house. Being a little younger than mum and dad, the furnishing was very 1950's and as I loved the art and culture of the 1950's, I thought them very 'with it' listening to music on their record player with uncle David singing to hit songs of the time. In their flat they even had a fridge, something quite novel to us. Most police homes had a cold slab in the larder to keep foods such as butter, milk, fish and meats fresh for a while.

In those days there was a corner shop on almost all junctions where there were housing estates. People went to the shops more often, buying food just to last for a few days. Supermarkets were none existent and the big stores in towns and Cities were mostly for clothing, shoes, furniture or household goods.

Because food was bought in small amounts children would be sent to buy milk or other fresh items. It was common, and considered quite safe for a child to go alone to the corner shop. At the age of eight I loved to be sent on an errand but one day I had a fall from my scooter when returning with a loaf and jar of jam. The grit from the croft I had to navigate on the way to the shop had got into the wound. I sobbed as dad sat me on the table and administered a red hot Kaylin poultice to clean the wound. The cure was worse than the cut.

The croft was a patch of land that had (before bombing in the war) had houses on and was now just a patch of rough land with a track worn across it by the many feet taking a short cut to the school, shop or the bus stop.

Going to the shop always made me feel that I was being useful to my mum as I liked to be her little helper, a facet of the Empress that would soon stand me in good stead for the role of helping care for a new addition to the family.

Reader... Have you had responsibility of care for another? The Empress within us is brought to the forefront with any 'mothering' we do for others. The role of Empress is important in so far as providing guidance, nurture and protection to the young or those with a weakness of any kind. If fate called you to be the 'Empress' for family or in society, then it is because you are special, you have the love within that is needed for this role.

4/ Tarot lesson, THE EMPRESS

Card No 3. The fourth lesson of the TAROT...Mother...Nurse...Competent Woman!
Song...'Love Letters in the Sand'...Singer...Version...Bing Crosby.

The Empress card depicts a woman in the fullness of life. She is Venus personified. She represents Motherhood in all its forms. The Empress is the Mother that produces the child, the woman that looks after the child, the woman that nurses the sick, the woman whom looks after the home or business. A woman of wisdom. She can make the rules and do the organizing but also shows the gentleness within us that we might all tap into, if we are given a responsibility of care.

There is so much for us to learn from our mother whom gives us birth, or from the person whom plays the roll of bringing us up, through our childhood. I also think of the Empress as lady bountiful. Our female roll model may be our birth Mother or our Grandma, or a foster Mother. If we are brought up by a man then the care side of his nature will be required to give us a balance, or this may be provided by a relation or teacher. The Empress card depicts efficiency and ruler in female form so can show us the path of being gracious as well as teaching us to share, in short this card tells us we need to follow the rules of our elders and we will be rewarded with many blessings. In her roll of Mother Nature, Mother Earth, the Empress tells us to look after the planet and it will provide for us!

The role of a good mother in the ideal world would be instinctive but if as an individual we have a neglectful mother then we may need to learn from a motherly person, perhaps an aunt or grandmother. The mothering instinct is in most of us (both male and female). It is a survival instinct of human kind, but sadly drugs, alcohol or other addictions can hinder this natural instinct. This is where our need for good social services must come into play if we want to uphold a civilised society.

The young must be guided and learn how to apply that natural caring instinct for the sake of the next generation. If we are lucky enough to have a person of care to look after us and be with us in our formative years then we can promote a caring attitude in our society wherever we are able. By so doing we might just be able to cure some of the problems we are faced with in this world of today.

Children deserve to be nurtured and if we are to produce a future population of right minded adults that add creativity and caring to society we need to create that 'right' environment now, at home and in our schools. It was at my mother's knee that I learned to care and share and be creative. I wish every child may have such guidance from a parent or guardian.

Reader... Nurture your inner child with merriment and laughter whenever you can. Be an example to all the young children you have contact with. Find inside you once again the child you once were, the child within us all.

Chapter 5
1957 - 1958

My Father was a strong influence on my young life with his Leo personality always present. He was very handsome, tall and slim and always dressed smartly in his Police uniform. Mum was always ironing a pile of shirts but he would often iron his own trousers. A piece of wet soap was smeared on the inside of the crease of the trouser leg then turned right way out, a clean damp tea towel was placed on them then the iron so the crease would look as sharp as the day they were new on. He was a figure that commanded respect, and he did indeed expect respect. The police in those days were called a 'force' and they were not only the law enforcement but also by most people, viewed as community helpers. The television programme Heart Beat very much reminds me of those far gone days.

Before bed time I would be allowed to listen to a radio show for children called 'The Ovelteenies' on the radio. We would sing along to the theme tune then mother would read a story. If dad was home, he would carry me up stairs. With a one, two, three, he would pretend to throw me into bed. Dad would tell me a story about two sailors, Mick and Patrick. These imaginary sailors were described in so much detail to me that I can almost visualise them to this day. Mick, with Patrick would have amazing adventures in far away places with strange names. Later in life I realised these were some of dad's own adventures from his days in the war on the Merchant ships.

One evening there was a knock on the door and mum sent me to answer it. A small strange looking figure stood on the doorstep looking dishevelled and rather dirty. His appearance startled me at the time, not because he was half my size, (I had seen some tiny clowns at the circus) but because he was bleeding from a head wound. In his hand was a blood soaked trilby hat. His voice was strange, he seemed to be chewing gum, and at first I could not tell what he was saying. After a moment I realised he was saying his name and was asking for Bobby Smith. Dad was at work so I shouted mum, she and grandma Smith who was visiting both came to the door. Mum was all of a dither but gran took over and brought the poor fellow inside and tended to his head. After cleaning the wound, she bandaged his head and Mum gave him a cup of sweet tea.

'Lucky you were here Alice!' Mum said when the little fellow had gone. Grandad Smith had brought grandma in his van and would be letting dad use it for a couple of weeks whilst they were away on holiday.

This was not the last we would see of little Mr Foster as we thought his name to be. He would come round to thank us over and over again. By this age I had learned there were some people we must be extra kind to as they had troubles we were lucky enough not to have. Later I was to learn that Mr Foster was not the nice poor little old man that we had helped, he had a much darker side to his nature! Playing out in the street one day I saw Mr Foster come round the corner and went to say hello. As I had spoken to him a few times when out with mum, by then I could tell more of what he was saying. It cannot be repeated in print what he was saying as the language is such that would have made the prisoners of 'Cell block 10' blush! Apart from the swear words most of what he was saying seemed to be about certain ladies of the silver screen that were strutting about naked. When I told my mum what he had said she made me promise to avoid him in the future as he had seemed to be trying to attach himself to me in some way. A few years later I did encounter him in spirit form but thankfully I would be able to fend off the negative entities by this time.

The man next door to us, Mr Rutland (Al), was prone to nightmares and every now and then he would wake up screaming and shouting. Being a quiet child my parents would often forget I was listening. One day after we had all been woken up in the night, by Mr Rutland screaming, I overheard dad telling mum he thought Al had got shell shock from the war. Though this was the cause of his nightmares, dad was running out of tolerance after a full week of screaming waking us up.

One night when the screaming started, Mrs Rutland, (Annie) came round for dad, asking him to try and calm Al down. By then mum was wide awake and went to the bedroom window to watch for dad to come back. The noise had woken me up too. 'Think things will be quieter now, so you two go back to bed, I'm going to make myself a brew', said dad. As he returned to the bedroom he stood drinking his tea and looked out of the bedroom window. He had left the light off so that mum could get back to sleep.

As dad stood there he saw a shadowy figure creeping along the line of cars parked in front of the police houses. He watched for a few moments and saw the person going to try the handle of each car in turn. They were all locked! As the man went to the van parked in front of our house dad watched. The man tried the passenger door (it was locked) then the he went round towards the driver's side door. Dad had to spring into action! Knowing that the van door had a broken lock he raced downstairs after alerting mum.

Not being fully asleep mum watched on as dad grappled with the would be thief. The man pulled out a knife but Dad managed to wrestle it from him. By now mum had her dressing gown on and was at the front door. 'Go and telephone the police!' Dad shouted. I was out of bed now and standing on the stairs. Mum told me to stay in the house and shut the door as she rushed off. She had to run two blocks down the main road to a call box as even police houses had no telephones at that time. Dad found the headlines in the paper quite funny after the trial as the young man had said to the Judge 'We only live for a laugh!' Dad did not see the funny side at the time but did say that it was one time he did not mind Al next door screaming to wake him up.

In 1958 dad was on duties late and had witnessed from close by the terrible air crash on Winter Hill. The sights of this shocking event would live with him for ever as would many of the accidents he had to attend. He never liked motor bikes much as he had attended many that had crashed during his time in the police. Later in life these and his war time traumas would come back to haunt his mind. When I first met my husband, my dad would never let me ride his motor bike. As a young woman I would never go against his wishes, though he would eventually get used to the idea of my riding, but only because my husband had, by then taken advanced driving instruction.

My father was ambitious and when the word came out that the police wanted volunteers to go to Cyprus to help the Army tackle the political troubles there, he was eager to go. My brother John was just a few weeks old and Mum did not want dad to go, but before long the matter was settled. Reluctantly mum gave him the go ahead when he told her there would be chance of promotion. He also knew he would get extra wages that would make life a bit easier for us all.

Mum did not want to hold him back as he wanted him to reach promotion to sergeant. It was said then that a bobby on the beat could only get promoted if someone retired or died on the job. Also the thought that they may be able to buy a washing machine was a big persuasion, as up to then mum used a boiler and wringer in the washhouse out in the back garden.

We had a lovely milk man that dad and mum were friendly with and it was arranged that he would take me and mum to stay with grandma May and grandad Ted for the three months when dad would be away. There was some weeping as mum kissed him goodbye. Dad said he would write and when he got home we would all go on holiday.

My temporary new school in Manchester was the same one mum and her sister Joan had attended more than 20 years earlier in the 1940's. Old Moat Lane junior school, would bring me much to be glad about! Although I was the new girl I quickly made a friend, (Kathy). She had a bike called bluebird and would let me take a turn on it on our way home. The teacher was Mr Jones. He was a happy, quietly spoken man but the children were very respectful of him as he had a commanding presence about him. To me he was an Angel as apart from his amazing violet aura Mr Jones would introduce me to the joy of adventure books. He would end the school day with a chapter of 'Just William.' and would read it to the class in a very amusing way, doing different voices for different characters. My reading and writing skill, came on leaps and bounds whilst at Old Moat.

The rest of the time we spent at Manchester was mixed with tears and joy. Sad that dad was so far away but happy that he would be home for New

Year. This was not to be! A letter came for mum and when she read it she began to cry. Dad had extended his stay in Cyprus for another three months! Dad had included a birthday card and letter for my tenth birthday in with the 'sad' letter and photographs for mum.

Later, John and I were dressed in our best clothes and a Christmas photograph was taken to send to Dad. My big delight was a red satin dress with flesh coloured under slip and a raised pattern of red flowers that I had received as a gift from Auntie Joan.

For the photograph John was in a pale blue outfit gran had knitted for him. His chubby little cheeks had dimples when he smiled; John was the happiest baby you could behold and started speaking early. When dad came home he was already saying a few words. He could say 'cup o tea.' in his baby voice.

Dad had brought home some gifts for us all including a strange shell for me. It was a large 'lucky money' cowry shell. I have always felt lucky as whenever I have needed a small boost of cash I could whisper to the shell. Invariably something turned up! Perhaps it is just the positive belief that works, as these days I ask the Angels to help whenever I am in need or have lost something and this almost always works for me.

I thought, dad (my Emperor) was glad to be home and was delighted with the way John had grown. Dad could be a stern rule maker of the house, a typical Leo personality. He could also be the very gentle 'pussy cat' Lion too! The next few months went by with dad deep in studies towards his sergeant's exam, mum busy with baby John learning to walk and to our delight TALK. For me there were a few more adventures for me with a new friend Lesley.

Mum was now the proud owner of an electric Twin Tub washing machine though the old ringer was still needed as spin dryers were a separate commodity. She seemed happy at home spending her time with John. Dad and gran May had bought John a beautiful (coach built) baby carriage that mum was proud to push out. We soon settled back into our police house.

With a new decade looming, dad was hopeful of promotion, although it would mean moving house yet again. I went back to Castle Hill school, into Mr Porter's class. Thankfully Miss Hunter never crossed my path again.

Mr Porter was a nice teacher but there was a growing fear within me about something that had been whispered about in class… The eleven plus! I had no idea what this was exactly, but from the other children I knew it was BAD news. Some kind of test! Mr Porter never shouted although there were often red lines drawn through my work. I still loved to read but my spelling had not improved much since before dad went away. Mum was busy now with baby John and had no time for reading. Dad was out a great deal as he was doing something called 'acting Sargent' in training for when he became Sargent full time when a place became vacant.

Reading was the last thing on my mind at this time. After school activity for me, was now climbing trees with Lesley. We were together running quite wild if the weather was good, (both real Tom boys). We played acting games where we would take the role of the hero such as Ivanhoe. Despite wanting to be dressed like a boy during the week day evenings after school, on Sunday I would follow the 'Pony tail girl' fashions, with my pea green or shocking pink ankle socks and hair tied in a matching ribbon. On rainy evenings after John was asleep I would still do art or crafts with mum.

Dad would often ask me to read the words in the credits after 'Robin Hood' that came up on our new 'twelve inch' television. This always made me worried and at times I was glad when the clock struck six as children's hour had finished. At six the news came on and it would take dad's attention away from me. At the back of my mind there was still the big question, what would happen if I could not pass this eleven plus test? My dad was so keen on his own achievements, he was my hero, and I knew he wanted very much for me to do well. These thoughts made me feel like I was bound to disappoint him.

5/ Tarot lesson, The Emperor

Card No 4. The fifth Lesson of the TAROT... The Father, Protector, Leader.
Song... 'Volare'...Singer ...Version...Demenco Modinio ...1958

On this card we see a bearded man sitting on a throne. He often has a shield with an Eagle on it. In his hand is a sceptre, symbolic of generation. His posture indicates the number 4, which is linked to Jupiter, as well as the number of the elements and the cube representing firmness and fulfilment. Just as the Empress represents the mother in the person's life, the Emperor card is mostly about a Father influence on life. The lesson one may learn from a Father or a person who may be a surrogate Father figure to us, such as uncle or Teacher and later in life a Husband or even a Boss. The Emperor also represents male strengths and government and also kingship.

We could learn lessons from both parents but the traditional Father figure is portrayed in the essence of this card. The strictness and authority aspect of the card reminds us that there are rules set down by those elders in our lives. For many the first figure to give us the rules of the home is our father. The government, the school authority and later the person or organisation we may work for, then follows through with other rules of conduct they wish us to follow. In divination the Emperor, like the Empress depicts someone to make the rules to protect and guide us. All the cards have a dual aspect just as all humans have a light and dark aspect of their nature.

The negative side of the Emperor would be the abuse of authority. We must all learn the rules of the home and of the country we live in if we want to fit into civilised society. The positive aspect of this card is caring protection and guidance to the young. The protective leader of the clan or in ancient times, the tribe. In the culture of the American Indians the Emperor equivalent was the Chief.

Reader... Do you need to find the 'Father', protective hero aspect of your nature? Leadership, guidance and protection are all roles that are required for an orderly society and roles we may need or be required to channel at some point in life. At these times set your mind to 'forthright fair and orderly' mode.
In work or group situations be confident.

Chapter 6
1958 - 1960

At home, now back in Bolton, my new class teacher, Mr Porter asked me to sit next to a boy named Ian. His family were from the West Indies and came over to Britain in the fifties as part of the Wind rush project. The poor lad did not do too well with lessons as he struggled to learn English and his nose ran constantly. He probably hadn't got used to the climate here. Ian had no handkerchief and would keep wiping his nose along the sleeve of his jacket. Another lad, Kevin had started at school at the same time as Ian. This was just as I had returned from Manchester. Kevin and I made friends even though he was soon moved into the top class along with my friend, Lesley. Lesley and her family had moved in round the corner, in the house next to the one the Mainwright's had lived in.

The man who had lived there before had now retired from the police. Although Lesley was in the top class she and I would stick together at playtime and on the way home from school. We would go horse riding together at weekend. Kevin would often tag along as he lived in a new house close to our street and near the stables. Lesley said she hated boys, Kevin having a horse, she made him an exception.

Lesley would set the rules of our out of school activity and was always thinking of how we could have an adventure. I knew even then that she was very clever, her dad was a detective and from her behaviour it seemed to me she wanted to be one too. Lesley and I went everywhere together and I'm not sure she liked to share my company, when as a 'new boy' Kevin stepped in along with us. He seemed nice and I thought he was rather cute. He had striking blue eyes. There was something about his aura that caught my attention.

From my dreams an inner knowing about future events came to me. I had no knowledge or belief in reincarnation at that time. One day, walking home Kevin said he had been in the WAR. Lesley laughed and began to taunt him. Not fazed in any way, as we walked, he told us more about his past life. He remembered being in the Air Force as a pilot and described this in great detail saying he remembered being shot down over the sea. 'You just saw that on a film.' scoffed Lesley. Kevin politely kept on with his story. He told us he was married and remembered his wife and child and the house they lived in, plus the other Airmen he had known.

I thought Kevin seemed to be telling the truth and even Lesley began to take him seriously as he gave us a most remarkable description of his past life. The three of us walked home together after school each evening for the whole of our last junior school year. He never wavered from his story. He often said he would one day find his wife and child to tell them he was now okay and alive.

Kevin took us to the field to meet his horse named Diamond. We were mad about horses and Lesley never gave a thought to the danger of riding without a saddle or hat. For my part I would just feed him a nice bunch of clover. There were fields across the main road from our homes where Lesley and I went riding every Saturday morning from the stables near the ancient cottage of Richard Cromwell.

Later in life when I began to learn more about the paranormal I would have liked to talk to Kevin, but I never thought to ask his surname. Apart from his tale of a past life all I remember is that his father had bought him the horse after winning the Football pools! Wherever Kevin is, I hope he had a full and fruitful life, after all, if his story was true he gave his past life for the good of our country and for our freedom.

Around this time Lesley and I got into quite a lot of mischief as we liked to think of ourselves as 'The avenging Angels.' Lesley had got the idea out of the comics we read. My Mum made us black capes and eye masks to dress up. We acted as if we were invincible! Each evening after school we would go across the main road and through a small wood then over the field down to the Mill pond. We would watch the older boys and follow them to the edge of a Mill pond where they had made a long rope swing that went out over the pond. We would wait and watch from behind a tree and when they went home we would have a go on the swing. One time they came back and caught us and from the other side of the pond one of the boys started to shoot at us with a pellet gun. We ran like crazy and just escaped being winged.

Another time we went down to the ice on the Mill pond. Lesley wanted to skate on the pond. It was good luck that she did not drown as the ice started to crack. I confess I was too scared to venture out past the bulrushes near the edge but managed to hold out a tree branch for her. The river was another place we loved to frequent. We would pretend our home was a hollow tree as we imagined we were in an episode of 'Robin Hood' off the television. I remember the male star in it was an actor named Richard Green. We were literally running wild for a couple of hours each evening after school. We would roam across fields and through woodland most of the day during the weekends, and school holidays. We got away with it, probably because our mums both had our younger siblings to keep them busy. They could hardly keep up with all our pranks.

Mum always warned me of the danger crossing the road and of going into deep water but if Lesley's mum had warned her, then I can only think that her love of adventure outshone the need for safety.

Nothing seemed to phase Lesly and I was quite in awe of her but life was not all play! My teacher, Mr Porter had been having driving lessons from Jack who had asked about my school work. Mr Porter said I was below par when it came to maths. He thought my reading had improved and I was in the middle group for English but changing schools so often the math had come out worse for wear! Dad decided I would go for tuition to the home of a retired Headmaster he knew, Mr Brown. Mr Brown was kind and had a mild manner of speech.

Mr Brown, taught me a few basic sums as he puffed away at his pipe. His little cottage was full of smoke and all I can remember is that the cottage felt as if it were full of ghosts that seemed to whisper to me, making lessons difficult, and everything was strangely brown like his name.

It was at this time my dad (soon to be Sergeant Jack Smith) had been on some flying lessons with Mr Ron who used to live next door. Gran May had paid for them because word was out that the police were about to do a trial use of helicopters to watch traffic from the air. It may have been with the new motorways that were being built. We had been back in Bolton just six months or so when Dad got the promotion he was after and we were on the move again as his step up the ladder dictated. Once again we moved in a snow storm, just before Christmas 1959! The next house was on the end of the police estate in Hutton near Preston. The estate was next to a wood just off the Preston to Southport dual carriageway. In the 1950's this was the main route to Liverpool.

Leaving my friend Lesley had been upsetting as I did love some of the tomboy things we did together in Bolton. Whilst I would miss her, at least being next to a wood there were plenty of trees to climb. Lesley and her family had moved too. They were not as lucky with their move she informed me by letter. Not many trees in Crosby! We kept in touch for a while by letter and we did one exchange holiday at each others homes during school holidays. Though we missed the adventures of the trees and fields next to the old mill at Bolton we had a great time on the beach picking up pebbles close to her new home.

Lesley still had a lot of mischief about her and she said that we should go into a small playground that was directly over the fence at the back of their house. Lesley said we must get up very early before the gate keeper would open the gates at 9 o-clock in the morning. Lesley had got on the wrong side of the gate keeper the day before I had arrived and wanted to do something to annoy him to pay him back for telling her off. The exact way she would do this was not told to me until we had climbed over the fence. It was a misty morning and I had a feeling of foreboding but went along with her. There was a loud chirping, and screeching from all the birds, a kind of mournful chirping choir. Lesley said the birds were warning each other that there was danger from a prowling cat. I had never heard such noise even though we lived next to a wood. There was a mini golf course with little metal flags at each hole; Lesley moved them all around so that the man would have to restore them to the right place when he arrived. If there was any more trouble for her then I never found out about it.

After the 'gate keeper' event we did not dare to go over the fence. Lesley knew she would be the main suspect for the 'crime'. Her mind was so active that she often would wake me in her sleep walk. Her mum had to gently guide her back to bed. By the end of the week the thought of home was a comfort. Although my fear of darkness has never left me, when asleep, it seems that I need to sleep until morning.

After a while the letters back and forth between myself and Lesley dried up. She had often corrected my bad spelling and I did feel quite affronted by this at the time. I do hope that by now she has had the wonderful, exciting life she craved. The last news from speaking to her mum was that Lesley had a very good job after university. She was working as a buyer for Harrods Store in London. Over the years I have often wondered if she remembers the conversation about reincarnation and what are now her thoughts on the subject. If ever anyone has been here before then it would be her.

When we first moved to Preston it was school holiday over Christmas time. Just after New Year 1960 I caught a virus and so would not start school until the second week of term just a few days after my eleventh birthday. I had missed the exam set for the eleven plus and would go to take it before finishing the last year of junior school in Penwortham. This was a little daunting as I had to go by myself on a bus for the first time.

At the bus stop I realised I had not brought the required pencil. Seeing me in tears an elderly man with a bright white aura came up to me and asked why I was upset. He gave me his handkerchief and a pencil and saw me onto the bus. Later I found out he was a retired headmaster of the local boys Grammar school, though at the time I truly thought he was an Angel. Yet again, I seemed to have someone just turn up to help after me!

Starting at the next school I had begun to feel somewhat self conscious about myself. Taller than most girls of eleven and quite thin too, I felt shy as I was introduced to my new classmates. The teacher was a kind and friendly looking man in his late fifties from what I remember. The first few weeks I struggled to catch up with the other children as by then I had missed two weeks before Christmas and two weeks after. It was decided I should be sent down to class two, to join the less able children. My Dad was upset about this and to his further annoyance the results of the eleven plus were out and I had failed! The word **FAIL** had never come into my world before and though Dad tried to hide his disappointment, I felt the negative vibe from him. He did however get me a second hand two wheeler bike (the carrot he had dangled before me as an incentive to try to pass the exam) that he had promised.

All three teachers over those past couple of years were, I think, my Shaman! All friendly, learned men with kind hearts. Mr Brown in particular had a sort of healing vibe in his aura. However, the person making me think about deeper spiritual things the most, was just a little boy with his memories of a past life.

Reader ... Have you any memory of your own past lives, or ever felt affinity with someone instantly at a first meeting? If you have then you are probably an old soul that has been brought back to the material sphere to help or guide others.

Reader... This is the RUNE Gebo

The RUNE Gebo is said to represent partnership, interaction, unity with the self, with another or with nature, the universe, with God.

6/ Tarot lesson, THE HIEROPHANT/POPE.

Card No 5. The sixth lesson of the TAROT... The Pope, High Priest, Shayman, Friendly Advisor.
Song...'Heartbeat'...Singer...Version ...Buddy Holly...1958

The Hierophant is the spiritual part of the nature of man. He represents the Teacher, the Friend or the Shaman. A healer, priestly honest man we may trust to give advice, a person that gives gentle guidance. It is the kind of energy we may think of as that which was said to have been given out by Jesus around the sick. It is a widely held belief that the image on this card may have originally been a depiction of Jesus. We know the head of the Roman Catholic faith is the Pope and as such he is said for his followers to be the earthly representative of the Lord of Christianity, Jesus.

The image on this card is of a regal looking man sitting between the Pillars of Hermes and Solomon, wearing a headdress and long flowing robes. On most designs he has his arms crossed with two fingers raised in an esoteric gesture in front of him and he leans on a staff/ wand/ cross. Two people are sat at his feet as if waiting on his words. His expression is one of serenity as if speaking words of inspiration.

The lesson from the Hierophant is to try to tune into our own God. Believe we can get help from a higher force, our Angel. Our guide or from another human we think of as having the answers! He is the opposite or male equivalent to the High Priestess. The two are the Ying and Yang of the God energy. In life there may be times when we find it hard to tune into our higher self for an answer to a quandary, it is then we may look for someone to give us true guidance, it is then that the Hierophant may be looked for in earthly form. Wisdom learned from the teacher or close male we trust.

In some Tarot designs the words printed at the bottom of this card is 'The Priest' said to represent the godly energy that was used by Jesus for healing and for his affinity with children. In divination he can be an actual doctor, teacher or a man of orthodox religion such as Vicar or Minister. In most cultures there is a figure in the community or tribe that is the wise man, the Shaman or doctor/ healer. A kind of emergency 'go to' person that gives out help of all kinds. In modern culture for the world of today there are many titles that would fit the description of the Hierophant but the most apt in my opinion is the trusted Teacher, Doctor, Minister or Herbalist.

In divination the card will most often represent a gentle kind of man. A friend or even sometimes a good partner or kindly boss. In reverse the card can represent a break with faith, or an outwardly unassuming man with a more selfish motive. It was during the next section of my life I would meet my first unusual male friend, my first Hierophant!

Reader... Do you give or take advice when needed? Could you be a natural healer? If you think you may have a natural gift for caring or guiding others, then take time to draw in the 'God' energy' from the sound and colour vibrations of the natural world... Take in the energy first and then you can direct it out through your thoughts in meditation. Many 'seers' believe that this universal energy can be tapped into if we step back from all the 'white noise' and stress of everyday life.

For me it only takes a moment to draw in some extra energy by visualisation. In my mind I put up a blank screen and then let the rainbow spectrum fill my 'Earth' body and expand the rainbow out into my aura, the astral body. This is called cleansing the aura. The violet light is particularly energising. This should be done before healing or attempting to use the Tarot or any means of divination in order to allow a pure view. Try this yourself to just lift your spirits.

Reader...This is the RUNE Teiwaz

The RUNE Teiwaz is another protection symbol as it is said to represent the Warrior. It is the spear that defends and as such was thought to be the male leader of the tribe or family, a masculine strength.

Chapter 7

Early 1960's

These years were to change me for ever! I would no longer be the fairly quiet shy little girl of the 1950's. By the eve of my engagement on 5th November 1967 there would be many frogs to kiss before meeting my prince! There were also many ghosts and strange events. These events seemed to gather momentum during my thirteenth and fourteenth years.

The growing up period of anyone's life, the 'puberty' years, are probably a little painful for most of us, for me this period of life was to be the sharpest learning curve of my entire life! Not only learning more about boys, men and the art of flirting, but learning there are more aspects to this world than those taught in school! For most of the time life was probably what can be termed 'normal', but for the poltergeist/ spirit experiences. These could never be termed normal! Mum and I became convinced that the house had some kind of supernatural entity because of all the strange activity. Dad refused to believe it. The strange energy that pervaded the house during the hours of darkness would dissipate in the light of day. Dad was so focused on his new job and working long hours he was often asleep or out at night.

The only good thing I had found from the embarrassment of being sent down a class in the last year of junior school, was that I would sit near cute blond James from our estate, in the same class. I had developed a little crush on James after meeting him at the 'police' children's Christmas party. The crush was not to last long, as he for ever blotted his copybook as far as I was concerned, when he asked me if I would show him my bottom!

A good thing that came from being in class two was a friend I made called Norma. She and I would soon find we were to be in the same class as we went into Penwortham Secondary Modern school. Norma, and Rose, (my other new friend) would become like the three musketeers throughout the rest of our school days. We still keep in touch to this day!

Norma, Rose and I would spend many of our Saturdays together. We would mostly spend the afternoon at Worsley's Dance Academy though that depended on what film was on at the Cinema. We loved 'The Young Ones' and 'Summer Holiday' with Cliff. They were not as keen as I was on Elvis. They thought it more patriotic to like the English pop stars. My heart belonged in 'Blue Hawaii' with Elvis! From other trips to the Cinema with Peggy during the 1950's, I had been enamoured by the more 'Rock and Roll' Elvis. To this day there is a little of the 'Rock Chick' still alive within my aged bones and my hubby and can still be tempted to get up for a jive to 'Jail House Rock'!

The dance classes were a mixture of bliss and embarrassment. Bliss if asked to dance and the feeling of bitter rejection if not asked. In those days it was not the done thing for a girl to ask a lad to dance. My own dilemma at the time was being five foot eight and a half, when the boys of my age were almost all five foot five. I had to reach up to make the required ballroom hold. The dance teacher was quite strict on the rules of the dance hall. Our main thrill on dance afternoons was on the way home where we would stop off at the coffee bar near the bridge at Broadgate. Older boys and girls would gather there around the juke box and we would sit and watch. Later the television series 'Happy Days' would remind me of these 'coffee bar' excursions!

Mum was at home in the early 1960's looking after my brother John and also two other young children, as their mothers worked part time. I don't know how she found time, but we always had home cooked meals at tea time.

Friday; mum made apple pie, and a sandwich cake smothered in icing sugar. The wonderful smells would greet me as I came in from school. Mum and I would sit and have a cup of tea and she would ask me to look at the pattern of the tea leaves left at the bottom of the cup. 'See what you can see? She would say. This was all a bit of fun for me and we would ponder on what the patterns might indicate in relation to our lives and the family. Never in a million years could I have thought that things I would see and describe could really connect at a later date with events that happened. Being a fairly level headed Capricorn my early psychic experiences were always a source of puzzlement. For many years I would look for a rational scientific explanation for any psychic and paranormal happenings. Later I would look for answers from many books.

By 1962 my Grandfather Ted was very poorly and there was a dark cloud over our visits to Manchester. At the time I had no experience of anyone so sick or of death apart from at the Cinema. I knew Ted had a bad cough from when we lived at Manchester but now it became obvious that there would be no recovery. We went to stay and help out by taking turns to sit by the bedside. When it was my turn to sit by the bed Ted was delirious and rambling and trying to get out of bed all the time. By now he was just a pale shadow of himself and seemed not to know me. This would be the last time I would see him alive. The next day Ted passed away in his sleep. The Woodbines had finally got the better of him.

On the morning of the funeral I was to look after my brother in the sitting room. No one told me the coffin was in the parlour, though I had been told not to let John go in there. Mum and gran were in the kitchen making the food when John escaped me and ran to the parlour. I tried to stop him opening the door. 'What is that?' John cried as he looked into the coffin. In shock we looked at the white shrouded figure and deathly unrecognisable face. I quickly led John out.

To my eyes this was not Ted. I was not upset at what I saw but the sight had confirmed my belief that the body is just a shell, a cloak for us to wear whilst in this life. My worry was that John might be upset or confused.

After the funeral the house was full of relations and puzzlingly they seemed quite jolly! It was like a real Irish wake! John must have had a slight notion of what he had seen but he and I never spoke about it. He did not understand and I was too shocked at the sight of the body that looked nothing like the alive Ted! Granny put on a brave face. Our granddad had gone and after the wake, a strange quiet heavy atmosphere settled on the house.

Back at home life went on as normal but we would go to see granny every third weekend if dad was off work. Life was full through the week as there was much going on in the world to take our minds off family matters. Dad loved his job as a police sergeant on traffic but soon he would be chosen to be the first police 'Eye in the Sky' on watch from a helicopter. His flying lessons earlier had clinched it for him thanks to grandma May. With our move to Preston my parents had made many new friends and would go to police events together. There are photographs of them both dancing together and in a group photo with the other two Sergeants, their wives and all the other Bobbies and their partners at a Christmas dance. There was much comradeship amongst the men in Lancashire Police Traffic division. There was a great feeling of belonging on the estate, all the houses being occupied by police families.

Now at Penwortham Secondary school, the fifth school I had attended, I was to catch a bus on my own each morning. With a ride of four stops to get there, I was glad I would soon find a companion to go with. Pam, one year older than me, had moved in round the corner from us. I went round to ask if she would like me to call for her on my way to school.

Pam was the kind of person who didn't like to hurry. To say she was 'laid back' would be the under statement of the year. She was still wearing her old pale blue jumper from her last school. Our uniform should have been dark blue. When the teachers remarked on this Pam just shrugged. She also ignored the rules for wearing a beret hat. It should be worn on the top of the head at all times on the way to and from school was the mantra the head mistress used.

Each morning when I called for Pam she would be savagely back combing her hair to make it into a perfect Bee hive shape. This would often make us late and we had to run hell for leather to catch the bus at 8.20 a.m.

Evenings would see Pam and I starting to hang out with a few other teenage kids from our estate. The favourite place to do this became the big old Oak tree on the corner, a few yards from my front door. When we joined the 'group' all the talk was about the Cuban crisis going on between

America and Cuba, with the Russians somehow involved. As the situation got worse and tension mounted our parents watched the news, whilst us kids would talk about what each of us would do if Russia decided to go nuclear. One lad said he would grab a blond, pinch an E-type Jag and drive into the sunset. Fear had gripped us all. Thankfully president Kennedy of America saved the day.

Before long I learned Pam was keen to become a hair dresser. She was not remotely interested in any studies and to my shame I have to admit her attitude did rub off on me. We would avidly browse through hair magazines looking at styles. It wasn't long before I too had the required back combed Barnett, so we were often on the later bus to school. We were reprimanded by one particular prefect, Natalie, on playground duties on a regular basis. Disrespectfully, we called her 'Nag bag Nat'. Each day 'Nag bag' would be waiting at the school entrance and loved to threaten us with dreaded punishment if she decided to tell Mr Wood (the most feared teacher of the school) Each morning 'Nag bag' would sneer and get out her little book for naming girls that she thought, should be 'shamed'. (More about her later in my story.) The reprimand was not only for our late arrival but for wearing our hats on the back of the head, (so as not to disturb the beehive). All told, the telling off we got most mornings only served to turn us into slightly petulant teenagers.

We became more interested in music and fashions than into school work, but a fear of failing pulled me up just in time before exams. Pam seemed to have more spending power than me so we would go into town at the weekend and visit the record shop. This was a new experience for me and I was fascinated to see that one could go into a booth and listen to a record before buying it. Pam bought a new record most weeks and we would call for another friend Sue whose sister Kathy, worked in the record shop so that the three of us could go into town to listen to the latest hits. We were in admiration of Kathy, not only because of her dream job but also of her fashionable clothes.
Before the Beatles popularity, Kathy was mad on the Everly Brothers. We would hear the tune 'Kathy's Clown' belting out of the window as we passed her house at the end of our road. Sometimes we would listen in

their sitting room whilst waiting for Sue. Living close to each other we would spend our after school time together. At school I spent time with Jan and Norma but as they lived near School they spent their evenings together. Jan was good at sports and this won her a place as a prefect during the third year. It was great when she was on playground duties as she let us classmates into the locker room to listen to music on a transistor radio.

At school we were not too impressed with the lads in our class. For one thing they were rather unmannerly and loud. It was a painful experience when there was a dance class prior to the Christmas festivities. The third year girls were all sat along one side of the hall, the third year boys along the other. Teachers in the middle of the room demonstrated how to do a waltz. The boys were asked to choose a partner. The girls must be polite and accept the offer to dance (no choice) with any boy that asked them. This was okay unless you were the unlucky girl who did not get chosen. For my part I would rather have not been chosen than having been picked by a boy a foot smaller with large boots and no rhythm. Worse was to come later when my mother arranged a dance class in town with 'big boots'. Oh the embarrassment!

We were on a family visit to Manchester when gran got some exciting news. Her brother Jack Morris, who lived down in Ken, had phoned to tell her he had won just over £16,000 on the football pools. Back during the war years, gran had housed Jack's wife Dora and their two children as the bombing down south had become severe. They had lodged with gran for almost two years. Though Manchester got its fair share of the bomb raids, it was considered more 'safe' than Kent. Jack was the youngest of the Morris family and had met Dora when his ship had docked at Southampton before the war.

We were all thrilled for Jack as he was not well and by all accounts Dora's health was even worse. Gran told us that Jack was coming to visit her soon and bringing Dora and his family for us all to have a night out in Manchester together. Uncle Jack wanted to splash the cash and in the 1960's the amount he had won could set someone up for life.

That night sleeping in gran's room with her, I had a dream that I was in a beautiful garden with blossom trees and I saw a stream flowing into a pond full of golden fish. The dream was quite vivid. There was a Pagoda house with a path leading up to the entrance. The dream ended as I got to the open door at the end of a winding path.

When Jack and Dora travelled south, gran wanted them to stay with her for a few days and we were invited to come for a celebration party. We had a right old knees up and it cheered gran no end seeing her brother. Jack was always the joker of the family and he had not changed at all. He was amused when gran put on a 'Twist' record and I showed him this new dance. We all had a great evening and the next day we went to see the new film '55 Days in Peking'. The film was shown on a new cinema screen with surround sound and a curved screen. After the film we went for a Chinese meal. Never having been to a Chinese restaurant before I was mesmerised. The colours and clothes were a big delight to me. I felt somehow, this culture had resonated within my soul, as my dream had taken me to a Pagoda garden like this before.

A few weeks later, gran and I were to visit Jack and Dora for a short holiday. Dad would drive us down to Kent in his battered old car. Dad, mum and John would holiday on the South Coast. The car was an old Ford with a faulty back door catch that might fly open. No time to fix it so we all got in. Dad tied a rope from one door, over three pairs of legs to the other door. Gran May sat back right, John in the middle, mum behind me. Because of travel sickness I went front left. Off we went!

After a few miles a torrent of rain poured down. Gran May mumbled that her feet were getting wet. Dad said not to worry we would stop as soon as we passed Birmingham. Traffic was slow, the rain was lashing down. May said again, that her feet were wet. Dad said not to worry we would stop soon. When we eventually found a place to stop, we saw the foot well was five inches deep in water. Poor gran had not liked to complain but her feet had been under water and her shoes were ruined.

Reader... This is the RUNE Ansuz

Tradition has this Rune as the messanger. The God Loli is the ancient bringer of news. He is known to the American Indians as well as the Norse people.

7/ Tarot lesson, THE LOVER, or LOVERS

Card No 6. The Seventh Lesson of the TAROT... Choice, Unity, Bonding, Partnership.
Song... 'Let's Twist!'... Singer...Version... Chubby Checker

*The Lovers of the Tarot are depicted in the Garden of Eden. The traditional image is of a man standing between two women at a crossroad. One woman wears a circlet of gold on her head, the other has her hair hanging loose about her shoulders. A Cherub holding a bow and arrow flies above them. This represents the **choice** between **Vice** and **Virtue**. From the bible we see Adam with his choice before him. On some more modern cards there are two Lovers standing together hand in hand, or side by side. An Angel hovers over them. We note the plants and animals on the card. In the tree we see the snake, often depicted hanging from a branch of a tree quite close to the two figures. The snake on the card is there to remind us there is always temptation. The snake has long been a symbol of sexual energy. As we become aware of our own sex drive during puberty we face the trials of searching for a partner. With choice, the interpretation of this card can link to attraction, with problems to overcome for a young person in choosing a mate during his or her promenading years.*

For all partnerships there will be decisions and we must take care not to let one stinging word spoil a precious moment. The negative aspect of this card would be failure or a foolish choice with reactions leading to restrictions of our chosen path. We may need to kiss a frog or two in order to recognise our true partner when he or she comes along! Perhaps we are reminded that lovers will always be tested in order to make stronger a true bond, or to break a weak one. A taste of false love will make us appreciate the real thing if and when we find it. After all we know that the old saying is 'The path of true love never ran smoothly!'

The choice if this card is chosen is not always about romantic love. The traditional interpretation is about right and wrong path. There may be many prospective partners we could meet and unity is just one aspect when this card appears. A close friendship bond, a love tie, or a business partnership, if of significance may link to the meaning of choice in divination. We may also face choices throughout life that link to partnership. Where to live, if or not to have children, who is to be the bread winner? If love should fail we have to decide if to stay, or would it be better to go?

So then, we understand that the Lovers card indicates a choice that may affect two persons initially, then may have bearing on others around them. The choice of partner might affect the rest of our family and friendships. When making a decision it will often have 'ripples on the pond' effect. Reader... Have you been tempted to take the hard road rather than the easier one? What have you learned from any mistakes you made? After reading Tarot for many people that have had a troubled love life I have to say that it's no use clinging on to a relationship if feelings are one sided. Both lovers must be equally committed to each other.

Chapter 8

1962 - 1964

One rainy afternoon several girls from my class were huddled in a doorway at the back of school, all ears towards the small transistor radio one of the girls had brought. The D.J. announced the new sound of the sixties would be on next, this was a début record of a group of Lancashire Lads named The Beatles. 'Love me Do!' was the song. From that moment on the name and style of the 'Fab four' would sing out from television, radio, and record player all over Britain.

What a thrill it was for us girls to know that four cute boys from 'our' Lancashire had become overnight music giants. The Mersey sound had arrived. The world would never be the same again! George was my favourite but we were all in love with a Beatle! Mod or Rocker was the big question at school in the early sixty's? Loving Rock and Roll made me a Rocker, yet the buzz of the 'Mersey Sound' blasting from transistor radios everywhere was 'FAB!'

In the third year of Secondary school the fashions and culture changed with the advent of 'THE BEATLES'. On our trips each Saturday in 1961/62 we would dress in the full skirted dresses with the 'can can' underskirts. Later top model, Jean Shrimpton, was our inspiration. Pointed toe shoe and shiny slacks were a fad, but by 1963/64 the model we wanted to copy was Twiggy. 'Mini skirts' had arrived! I had acquired a Gold leather look, long line jacket. The trip to town had been to purchase school uniform but in C & A, I managed to persuade mum that the jacket was a life or death issue! Whilst on a visit with gran to Uncle Jacks, we went to Torquay and he bought me some brown shoes and slacks with a gold thread running through, so the jacket was a perfect look.

Whilst in the shop in Torquay the band 'The Kinks' had turned up in the shoe department at the same time as we did. They were all trying on Chelsea boots and acting the fool with each other. It made my day, but the assistants were looking a bit frazzled as they tried to serve them all.

By the third year of secondary school we all wanted the new trendy gear that had the flavour and style of Carnaby Street. A must for weekend outings was the black polo neck sweater, a leather or leather look skirt with hem line about five inches above the knee. Another must for the trendy girl was black high leg boots with pointed toe. Mine were stiletto with zip down the outside of the leg with a small chain and a silver coin on the end. White plastic boots only became a trend in the second half of the 1960's and as these were more a 'mod' trend I never wore them. For me the Rocker image would only take a back seat, when hippy psychedelic garments of the 'Flower Power' era arrived! An alternative to the black polo was the white shirt blouse. This was handy as a school shirt would do if one had no polo sweater.

At school the 'rule' of skirt length was no more than two inches above the knee. Letters were sent out to parents stating this. Mothers all over England were probably keeping a close eye on their daughters to make sure this rule was followed. Daughters all over England went out of the door each morning with skirts of the required 'respectable' length and on the way to school would turn over the waistband of their skirts to the 'trendy' length of six inches above the knee. It was considered worth a reprimand from the teacher in order to appear 'with it'! Another style from the early, to mid, 1960's that any trendy teenage girl would not be seen without, was the bouffant hair do. An essential tool for this was the back comb. Each morning Pam and I would do the back combing for each other, necessary to get the desired hair lift.

The school beret had to be pinned to the back of the head so as not to squash the beehive effect. Mum was not a fan of my hair style and had once talked me into letting her do a home perm for me. The perm was a disaster and I had to go to school looking like a grannie. After many of my complaints mum paid for me to go to have a professional cut. On my return she remarked that my 'Cilla Black' hair do was shaped like an orange. Though she probably never meant this as a compliment, I took it as one at the time.

Friday night was the youth club disco. Saturday was the local village hall dance. The events were quite different. The Youth club was 'tame' as it was overseen by an adult and generally frequented by just school children. The dance was for sixteen to twenty something's and often a quite rowdy affair.

We lived for Saturday and would often go to watch a friend Colin play in a band, with his brother Rob and two other lads from our estate, all squeezed into Colin's dad's van!

It was around the start of the Beatles era that my dreams became more 'real' and more dramatic. One dream that would reoccur for the next three decades was about flooding. In the dream I would wake up as heavy rain was beating against my window. On looking out, I would see the water level outside rising quickly. I would go to the landing and small animals such as mice, rats and hedgehogs were running up the stairs to avoid drowning. It would seem the house was empty and I would start to panic. How to get out? I pulled out the top draw of my dressing table to use it as a raft, thinking to get out of my bedroom window. At the point of pulling out the draw I would awaken. This dream remained the same whilst I lived in that house but changed later, with the lay of the land around my next three homes, but more about that later! Today we know the sea levels are rising and we are said to be in the grip of global warming. I hope not, but think now these dreams were prophetic of what the future may hold for our part of England in years to come!

My interest in boys during the first three years of the 1960's was limited to a shy flash of eye contact at the Christmas party at police headquarters, or a shy smile at the Saturday dance class. That was up until a family holiday to Pontins holiday camp in Wales. By this time the new dance craze, 'The Twist' had become all the rage. At the holiday camp there was a large ballroom. A dance class took place each afternoon for adults then at a later time for children. After the evening meal in the camp dinning hall, there would be an hour of dance and music for the children, held in the ballroom. Later the adults would start to gather for the ballroom style of dance. The dance teacher was a guy named Raymond. He was in his late twenties and looked a bit like Cookie from '77 Sunset Strip', a hit programme on telly at the time.

During the day, Mum and I looked round the camp site whilst Dad and my little brother John went to swim. In the window of a dress shop I spotted a 'Twist dress' that had become the in fashion for all trendy girls.
'Please Mum!' was my cry for the next few days. Mum eventually gave in to my demand and bought me the dress.

My new 'Twist dress' was very fitted with a section at the knee that flared out to accentuate the movement as one attempted to do the hip swivel of the dance. It had to look as if stubbing out a cigarette under both feet! This was done to the music of Chubby Checker. Dad was not too happy when he saw me dressed for the evening dance. He said my dress was too old for me, but Mum had the last say, and we all went of to the ballroom, me feeling very pleased with myself. The dress got me a lot of attention from Raymond but we were under the watchful eye of Dad. The evening may have turned out more like 'Dirty Dancing', me as 'Baby' but, there was to be nothing more 'flirty' than a 'Cha-Cha-Cha'. That evening I felt no longer the 'ugly duckling', a swan was trying desperately to break free!

Back on home turf the 'Twist Dress' was only allowed at the police youth club worn with 'Bobby socks'. Then 'cool' Raymond became a distant memory. As always Mum had the last word when I wanted to go to the Christmas party in stockings rather than short socks. Dad reluctantly gave in and I donned my first pair of flesh coloured silk nylons along with the required suspender belt. The club was highly supervised by dad or another bobby to make sure the teenagers were kept under control. I got a few admiring looks from the boys, but there were none that took my eye as they all seemed far too young after my brief flirtation with Raymond.

By the time I had reached the important and much desired milestone of my fourteenth birthday just after the emergence of the nylons I was asked out by an older boy, Rick. His father was one of the superiors in the police. Whilst I was thrilled to be asked out I can honestly say the young man in question never made my heart flutter even a little. The proposed date did put me in a quandary as I had never been out for the evening alone after dark with anyone before. What would dad say?

After me telling Rick to ask my dad if I could go out with him, there was a knock on the back door. I waited in silence as Rick politely asked. Dad looked up from the newspaper with a deep frown. 'No!' Was his reply 'do you know my daughter is only just turned fourteen?' To give him his due Rick stood his ground, whilst I was wishing it would swallow me. 'Girls of fourteen are very grown up these days Mr Smith!' He said. I thought my dad would explode. He just growled 'Get out!' in an unmistakable termination to the conversation.

Though I was not too bothered about Rick or the none date outcome it would be some months later before my first date with a boy, and I would never ask any boy to my house for the next year or so if dad was at home.

When dad was on night duties mum and I would go to bed around ten o'clock. By now we had become quite convinced of there being some strange energy in the house. Of late there had been an increase in the clunks and bumps during the hours of darkness.

One night a few weeks before Christmas we went to bed as usual. Mum always took the poker to leave next to the bed when dad was on nights. Mum felt the house was more vulnerable for burglars being close to the main Preston to Liverpool Road. I slept on dad's side of their bed, John would sleep on a (folding) Z bed at the end of the big bed.

One particular night we had gone to bed early as both mum and I would like twenty minutes read before sleep. After a while mum switched off the light. Mum had checked the door was locked. As soon as the light went out there was a noise as if someone was climbing the stairs. It sounded as if a heavy man with one wooden leg was climbing up and down the stairs. 'What on earth is it?' mum said. My heart was thumping and we were both shaking as the noise became louder and then softer as if whoever it was kept on going up and down. Mum quickly switched the light on. The sound receded a little but we thought we could hear breathing. Each time mum switched off the light the noise grew louder. When the light was switched on the noise abated. This went on a few times then we decided to leave the light on.

When we got up at first light after being awake all night we expected to see signs of the activity but found nothing amiss. When dad came in we told him of our midnight visitation and he laughingly said it would just have been the house settling and we should not let our imaginations run riot. In the cold light of day, we tried to convince ourselves that dad was right and it must have been the house. In truth we both knew there was more to it but we had to face the next night and so it was better to kid ourselves there was nothing to worry about.

The next night mum did the usual checks. Doors all locked, even the bedroom door, poker by the side of the bed. We climbed in and all was quiet until mum turned off the light. The noises came again and this time seemed to be footsteps right up to the bedroom door, then a moment of quiet, then thud, thud, thud! 'Oh God!' mum cried, 'what in Hells name is it?' It had sounded as if someone was bumping on the bedroom door with the flat of their hand. Mum switched on the light and the noise stopped. We lay huddled together and left the light on. After this we always left the light on. Still, now and again we would hear the footsteps on the stairs and a single bump on the door. We didn't talk about these things too much; It was as if by talking about it we may give it more power. Dad claimed not to ever hear the night noises and in deed there was not as much to hear whenever he was at home.

Mum and I had little sleep each third week as dad was on night shift. We still could hear footsteps on the stairs but less often now with the light left on. An added safety precaution was the clothes pegs wedged under the gap at the bottom of the door. Though the bumps on the door had stopped we would hear the sound of creaking and sometimes breathing, outside the bedroom door. It was extremely unnerving.

One Christmas eve when dad was on nights we were in bed after filling a pillow case with toys for John, his Z bed was at the foot of the big bed. We had waited, staying up late, until we knew John was fast asleep. After a few moments reading, mum switched off the light. Almost right away we heard a rustling as if John was rooting through the packaged gifts. Mum switched on the light. The rustling stopped and John was still fast asleep. This happened many times before we were once again forced to sleep with the light on or just stay awake.

Mum was always the go between for me when I wanted to get round dad. She would often persuade him to let me go to evening events such as birthday parties or the Cinema. There was a dance each Saturday night at St Mary's church hall in Penwortham. Pam and I were desperate to attend. This time it was mum who but the blocks on for me! 'No you are too young to be out so late at night!' Not until you leave school.' was the response mum gave when I asked her if I could go. I tried persuasion but this time mum was not for giving in. My plan was to bide time for a week or two then try asking again.

Promising not to be out late if I could attend the dance I tried asking again. Mum was not to budge! To my shame I came out with a nasty remark that was like a slap in the face to mum. We had both raised our voices and as I shrieked the remark at her there was a **whoosh** and **crash** as a heavy framed photograph flew off the sideboard and across the sitting room to land between us on the kitchen floor. The photograph showed Ted and grandma May next to mum and dad on their wedding day. In shock we both looked at each other. 'There must have been a gust of wind.' said mum. I thought this was an absurd suggestion as the windows were closed. 'It can't have been wind as these other little cardboard framed photos would have blown off too!' I pointed out. We both knew there was something weird going on!

Dad brought home a tiny little puppy. It had been found and we were to look after it until it was claimed. We named it Pip. Mum told me she felt safer with a dog in the house but she changed her mind when each evening when dad was at work, it would sit growling at an unseen object in the corner of the living room. Pip would cry each night if we left him downstairs when we went to bed so in the end, he it slept with us. Once again when dad was on nights there seemed to be an odd energy in the house. There was again a weird noise on the stairs. Pip was shaking and would not stop a low growling even though she was in the bedroom with us. 'I can't stand any more of this!' I said and pulled the pegs from under the bedroom door and unlocked it. 'Don't go down', mum pleaded in a loud whisper.

I just had to see what or who was causing the disturbance. There was nothing in the sitting room. Nothing at all was visible downstairs, but the house still felt somehow alive. With a strong feeling of someone watching me I hurried back to bed! Would this thing, haunt us for ever? Things would quieten down for a while but then the noises would start again. Mum was on the ragged edge even before we got into the bedroom and said it was a haunted house and yet dad would have none of it.

We got used to less sleep when dad was on nights as it was hard with the light on and if it were off, the noises were too scary. By the run up to Christmas 1964 we would have another visitation and this time it was actually in the bedroom. Mum had a basket weave stool at her bedroom table. Each time the light was off the sound of crackling would start, as if the stool were being sat on. When the light went back on the that would stop. Again this told us that darkness gave the entity some power. In my mind I thought of this 'ghost' as a man, though I cannot say why, it was just a sense, a feeling.

Determined to get to the bottom of all the nocturnal bumps, thuds and knocking, despite mum's objection, I would now often go out of the bedroom to look downstairs. The noises would stop the moment I ventured out of the room. The house would then feel at peace again. Who was this entity and why was he hanging around our home?

Many years later after I had started running a meditation group to raise funds for a charity, one of the girls, Margaret, told me she had had many dreams of a scary man hiding in the woods next to where we lived. Her family had lived on the police estate, just around the corner from our house on Lindle Lane. When I asked Margaret what she thought the man looked like, she said he was unkempt and dirty looking, with a straggly beard. That description would fit exactly with the image I had in my mind when we had been plagued with the phantom menace.

During this time, mum and I did not connect the 'spooky' happenings with our liking to 'read' the tea leaves. The two things seemed so different as in the daylight hours the house felt quite normal and cosy. Also, my reading of the leaves had now started to produce some accurate information. Were we dabbling with the dark side and attracting some kind of lower entities? That had not crossed my mind as we were still trying to find some kind of rational explanation for the noises.

Reader... Look after your body, it is the vestal that caries around your soul. Bravely go forth on to the next adventure in life. Conquer your fears. There is nothing to fear from a departed spirit. If you feel a presence in your home, then send the lost soul love and ask them to fly away to their freedom.

8/ Tarot lesson The CHARIOT

Card 7. The eight lesson of the TAROT... Progress. Movement. Triumph. Travel Song...'Love me do!'...Band...Version... The Beatles.

THE CHARIOT.

The Chariot is depicted facing us on the card and is pulled by two horses, (on more ancient packs two sphinxes) one black and one white. It gives the impression of arrival at an important destination. A man, sceptre in hand is thought to be riding to victory. This can indicate a new place or experience where customs and surroundings are new to us, initiation. We shall ride forward with confidence. The horses are reminding us of the two energies that are always with us, or the two sides to the one energy. Will we find the positive outcome or the negative one when we alight from the chariot? If presented reversed in divination, the outcome may be lack of confidence for any challenge ahead, or getting cold feet. A modern interpretation is that the person riding the Chariot represents us, the individual. In any new situation we have to face, we can either front it out, or act confident so as not to let ourselves down. There is nothing to fear if we are willing to adjust and adapt to the new place or new people we may meet. Life is always throwing up change and we must therefore embrace the next challenge.

The divination meaning of the Chariot is Progression, triumphant in the new challenge. Movement and discovery of the wider world also links to the interpretation. Meetings, interviews, travel and adventure into the unfamiliar. The Chariot is just the means of getting there. The body conveys us on our journey through life just as an actual vehicle conveys us to new places. Sometimes the Chariot can depict road transport or over land journey. The motto is to go forth and experience new places and people. Adapt to change! Change from child to adult, from single to partnership or work into retirement. Any challenge of life can be linked to this card. Be not afraid of change! Be the victor of your present incarnation. Would my new 'adolescent self' adapt to the challenges ahead?

Reader... If you are on the verge of some new chapter of life let the 'Chariot' lesson guide you to face it with bravado. Life is an adventure and as such a new experience will be of value. New places, new faces, and with each face a person we may share with, sometimes good, sometimes not so good but all a stich in the rich fabric of our life.

Chapter 9

1960's continued

During the summer of 1963 my Auntie Joan had been the topic of whispered words between mum and dad. I later learned Joan and her husband; Len had parted due to his infidelity. Not only had he been caught with a barmaid that worked in his pub, but during the argument that ensued he had hit poor Joan with a bag of cash. When we next went to visit granny and granddad we found Joan had moved into her old bedroom. Later Joan went back to Len for a short time but he had not changed his ways and before long she was back again with her mum and dad.

Granny bought Joan a record player to try and cheer her up. When we went at the weekends she would put on a brave face as I would show her the latest dance craze. There were lighter moments as Joan tried to pick up the threads of her life. She returned to her former occupation of hairdressing for a short time. I was amused when she told me of doing a special hair dye job on a group of local lads that had started a band. Later we saw the band on television. It was Freddie and the Dreamers!

Auntie Joan had never had any children, Len never wanted any! Joan and I had strengthened our bond further as she had often taken me with her on holiday. She and Len would always holiday at different times due to the fact he would not leave the pub he owned in the hands of outsiders. For a year or so after they parted life seemed to improve for Joan but then she became very poorly.

When later Joan came to stay with us mum told me she was recovering from a serious operation. Joan looked so sad all the time. Though she seemed recovered from the first operation, she would later have to undergo more surgery. Mum and I would go to Manchester some weekends and I would accompany Joan to the cinema or the Catholic church hall bingo session. Soon this would not be possible as Joan became gravely ill.

After granddad Ted passed away and whilst Auntie Joan lived at grandma's, mum and I had felt a strange atmosphere and heard noises in the night in our own home. Mum was convinced by all this 'poltergeist' activity that our house was haunted. That was until one weekend when we were at gran's. Mum wanted to clean up and make tea as a surprise before Joan and gran would be home from work. I was reading a book in the sitting room and mum was busy in the kitchen. Suddenly there was an almighty crashing noise from upstairs. Mum rushed into the room ashen faced and asked me what the heck I thought it may be? 'Come upstairs with me' mum pleaded. We slowly climbed the stairs, mum brandishing the poker in one hand in case we encountered an intruder. We expected to see the bedroom ransacked, furniture broken from the sound of the noises we had heard. Nothing was out of place! There was an unnatural silence and I felt as if the house was like the eye of the storm, deathly quiet!

Mum sent me next door to ask if the neighbours had heard any banging noise. The parents were out and the boy next door came to answer as I knocked. 'Did you hear all that crashing and banging just a few moments ago?' I asked him. 'No' he replied with a totally blank look on his face. Nothing was spoken about our experience when Joan and gran came home, but mum and I would never forget the noises and would puzzle over whatever could have caused them, for years to come.

Back at home and with the normality of school I had begun to notice some of the boys and they seemed to be noticing me! My first boyfriend, Stue (Stuart) was in the year above me and part of the attraction for me was his long pale blue hand knitted angora sweater. I craved a sweater like his as a short lived trend at the time was skirt just showing an inch below a long sweater. We never spoke at school but each evening would see each other at the Oak tree 'meeting place'.

From about 1962 all the teenagers on our estate would gather round the long bench each evening. Stue would arrive on his bike as he came from Penwortham a mile or so away. There was a sort of clan thing going on. Someone could only be part of the 'meeting place' gang if brought along by one of the established members. My friend Pam and I gained admittance to the gang through an older friend, Chris. At first Pam and I would stand on the edge of the gang and weigh up what was going on. It became clear that Stue had more of an interest in me than I first thought.

Now and again Mum and Dad would go to the police club. Pam and I would be left at home with John tucked up in bed. We liked to baby sit as we got a treat of a couple of shillings to go to the youth club on a Friday. The only thing we begrudged by staying in was missing an evening with the gang at the big tree meeting place. When the coast was clear of parents, Pam would go to see who was at the meeting place and if there were only three or four friends we would invite them in to play records and have a dance. To be honest there was more smooching than dancing went on!

One evening Pam just found Stue on his own waiting by the tree. Because he said he had come down just to see me she brought him in. Pam feeling a bit like a gooseberry went to help herself to a butty from the chicken mum had cooked for Sunday lunch next day. As we sat on the sofa I soon learned that quiet shy Stu was the wolf in sheep (or fluffy angora) clothing! In the vernacular of the time his problem was termed 'wandering hands disease'! I soon had more to worry about than his problem hands! Pam had helped herself to more than a picking of chicken. What would Mum say when she found half the bird gone? Soon the chicken and the fluffy jumper would recede into the mist of time. I must focus on studies! Extra concentration paid off as my position in class went up from twenty something to third that year.

Reader... Assess your life and take command of your routine to find time for play. Try always to keep perspective and balance so that you can make the most of your life. Sometimes we are hustled by others and just give in for a quiet life but there is more tranquillity in making your own pace and plan.

Reader... This is the RUNE Nauthiz

The RUNE Nauthiz is said to represent restrictions, obstacles, constraint. Need to learn and remember that the most fruitful plans/ ideas depend on divine timing.

9/ Tarot lesson, JUSTICE

Card No 8. The ninth lesson of the TAROT
Song...'Are You Lonesome Tonight'...Singer...Version...Elvis

The Justice card represents Balance, Harmony and Equilibrium. The image on the card shows a commanding figure sat on an ornate chair holding a weighing scale in their left hand and a sword in their right. The obvious link to the zodiac sign of Libra hardly needs mentioning and Libra is said to carry the scales of justice. The card may have origins in the ancient Egyptian service of weighing the heart of the dead before embalming and mummifying.

In life, we hope for fairness and all individuals that value truth and honesty, know that in the end if we believe in a God or just in good we should try to live by the rule of fair play. Even if we do not have any religion we would expect in a civilised society to have to live by the rule of law! Society begins to break down if we have neither, word of God or law to guide us. Many of us expect to get legal help if we have a crime perpetrated against us. But there is also the possibility of Karmic law in the way things might balance out. In many cultures all around the world and from ancient times there is strong belief in the law of Karma. Whatever we think of these two forms of balance there is a need for rules in order to get things done and to have a knowledge of what is expected of us by others and by society in general. It is this act of balancing that is in essence the meaning of this card.

When the Justice card appears reversed in a forecast we could think there is a need of balance in the life of the enquirer. Balance found or balance restored is what this card will often indicate. The law of the land is required and in every aspect of life there are papers or documents that we may need. We need a passport to journey to other countries, a birth certificate to register a new baby, a certificate of marriage or divorce and many other legal documents are required for a multitude of reasons. This card may often point to the need of the law itself. We often hear of the importance of a work/ life balance to maintain harmony and peace of mind. In keeping good health, we need to balance body requirements. A healthy diet, a balance of fruit, grains and vegetables. The balance of regular exercise but not to point of exhaustion. Infections or ailments can give us an imbalance. Ear infection, migraine, eye problems, or mental stress might need medical treatment to bring back equilibrim. This card is about the right path or right thinking, cause and effect. Would the next chapter of my life bring me a balance of ideals and potential?

Reader... Do you need to balance work with relaxation, or are you the peacemaker in family or with work disputes, needing to remind others of the importance of rules? Fairness and equality is the essence of this card.

Chapter 10
1963-65

As Christmas neared, along loomed a fourth year dance, my mind turned to who to invite. Stue was not now an option, but I could not go alone. There was a hoped for prospect of an invite to a fifth year dance, if some older lad gave me an invite.

It was inconceivable to me at that time to contemplate dance partners from my own age. Manners had always been important in our home and boys at school in my class seemed to do little but fart, swear and pick their noses. Yuck!

The two dances were held just before breaking up for the Christmas holiday. The first, $4^{th}/5^{th}$ Year. Out of the blue an older lad asked me to partner him. We had only spoken a couple of times at the local youth club but by the looks he gave me I was aware he had a fancy for me. He said his name was Alan, Al for short, and he wanted to be a chef. At first he seemed the perfect gentleman and I agreed to go to the dance with him and asked if he would accompany me to the 3rd year dance too. We arranged to meet at the youth club just before the first dance. He asked me to go outside with him to have a smoke. This put me off him a bit, as I had never been inclined to try smoking after seeing the brown fingers on Peggy also knowing what happened to Ted from his Woodbines.

The fact Al was a smoker had to be cast aside as pride was at stake. My friends all had partners for our 3rd year dance and one or two of them had invites to the $4^{th}/5$th year dance too. Not wanting to be the odd one out I must try to be pleasant to Al. That evening at the youth club he asked me if I would go into the bike shed. I refused! Strange as it may seem to future generations I was not sure what he was asking of me, but whatever it was I had a feeling it was something to avoid. In any case my dislike of spiders was another reason to avoid the shed. At school we had been shown a film about the life cycle of a rabbit and one about menstruation. We were also shown a diagram of a penis and one of a woman with arrows pointing to fallopian tubes etc. This was in a 1960's sex education lesson. It hardly prepared one for the question of physical intimacy with someone.

Because of the refusal I gave him Al spitefully said if I was not prepared to go 'all the way' with him I could not accompany him to the 4th/ 5th year dance. Not sure what 'all the way meant', 'Ok then you will not be coming to the 3rd year dance with me'. I retorted. My inner voice (the psychic part of the brain) told me I had not missed out on much with Al, but the practical side of my brain screamed out that I did not want to be the **loner** at the third year dance.

My short friendship with Al gone haywire, I was now left with the prospect of going alone. I realised Al was a sleaze ball but it was a big disappointment to miss out on the 5th year dance just a couple of days away. Before the 4rd year dance my friend asked me if I would invite a lad she knew, he was from the road she lived in and not at our school. Perfect! I had a date from the much admired boys of prestigious Hutton Grammar school. His name escapes me now but he was 'Prince Charming' throughout the evening, then once again, he too was a disappointment. When he walked me to the bus stop, not satisfied with a kiss he had to spoil it with an attempted grope. Could it be that all boys were dirty minded or was I being unrealistic in my expectations? After this I decided that even the Grammar school boys were off my menu!

The tea cup reading had become a long standing favourite pastime for us and by 1963 one or other of mum's friends would join us, also my new school friend Pat from round the corner. The shapes I could see would seem to form into distinct patterns and there were many and varied. Sometimes the pattern resembled an animal or building, sometimes a face, hand or foot. Often a name or initial would stand out. Could the patterns point to a meaning? If the pattern of a church was next to a horseshoe shape in the cup, we would expect to hear of a wedding. For me this was all a bit of fun and though I believed that there was a ghost or such like visiting us at night, I did not really think these tea cup symbols could possibly foretell the events of the future.

Never at that time did I connect the paranormal to my own psychic ability nor did I think the things in the tea cup would be able to tell us precise events of the future. When my mother's friend came back from a holiday and told us that the things seen from a tea cup reading previously had come true I thought it just an odd coincidence.

When mum and dad were watching T.V. my brother John and I would play a kind of 'psychic' game. We would use a pack of playing cards and I would choose one at random without showing John. He would be awarded points depending on the accuracy of his guess. I would hold the chosen card to my forehead and say to John to close his eyes before trying to guess. One point for the correct colour, obviously a 50/50 chance of being right. Five points for the right number but not the right colour. Ten points for the exact card. Two points extra for a face card. To my surprise John became so good at receiving the psychic message that I began to think the brain capable of being a transmitter and a receiver. This psychic training for the brain would later become quite useful for John as well as for me.

It was just a few weeks after Auntie Joan passed away that I had my first real psychic awakening as I now think of it! Never even with the bumps and noises in the night did I think it possible to see the spirit of someone after they had died. The popular ghost stories on television were just fantasy as far as I was concerned. The bumps and movement of objects in our home must surely have a rational scientific explanation. Dad always told mum and I that, there had to be a cause for the events we had described to him. Strangely the poltergeist only seemed active when dad was out. This was frequent as he worked long hours. 'No such things as ghosts!' he would say when we recounted the activity. He did think it strange that the carved head sculptures he had brought back from Africa during the war, would be constantly turning round. He would move them apart and turn them to face away from each other. Later they would be looking towards each other again. He would then accuse mum or me of having moved them as a prank. Mum and I had never moved from our seats and had certainly not gone into the front room where he kept the heads. John would be out or in bed and no other person had been in the house at the time!

As I described at the beginning of the book, my psychic awakening was the vision of my dear grandfather Ted. To this day the clarity of what I saw has stayed with me! Seeing granddad so clearly that night just a few weeks after Joan had passed away I used to wonder if mum was right, had I somehow fallen asleep without knowing it? NO! I am as sure as I can be that I saw what I saw.

The fact that the ghostly hand clasped mine for a few seconds makes me know. I was fully awake when I peeped from the covers. The relief I felt initially as I saw the familiar figure of my dear Ted was another reason I knew I had not dreamt it all. If I had been hallucinating, then surely I would have visualised Joan as she was the person we had just lost.

All these thoughts went round in my mind many times over during my teenage years. I began to read the bible as throughout my life many people had told me that it holds the answer to all spiritual quests. Other books found their way to me that also had a great deal of information about the workings of the mind and books about belief systems of religions other than the Christian faith I had grown up with. There were many new influences coming into the popular culture of the 1960's and by this time I was open to any new
knowledge that may help me have more understanding on the subject of the soul, and what is our destiny in this life and perhaps in the next.

For me around the time of all the poltergeist activity in our home it seemed as if I were living two lives. In one, the normal everyday school and social life with all the usual teenage interests and the other a kind of secret life of trying to follow my own quest! Reading the bible was quite a task that I had set myself and there was much in the bible that did not quench my thirst for spiritual knowledge. The bible did however confirm that even in the times before Christ there were people who experienced psychic visions. In the New Testament there were also things written about Christ that only make sense if we are open to the idea that Christ had foreknowledge of events that later proved true. Also the prophesy of the coming of Christ by John the Baptist was intriguing.

Most of us are now familiar with the story of Joseph and his dream premonitions thanks to Sir Andrew Lloyd Webber, but when I read about Joseph from the Bible, it held a very personal note for me. The dreams I have of a great flooding had become more regular and I started to have other dreams that I now know to be termed 'dreaming true'! In these dreams it feels as if one were actually standing on solid ground and the buildings and people are real even if you have never seen them in your waking life.

To this day my dreams contain people and places that seem just as real as the places and people in my daily life. The contours of faces and the bricks in a building look real, yet they are not known to me in my waking life. One such dream happened when my friend Val had come for a sleepover.

Mum and dad were going to a wedding. John was put to bed and Val and I sat and talked about all things of mystery and decided to do a bit of magic we had read about. It was said that if you wish to know the man you will marry you should pluck one hair from the crown of your head and drop it into a saucer of hot water. We were eager to do this trick and I remember the hair I dropped into the water curled round into a kind of circle. 'It could be the initial O or D!' I exclaimed. It would transpire later that 'D' was my husband's initial though I did not find that out when we first met.

When my parents returned mum came into the bedroom to tell Val and me about the wedding. 'I have brought you both a slice of cake.' She said. We were not too enthusiastic about this as neither of us liked fruit cake. 'It's not to eat, it's to put under your pillow', said mum. 'Why should we do that?' I questioned. 'Well there is an old superstition that a young girl will dream of the man she will marry if she sleeps with the cake gifted her from a new bride'. Mum explained. The cake was wrapped in foil and so we slept with it under our pillows.

That night I had one of my vivid dreams and during the dream I was swept up into the arms of a tall young man. His head was turned away from me but I could clearly make out his clothes and hair colouring. He had dark red/ brown hair and he wore a navy donkey jacket with leather patches on the elbows. When we woke up Val said she had no dream but asked me what I had dreamed. Disappointed somewhat to think I would marry a road worker and not some famous pop singer I recounted my dream. It would prove to be true a few years later when I saw the man who would become my future husband. Just three or four years later when I was eighteen my boyfriend, Dave would pick me up from work on our second date wearing a navy donkey jacket. He worked for the electricity board during his apprenticeship and the jacket was regulation attire.

Several times whilst living in the first house on the Lane a knock would come on the door and there would be a sad ragged looking person asking for food. In those days we called them tramps. Mum would give them a drink and food. One day she had just made some bacon butties and she thought the tramp would be glad of one. Later she was upset to find it in the hedge. On many occasions dad told us he had been asked by Tramps to be arrested so that they could sleep in a cell then be fed breakfast. This was a 'no-no' with the authorities but one cold Christmas Eve dad did break the rule.

Back in my last year at the school I had decided my future work must be in something artistic. Most of my friends went in for secretarial work but I knew this would never be right for me. How would I find work in an art office? I felt the need to have my own earnings and be able to contribute to the household funds. Fate would, once again lead me into the next phase of my life.

Reader... In lonely times, use the time as a gift. Further your knowledge, hone a skill or listen to music that you love.

10/ Tarot lesson, The HERMIT

Card No 9. The tenth lesson of the Tarot...Knowledge...Inner self...
Song...'Only the Lonely'... singer... version...Roy Orbinson.

The Hermit of the Tarot is shown as the cloaked figure of a Monk. He holds aloft a lantern in his right hand. In his left hand he holds a staff.

The loner element of the monk is the first aspect to take into account when trying to understand the meaning. The lantern indicates a bringing of light. The staff indicates a gaining of strength (staff of life). The staff is also the Rod or Baton of the minor arcana cards in the Tarot pack and so links to the fire element. The Hermit crab may be a link to Cancer the crab (Cancerian of the zodiac) as the original hermit was said to be the son of Neptune. Some give him his original, more ancient link to the zodiac sign of Leo. The Hermit of old was the man looking for wisdom. Study and knowledge may be the aim of his search, or stillness of the soul. This card in divination can indicate the person in pursuit of knowledge, either from books, a teacher or tutor. There could also be an aspect of life that one can only delve into if alone. The person living alone or of a reserved nature is also an aspect of the divination meaning of this card. We must all be alone at some point of life and must therefore learn to enjoy our own company.

Knowledge from the inner depths of our soul or knowledge available to us all, if we are open to it. Moments of quiet reflection can give us the peace we are looking for. This card reminds us to use our inner wisdom or study from the masters. Be silent, be prudent! In some circumstances this card can link to a period of isolation. Reversed the Hermit card shows a lack of solitude or wisdom for the enquirer. Whilst we may have to study during our schooling to get on in life we might also have periods where we need our own space. Solitude is not always a negative experience. Indirectly I would be touched by this 'Loner' aspect because of gran being now alone. There was an element of isolation in my life as I struggled to get good results from school. I often felt isolated within my thinking due to the spiritual pondering brought about by all the strange activity in my life.

Reader... Have you already learned how to be happy in your own company or do you need to find solitude in order to study or pursue a goal?

Chapter 11
1964 -1965

The last year of school life had begun with me coming to terms with the disappointment of having the form prize snatched from me even though my teacher had let slip that it would be mine. The fact that it had been given to another girl, 'the drama queen' of the class, was a bit of a blow. For my part I did not hold it against her, but was rather bitter that all the efforts I had maintained with school work had been wiped out. Why bother to try so hard if nobody cared a fig? Of course this was just a 'mind set' of my own that had built up at the time. Dad was absorbed in his work as lookout on police helicopter duties, mum was up to her eyes in young children and the form teacher had made me feel side lined. Although loving to read all the set books for the mock exams and still enjoying art, I made up my mind to 'zone out' during any lesson I was not interested in. With hind sight I know that this attitude did impact on my parents and to some extent my friends.

When it came to the dreaded time of the year for parents evening there would be yet another let down. A few weeks before, the art teacher Mr O had asked our class to make a model of anything we liked out of a Kellogg's box. This project was right up my street but just what to make? Dad came up with a great suggestion, an old sailing ship, like the old wooden pirate ships. Dad drew an outline on a sheet of paper and this made a template for the outer shape of my boat. The finished model looked like the Mayflower.

My ship had mast and sails made out of some old white pillow case and I painted the outer shell a brown wood colour and even put lines as if real beams. The project got me an 'A' that week. Mr O asked me if he could keep my piece of work to show at an art convention he was going to. 'Sorry sir, but I have already promised the ship to my brother.' I replied.

The following week and one week away from the parents evening I got another 'A' for a sketch of a girl dancing. The girl was just a figment of my mind, dressed in mini skirt and boots, she had long hair and in the background I had drawn a record player with music notes in the air. When Mr O saw it, he asked if I had copied the sketch from a magazine. 'No Sir.' I responded. This was true in so far as the whole thing was from my imagination. I had looked at fashion magazines to get the outline shape of the girl, not by tracing. 'Hum!' Reluctantly he wrote 'A' in the corner of the sketch.

Pencil sketches were my favourite hobby around this time. In return for my friend Norma helping me with math homework I often did her art homework for her. I had to make it look like she had done it or Mr O would suspect if the work was too good. In the last year I had also given a few of my 'Pop Star' sketches to one or two friends. Everyone that saw these sketches had raved about them. At a concert I gave one I had made of the singer P. J. Proby to his stage hand. He and another supporting band said it was fantastic but, pant ripping P.J. never sent me a thank you.

All the class had attended a work guidance talk prior to the forthcoming parents evening. After seeing a 'guidance' person individually, my classmates and I chatted about what work to choose for the future. For me there was no need to think, all I wanted to do was art of any kind. My secret dream was to run away to Paris and live a bohemian life in a garret in the artist quarters of the City. If this were not possible then my second choice would be to attend art collage but in my moments of realism, I knew it was better for the whole family for me to work and contribute to the home financially. During the last few weeks I had been doing shop work in a Saturday job. The job was very boring and a killer on the feet as the 'full timer' on the counter used me as a dog's body running back and forth to the store room to fill up the shelves. Still it was great to have some spending power at last.

Mum and dad came back from the parents evening looking quite downcast. They had asked to see Mr O, to get an idea of what he may suggest for me as an art work option. He had said my work was only mediocre and in his opinion it would be better to guide me in the direction of something in Care work, such a Nurse. When they told me this I almost screamed with laughter, for one thing I hated blood and secondly at that time my brother and his naughty little friends had put me off child care.

Deciding on work would have to wait as the next thing on my agenda was to earn a bit of extra cash to go to the Saturday night dances at the local church hall. Dad said I could go if Pam came with me and when he or her dad could pick us up at 10 o-clock. As most family friends were into bright colours and had admired the paper flowers I made for mum, I began to make them every evening to sell. The other things I could do that might sell for people to buy as birthday or Christmas gifts were my painted Eggs. These were little scenes of a Chinese ladies in a pagoda garden. Not sure if this was from the earlier experience of having a Chinese meal with Uncle Jack or from some kind of past life in China. My painting was done on duck eggs, strangely given me from our 'Fish man' who came each Friday in his van.

Dad would often refer to my nightly painting and flower making as being detrimental to my eye sight as I would be so absorbed in the work that I did not notice it was going dark. The miniature 'egg' painting I was often painting delicate bits of the design with a brush that only had one hair on it. The results did bring me a few bob but not the amount I had hoped for. As Christmas came there was the need to make things to give relations and friends as a gift.

Mum had been given some sheets of black shiny paper, and as in those days, the gift wrapping one could buy, had not caught up in design with the art movement of psychedelic colours, I thought I would paint my own. These were a big hit with all our friends and all our gifts were wrapped in it that Christmas. The designs on this dark background gave me an idea of another art project I wanted to try. This would be put on hold until much later, as in the new year I would need to swat for exams and the possibility for future employment.

My dreams had lately become more prophetic and clear, as if I were watching a movie. There were events in the family that would shake me as a night or two before I had 'seen' the person acting out the events exactly as in the dream. In truth it was impossible to tell anyone in advance, as when the dream came to me it would not fit what I had known at the time. One example of this was when I had a dream that gran had a lady living with her. In the dream I could see the back of a lady bringing bags into gran's hall. I just knew she was a teacher. Sure enough when we went to visit gran she had taken in a lady lodger, a teacher. This gave me more food for thought.

In one of my dreams, my friend Pam and I would be running down a hill, chasing after a dark haired man. Pam was dragging me along but to me it felt like we were wasting our time. As we ran my legs got more and more heavy, as if made of led. The meaning of his later became quite clear when we went to see the very first Beatles performance at the B.B.C. Pam's dad, Bill, managed to book a coach load of youth club members into the afternoon event. We could not conceal our excitement when we got the news. I did not link it to my dream until later. My favourite Beatle was George Harison, Pam was crazy about John Lennon though she did love them all.

At the concert I was a tad disappointed that the music could hardly be heard because the girls were screaming so loudly. At the end of the show an usher said we should file out of the front doors in an orderly manner. This was impossible as girls were in a frenzy, shoving and pushing each other in a hurry to see the band leaving. Pam was quite a strong girl and pulled me out of one of the front doors. I wanted to go out of the side door. 'Look!' she screamed as we emerged into the daylight. A short distance away there was a young man. 'GEORGE!' screamed a hundred crazy girls pointing to the man. Pam dragged me down the hill at breakneck speed. Part of the front runners in this mad 'group sprint', my shout of 'Stop!' had not the slightest effect on Pam. Her mind was made up! This **was** Beatle George! As we neared the end of the road George jumped onto a bus, he was safe. We must trudge back up the hill to get the coach home. Bill told us that all four 'Beatles' had calmly come from the side door and got into a Limo next to our coach. We could have got autographs plus a good gander at them all. The 'George' we saw was a decoy, but a very convincing one!

Pam did eventually meet all the Beatles when she went to arrange flowers at a hotel in Blackpool with a florist friend of ours. That was one event I sadly missed out on because mum and dad said I could not go that far on what seemed to them like a whim. For a time, I'm sure I must have sulked but earlier, Pam and I had seen all the fab four in the famous battered old van with 'BEATLES' on the side as it passed the end of our Lane. We used to sit 'band watching' every weekend, they even waved to us. We also had a wave from the 'Hollies', 'Gerry and the Pace Makers' and surprisingly the Rolling Stones. We felt lucky to live on the main road to Liverpool.

Reader... Do you embrace change? Have you found luck from a lucky charm?
Remember that the wheel has many spokes just as the tree of life has many branches. Each person you love you are connected to and so you and they are branches of the same tree. Firstly, your nearest, family branches, then friends, then those at work or in your community and onward to outer branches with link to all others you may meet during your life. You are part of the whole. Each can affect the other by what is said and done. Have love at your centre.

Reader... This is the RUNE Hagalaz

Hagalaz is the RUNE of power, liberty, a connection with the wild and is symbolic of hail. This RUNE seems to fit with my next chapter with the Tarot depicting the woman taming the Lion.

11/ Tarot lesson, THE WHEEL OF FORTUNE

Card No 10. The eleventh lesson of the Tarot... Rotation...Progress.
Song...'Return to Sender'...Singer...Version... Elvis...1962

The Wheel of Fortune card is often depicted as a large wheel with two or three figures around it. The pack I use mostly is the Egyptian Tarot and shows a tiny human figure at the centre of the wheel. Each spoke of the wheel shows a different letter from an ancient script. The card gives the illusion of movement. Most Tarot designs have inscriptions of Hermetic lettering around the rim of the wheel. A Sphinx, holding a sword is depicted sitting at the top of the wheel. A snake slithers at the left of the wheel and the Egyptian God Anubis lies as if holding onto the left side of the wheel on his back. In each of the four corners of the card there are figures, each holding an open book. Top left we see an Angel, top right is the mythical bird the Phoenix, bottom left we see a winged Bull, bottom right is a Sphinx. Each figure is sitting on a cloud. Perhaps these ancient symbols represent the different strengths we need on our journey through this life and many incarnations until we may re-join the original power source, the energy initiating life in our universe. The power I often refer to as the 'God Energy'. Reversed in a spread we might assume some kind of hindrance to or delay. In Gypsy tradition the 'Wheel' card is considered a lucky omen.

The Wheel of Fortune is like a Wheel of Destiny! Perhaps the individual viewing this card must glean the vastness of the mystical knowledge it holds. Plainly the card tells us that life is like a wheel! We are at the centre of our own wheel, our own life story. Each spoke in the wheel is a link to another soul living on the material plane of existence at the same time as ourselves. We are all links in the chain of life! Each of us has an effect on *each other by things we do or say as we interact with each other day by day in our world. Whatever the individual may 'see' in its complexity, we surely must glean a link to movement. If one chooses only to think of the material world, then we may remember the most important invention for the progress to modern living, the invention of the wheel. In symbolisation the card must be linked to the 'Tree of Life' where all of us are from the same tree, all connected to each other. He who may rise could fall and he who falls must rise' should be noted when this card is drawn. Note this card as 10 may link it to Iod, the tenth letter of the Jewish alphabet and as this is the letter of the 1st finger it points in command. The the finger of time passing, the finger on the clock, eternity, the ever rolling wheel. The Wheel of Fortune would truly spin in an interesting way during my last school year and into working life!*

Reader... Be at the centre of your life but be flexible in mind as we can expect nothing to stands still.

Chapter 12

1960's continued

The wrath I had felt towards dad, with him not letting me go to Blackpool with Pam to meet the Beatles, was soon diminished as there was something he suggested to me that did interest me at the time. He suggested I learn to play the guitar. There was a lad that we often saw at the youth club that gave lessons. Each Friday after school the Guitar lesson would begin. At first I was eager to learn and managed to get a few cords of 'When the Saints go Marching in'. However, this tune was not exactly one that I wanted to play and there had been a down side to the strumming during the past few weeks. My first two fingers had developed nasty lumps and my nails had split badly. Was this the price one had to pay for being part of the 'in crowd'? Although I enjoyed listening to a few bands my pipedream of being in one soon faded. Feeling like I had disappointed dad again I went back to my first hobby of art.

By the middle of 1965 there was a lot of talk about the World Cup which was to be held in England next year. It was a happy coincidence that all the police homes on our estate were to get painted and decorated after Christmas. From my colourful designs on the wrapping paper, I had done for Christmas, an idea was forming. Would mum and dad think it was too outrageous? Only one way to find out and that was to ask! 'Can I do a wall mural on the bedroom wall when it's been painted?' I asked mum. She had liked my other painting and said she would ask the powers that be- (police decorator) Not holding out much hope on this I was surprised when the answer was yes. 'Great, can you ask the decorator to do a very dark, or possibly black background for me to paint on?' I asked.

The decorator had no black paint but kindly used the darkest brown he could find. At the art shop I found paints I would need. I decided to do a depiction of 'World Cup Willy' as he was known, the England mascot. Because of the brown background there would also be a woodland theme with a large twisty tree in the middle and a jolly little Victorian car coming towards the room. The tree had a scary face like the ones in children's story books. The results were much admired by my family and especially John.

He loved football and World Cup Willy! The only down side to this project was the fact that word got out on the rest of the estate that the very eccentric Smith's had asked the painter to do the bedroom wall in BLACK. We laughed about it at the time but later I wondered if the neighbours linked the black to my liking to read the tea leaves and thought me to be some kind of Witch.

Regardless of this my gran loved the wall and asked me if I would do her a mural in her new home. This would not be until much later as my school exams were coming up soon. My 'World Cup Willy' resembled a Lion and so was quite apt for the English football team. Come to think of it, it's quite apt for this chapter in my book as whenever I think of my brother I always think of his birth sign of Leo, just like eight others in our family.

Mum and I were both Earth signs, so the vibe in our home was predominantly the Leo Fire element. Strangely the occupation of a police man would be ruled mostly by Leo. Eventually John would follow dad, plus our 'Leo' uncle and Stan, my brother in law into this occupation too. Our family crest should reflect Earth and Fire!

Dad and mum's social life certainly revolved around dad's work colleague's. It put me in mind of all the Lions in the jungle with the order from the top, King Lion, the Chief Super Intendant in his ivory tower (a detached house) at the end of our Lane. Down through the ranks to the young pups, trainees under dad's management. Dad was one of three Sergeant's in the Headquarters traffic section.

If there was a problem or tragedy for any family on the estate, news would spread on the grapevine within hours. We were like one big family in many ways, good times and bad were shared by all.

As in most families there was scandal and gossip on the estate and so just as everyone soon found out about our 'BLACK' wall, everyone soon found out that the television people were coming to film in and around the estate for a new police drama 'Z cars'. There was much excitement as we watched the film crew arrive early one morning. I would miss the 'goings on' that day as I had to get off to school.

At home that day mum was getting on with the usual household chores when there was a knock on the door. The Director from the film company had come to ask mum if he could use my brother John and his little friend Gordon to be extra's as they filmed a scene of a 'fake' police car driving around the square green in the centre of the houses. Mum went to watch as John and Gordon peddled their little three wheel bikes along the pavement followed by a camera man on a strange looking wheeled contraption as he filmed what turned out to be the opening scene of the new show.

It was some weeks later before we would see that first episode but before then we learned that there was a bit of a rumpus at headquarters and the police authorities had blocked the film makers to use the estate and the main police building in any future episodes. Why? We all asked. On the grapevine we were told that the police authorities were unhappy after viewing the first episode of the show prior to it being watched by the masses. What on earth could they object to was the question on everyone's lips?

We soon realised why when we saw that first part...After the lovely little part where we saw the children on their bikes the scene changed. The main character was entering his home after being out on police duties. His wife started to complain that once again his dinner was ruined and she was fed up with him always coming home late. The 'police man' was in the act of taking his coat off when she made a sharp remark. He shouted and threw his dinner onto the kitchen floor.

The scene we all watched seemed quite amusing to us, as we had often had a bit of a rumpus in our house, if dad came in late, although not quite as dramatic as the one shown on Z cars. It was deemed a bad example of police life by the police authorities but to us it rang very true to life. Mum and I were sure that many a dinner was wasted and more than a few probably ended up on the floor, though I only saw this happen once. Still we were tickled that John and Gordon had made an appearance even if it was only the once.

Just after the television people left there were two awful tragedies that caused us all to weep. The first one was when one of the police men of the motorcycle unit had been killed in a terrible accident. Because dad was on traffic he knew the man quite well, and by all accounts he was a very likable chap who left a wife and little children. Dad hated motorbikes as he had attended many fatal accidents involving them during his service, but this was especially upsetting as he knew the man involved. The whole estate was in a cloud of mourning and there was a kind of atmosphere of sadness hanging over the adults as they talked in hushed tones about the details of the crash. All we knew was that there was a Lorry involved.

Soon the sadness of premature death would come a lot closer to me as a lovely young lad, Colin that was in our circle of friends had taken poorly. All our friends gathered round the Oak tree that evening praying that Colin would soon be out of danger. He had been rushed to hospital that afternoon after he had collapsed on the school playing field whilst taking part in a marathon. We hoped he would soon be back playing in the band along with his brother and the other two band members.

Pam and I had been allowed to go to gigs with Colin and his band as his dad always accompanied them. The band also did sometimes play at the police youth club where we would dance and clap them like crazy.

My first boyfriend, Stue, had been to see Colin in hospital the evening after he was admitted. He told me he was very worried as Colin had been talking as if he were about to die. Stue said Colin had talked about 'kicking the bucket' and asked that all our gang would remember him. A shudder went through me at his words. Though he had told me this, it was still a shock when a few days later a friend called to tell us the sad news that Colin had passed away. His parents had known he was gravely ill for some time but had wanted him to have as full a life as possible in the time he had been given.

Colin had looked like an Angel on stage with his guitar and his white blond hair and blue eyes. I now hoped he was singing with them. Colin's death would again make me wonder what the universe had in store for us when we die? The gang at the meeting place gave each other strength as we each said a silent prayer.

Just after my fifteenth birthday whilst walking from the bus home with my friends Pam and Debbie. I glanced to my right by the woods, after a movement caught my eye. A man was standing down in the hollow of the ditch. The pavement was several feet above the ditch. To my horror I saw that the man was exposing himself. Looking away quickly I turned to the two other girls who were deep in conversation. A few steps further on I asked if they had seen what I saw. They had not seen the man. Pam wanted to go back and look but I said we should hurry home to tell someone. Mum was in the kitchen as we arrived and when told of the rude man she ran from the kitchen pulling off her apron as she fled. She told us to wait at home.

Mum was gone for a while and was quite breathless when she returned. When we asked where she had been she explained that she had run to the main road and waited until she saw a police car. She had flagged them down waving frantically with her apron. The police man had managed to apprehend the rude man right away.

The day after this incident a police lady came to our house and asked me to describe what I had seen. Because I was a minor I would not have to give evidence in a court. My statement was just one of several that had been given to the police about the same man. We found out later he had asked that several offences of the same nature be taken into consideration. Mum was praised by the police on her quick thinking as many children walked past or played in the woods and by her actions she may have saved them from trauma.

Our house being the first on the Lane past the woods there was a great temptation for John and his friends to climb the trees. By now my tomboy era had come to an end. One day, John and his friend had decided to climb the tree nearest to our house. We could hear shouting and when we went out to look what the noise was all about, to our horror we saw John hanging by his pants near the top of a tree. His fall had been halted by the fact a branch had snagged on his waistband. Mum and I could not look, if John had fallen further he would have landed on the concrete driveway. Luckily the branch was strong enough to hold him whilst the ladders were fetched from the wash house. Dad somehow got John down and all turned out well this time. We were glad of Johns growing interest in football as he became hooked on the game of Subbuteo. This was where tiny figures of men were flicked so as to aim at a miniature football to get it into the net. At least it would keep him out of mischief, if only for a few hours.

In the Summer months we were lucky to have a paddling pool in our back garden. Dad fashioned it from four old railway sleepers made into a square with a piece of tarpaulin covering it so as to hold the water. Johns friends would come round for a paddle. To make sure they were safe I would sit on the edge. One hot day when the children had gone home, by the pool, I watched seven Magpies land in the garden. Seven for a secret never to be told, I thought. My thoughts turned to the numbers.

Seven colours in the rainbow, seven deadly sins in the Bible. Then I noticed there were seven beautiful plump ripe peaches hanging on the reach tree near the pool. I remember thinking how strange it was that my birthday was also on the seventh. It was seven o-clock that evening when the news came in about lovely Colin. Seven was the number of mystery. I knew this from the Anderson and Grim fairy tale about the seven brothers that were turned into Swans by a witch. I had heard the Irish believed the seventh son of the seventh son was psychic.

My gran was the seventh child of Mary Ellen Morris, nee Muldoon. It was after this that I tried to find out more from books about the influence of numerology. From the earliest written word, we find evidence that mankind had a desire to put things into order. The use of numbers has enabled humans to progress with design in structures of architecture. Numbers enabled mankind to work out progression of stars and planets in the sky, thus enabling mariners from very early times to map the geography of the Oceans. To me there is a kind of magic to numbers. Certain numbers have followed me in my life and have had a mysterious link to myself and my life partner.

In reading the playing cards, or Tarot, there is a traditional meaning to each number from one to nine. In respect of the Tarot, we have the meanings interpreted by the artist that has designed them. For those wishing to become adept at 'reading' the cards as a form of divination, it is possible to glean a meaning from the picture on the card. Each card though, has numerous 'deeper' meanings, as we scrutinise them in more depth. On many Tarot packs there are no pictures on the Minor Arcana and so we must use the traditional meanings, by learning a little of this magical numerology.

Reader... Order, planning and strategy is the main lesson of the Strength card. Have you learned to use this kind of strength to help along your path of life?
On the note of numerology... Have you a number that has been predominant throughout your life?

Well, this is the half way mark in my story. Thanks for time travelling with me back to the good old, or some not so good old days. You will see that I have included the sad times as well as the happy. Remembering the faces of the wonderful people from the past has given me joy. We never really forget our childhood and there is so much joy in remembering.

Life was so much calmer as I remember the 1950's and 1960's era. Not as much noise. No mobile phones pinging or computer bells ringing and not as many vehicles on the road. No central heating in most homes but we did enjoy the comfort of the flame of the open fire and family life around it.

As time moved us on into the 1970's, my story would continue to bring some amazing characters to influence my life and touch my heart. The 1960's however would always be my golden era as it was a wonderful time for me. A great time to be alive, a time of youth and music, a time when fate brought my soulmate and I together and when my psychic apprenticeship began with one or two further strange events.

Below is a simple layout for a beginner when reading of the TAROT cards or the RUNES.
After the 'seer' has shuffled the cards and cut into three piles, he or she thinking on their Angel or spiritual helper the cards are shuffled by the enquirer and six are chosen at random. A card or rune for each position is chosen at random from the set without the enquirer looking at the symbols.

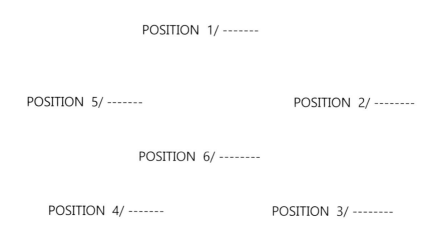

POSITION 1/ -------

POSITION 5/ -------   POSITION 2/ --------

POSITION 6/ --------

POSITION 4/ -------   POSITION 3/ --------

Position 1 The first card or Rune chosen ...
This will indicate issues from the past that are still relevant/ important to the enquirer today.

Position 2 The second card or Rune chosen...
This card or Rune can represent matters in or close to home.

Position 3 The third card or Rune chosen...
This card or Rune can represent material matters/ finance/ work.

Position 4 The fourth card or Rune chosen...

This card or Rune can represent events that will be of interest to the enquirer.

Position 5 The fifth card or Rune chosen...
This card or Rune can represent aspects linked to persons close to or related to the enquirer.

Position 6 The sixth card or Rune chosen...
This card or Rune can represent the main aim or potential of the enquirer.

There are many other layouts and the more adept reader may want to design their own layout. Most 'seers' design their own casting cloth or board/ table to give a deeper connection to their own vibrations.

12/ Tarot lesson STRENGTH

Card No 11. The twelvth lesson of the TAROT...Strength
Song...'Please Please Me!' ...Band...Version...The Beatles...1962

This card depicts a watchful sitting Lion. Behind him is a woman wearing the mask of the lion. She appears on some cards as stroking the head of the Lion; on others she is depicted trying to open the mouth of the Lion. If we think about the message from this, we could say the woman has to soothingly cajole the Lion. Perhaps we must all sooth our own inner sleeping Lion or he may growl or attack others. We may need to sooth our own temper or that of another. Male or female we must all try to balance our Ying/Yang! In reverse for divination the Strength card can indicate weakness.

It is good to have the strength of the lion but we also need some constraint in some circumstances. Thus we see may have to subdue our own inner Lion, but now and again this card may tell us we have to deal with the 'Lion' in part due to the nature of another. i.e.; his or her wrath or power. We can do so by the softly, softly approach. This card can also tell us we can gather our own strength for whatever we may need it for, healing or battling with an issue.

The nature of the hunter may also be acknowledged with this card. There is a time to pounce and a time to just wait and watch. There is a connection to authority as we know the lion is KING of the jungle and at times life can seem like the jungle. We have to bow to those in authority or face the consequences, be it the law of the land or the law of the firm we work for or just the rules of the house as decided by Father or Mother. Also we may need to remember the saying 'if we want to play with the big boys (the

Lions) we have to behave like the big boys, be a 'Lion' or pretend to be one.

What does the mask that the Lion is wearing on this card tell us? Perhaps we must all wear the mask at some point in life metaphorically speaking, as we cannot always show our feelings for fear of hurting someone or offending in some way, or just because we need to wait and find the right time to reveal our inner self. Often it could be a good idea to coax the strong minded person (the Lion) as we cannot risk his attack. Mostly the Lion card tells us we are gaining, or can gain inner strength when needed.

Could I learn to control the Lion within and learn when to wear a mask for self-preservation?

Reader... Have you already learned to be the strong lion that quietly watches and waits for his right moment? Sometimes strength has the insight of persuasion.

Part two...Looking for Enlightenment.

After the war and during the early 1950's there was a kind of quiet calm as peoples of all nationalities were striving to get back a semblance of order in their lives. For many there had to be a time of grieving; mourning for a fallen hero or a relation caught in the crossfire. Many had to build new homes or new lives for themselves. For some the grief would never end but they had to find a way of living with it. The time for this repairing of shattered lives seemed to slowly give way to a new more up beat era as we reached the middle of the decade. There was a kind of build up of energy that could be perceived in the art, music and culture of that time. By the end of the 1950's it felt as if a new era of possibilities had arrived.

It seemed as if a giant Cosmic Clock had started to tick with the beginning of the 1960s, and as the fingers of the clock ticked into that new decade it brought a kind of raising of the collective conscious. This can be seen in all of the arts of that time! This felt like many individuals were picking up, or tapping into a great surge of magical energy! It was like a universal dawn was breaking through all the pre set boundaries.

Looking back at all the momentous events of the 60's I feel there had been some kind of chasm opened up from another dimension and this torrent of divine awareness permeated the mind and hearts of many, though sadly not all individuals. The result of this is evident in the behaviour of many young people of that time. It was as if many of the young were no longer willing to accept the injustices of the past, such as racism, class division, gender inequality and sexual prejudice.

For those still clinging to the old establishment a person wearing a 'Ban the Bomb' badge was seen as subversive. To those minds able to tap into this new wave of cosmic energy the thirst for enlightenment became ever more pressing as they were fighting what they perceived to be an immoral and corrupt order in the old rule book. This led to protests and marches and all kinds of new thinking on religion and philosophy.

Now we may ask why was the positive philosophy of 'Peace and Love' of the 'Flower Power' generation not able to be sustained and built upon? My view of this after living through that time and being in part 'tuned' into that strange wave of energy, is that the force of evil, or hate that had abounded during the two world wars, sensed it was losing power. We may see this as the work of the Devil trying to hang onto those in his clutches, or is it just the human ego?

Those in positions of power are often reluctant to give even a measure of it away, often driven by greed! It is heartening to me that the music and art of the 1960's has endured and to a small extent left its legacy in the world of today. May be I am guilty of looking back at the 1960's with a golden glow or 'rose tinted specks'. To all who may ever read this I would say in the words of the bard of the 1960's, let us just 'Give peace a chance'!

In the unfolding Aquarius age ahead my prayer is that we may we see a new cleaner, greener, more tolerant world of sharing, compassion and harmony. At the time of writing, this wish seems a long way off but there are many individuals that are working in light. We can hope that this light and goodness shall bring about a shift in collective consciousness towards this goal.

The Aquarian age is still only in its infancy and as this is so we can only hope to see the very first tendrils of light entering the collective consciousness during our lifetimes. It is my thinking that we must all try to spread light wherever possible, by means of each of us doing only what comes from the place in our hearts where love is found.

There is much work to be done by politicians with the work of diplomacy, to fight injustice and at the same time ensure the safety of all their citizens. We must all hope that those chosen for high office will rule from this place in their hearts where love and responsibility is king rather than ego or greed.

My grandmother, May, always said that there were no winners after a war, only dead people and those that mourned them. Having been born in

1899 she had lived through two world wars and had first hand, knowledge of the grief they left behind.

Reader... This is the RUNE Isa

This RUNE represents Ice and winter, a waiting time, a time of reflection, delay that gives time to think, take stock of our true inner self ready for spring or ready for when we can go ahead.

Chapter 13

1965 – 1966

In most work situations a youngster will have with them an older person designated to show them how the work needs to be done. At College the tutor will teach the basic grounding for working in a particular chosen field. These years in the life of a teenager are what can often influence the rest of our lives. The tide of life turns as we are thrust into a new environment and meet new people of all ages. This was certainly true for my future path in life.

For me the people I met on the very first day of my work life would have a lasting impression on my long term future. It would seem at the time these were just chance encounters and chance snatches of conversation but as I was already questioning my beliefs and the faith I had grown up with, these events, looking back, did indeed shape the rest of my life! Fate often brings in and takes out of our life both people and possessions.

Weeks away from the end of my last school term the several jobs I had applied for in desperation, had not the remotest link to art and had only yielded two interviews. Deep in thought and blanked off to the scenery and other bus travellers I was startled by a young man almost throwing himself into the seat next to me. I knew 'Sooty' from our estate and the youth club. After I explained my job search he offered to have a word with his boss at a printing firm. During our conversation, I learned that a girl in the art office was leaving and the vacancy had not yet been advertised. 'My teacher thinks she may be able to get me a part time placement at Art college if I can get work with a firm where the job links to the art course; It's only one day each week.' I told him. 'Not sure where you might stand on the day off thing!' he added. Luck (or my Angel of Fate) had played a part once again in my life and if I could work at something I loved then that would be good enough for me!

School rules were set so that if you were over fifteen and exams were finished, when a job offer came up one could take it. Our school prided itself on the fact that the majority of leavers had a placement at college or in employment. Because of my having dyslexia (an unknown issue at that time) confidence in my own abilities had been somewhat eroded during school years.

The fact I had managed to secure a job in my favourite subject, this news would be in the school magazine for all to see, gave me a much needed boost of confidence. My interview with Mr Hean of the printing firm, Gregson, Grantham and Hean, went like a dream. I secured the job, and had been told that I would be able to attend art college on Wednesdays and make up the time by working Saturday mornings. The college accepted me partly on my sketches and because I was prepared to do a work related evening class of 'Typography and Design'. The down side of my work situation would be the early start. My alarm clock would need to be set for six a.m. in order to get to work for seven. I would be working for 40 hours a week, not counting the six hours on collage day!

My last day at school was the last day before the Easter holidays. Though I would miss my friends I was glad to be free of the rules and the subject I hated (Pitman short hand with typing). Most of the girls plus one boy in form 5B had lined up office jobs with the going rate of pay set at £2.10 shillings (pre decimal money). My wage would be the massive amount of £4.10 shillings! As I left school on that last day skipping down the lane whooping all the way with elation, I flung my hat (school beret) over into a field and tied my tie round the school gate post, such was my delight!

Because of the early start getting off to work and never being one to eat right away after getting up, mum would often make me a piece of thick toast as I got ready. By 6.30am I would be eating it on the bus. In town the bus stopped at the Cenotaph for five minutes. This would prove a nerve wrecking wait as Mr Hean expected me to clock on at seven.

Watching the bus driver and the conductor having a smoke break, I was on pins, the waiting with time ticking on. The Prison was where I had to alight. This was about five blocks from work so there was no option but to run like the wind. Even then the card from The clocking machine would show I had arrived at three minutes past seven. This was okay as my wage would only be docked if late by ten minutes. Once or twice if I missed the first buss into town by a whisker, there would be a few shillings less in my wage packet. It was customary in those days to hand your wage packet unopened to your mum, then she would give you some 'spends'.

The art and photography room was upstairs and downstairs a large workshop housed two massive old fashioned Letterpress Printing Machines, plus six 'new' Lithograph Machines plus a massive long book binding table. Around the table sat six women. The printing machines were operated by men. Two of the men seemed very old to my young eyes and in deed I later found out they were both in their eighties, one of them had their 90th birthday shortly after I joined the firm. It was astonishing to me that they were still working. The skills needed for the almost obsolete Letterpress were disappearing. The two old gentlemen were, Mr Gregson and Mr Granthom. They had set up the firm together many years earlier and Mr Hean had later invested with them. He manned the office along with a secretary.
From old copies of the official Preston Guild paper you would find Gregson and Granthom, were the chosen printers of the Victorian era.

Working long hours and getting home late did give my life restrictions but the independence of having a little money of my own was wonderful. Each Monday and Tuesday would drag on as I waited for 'Wednesday Art College'. Wednesday was a was a kind of freedom, although I felt like an outsider as the only girl in a class of older boys. I would now observe the peculiarities of the male gender at close quarters. It was my time to watch and learn. It was great to see all the 'mod' trendy students and the 'Carnaby Street' fab clothes they wore. For me dressing up 'Hippy' was part of the Arty set vibration that I so much wanted to be part of.

Now at work in the art room, I was also the only female assistant and my persona here would be quite different to the one I adopted for Art College. At work I preferred to blend into the background, so liked to take my lunch downstairs with the ladies of the bookbinding table. They were all extremely friendly and welcomed me to sit with them on my first day. Soon we were chatting away about all manner of things. All the ladies except one belonged to the same family. On that first day, sitting with them they were talking about things that they had been doing over the weekend.

Evelyn, the oldest lady asked me about my weekend. I mentioned mum and I had not slept too well as we were getting all sorts of noise at night, and that we thought the house may be haunted.

When Evelyn asked for more details I recounted all the strange nocturnal activities we had experienced over the past year or two. When I added the details of the spooky visit I had from the spirit of Ted, expecting them to be surprised at my revelations, I was astonished that they seemed to readily accept what I was saying.

'We are all members of the Spiritualist Church!' Evelyn announced. 'Our family are all descended from the 'Witches of Pendle!' she added. 'You do realise that you are the one causing all this activity in your home don't you?' she went on. Startled by the fact their family had knowledge of such things I did not know what to say. When I added, 'The noises seem to come from the stairs!' Evelyn asked if I had seen any ghosts or spirits as a child. I told them about the old lady that had appeared from nowhere at the end of my bed when I was about seven or eight. Evelyn then explained that there were persons at her church who were mediums, these individuals were able to tune into spirits and that often they were born with this ability. It was usual for a person of mediumistic ability to 'see' their spirit guide at some point during their childhood. Later they may realise that they could learn to control the psychic energy so that these entities could not cause such disturbances. When I asked how they managed this, Evelyn said she thought I should channel my 'gift' into some kind of psychic work so that these energies could be used to help others and thus not run riot. Mentioning that I could 'read' the tea leaves but did not always know how to interpret the symbols she offered to give me a book on all possible psychic tools and practices.

The conversation had to some extent made me think that I could be more in control of these spirit visitors than I had previously considered. Within a few weeks I had learned from the information in the book, many of the symbols that were accepted as 'signs' of future events. I figured that the Bible story of Joseph (of the coat of many colours in the old testament) was an indication of how symbols worked. From then onward the many friends calling in for a reading seemed to bring a clearer energy and there were less nocturnal noises than before. I was relieved that my new work friends thought all things that I had experienced were quite normal. Soon they were eager to test my skill in the art of Tassiology (tea cup reading) and now and again it became a lunchtime activity to see what the leaves could predict, though I still inwardly questioned what it was all about.

During the first few weeks at work I had been shopping for some bell bottom hipster pants that were very much in fashion. Bell bottoms and polo neck sweaters or 'Mod Gear' was the required 'uniform' of the 1960s College students attending for Art. The time, place and date for me to start College had been sent to me, plus a list of things to bring with me. Another shop for art equipment, then the day dawned.

At the door of the art class I took a deep breath. It was 9.15 am, the exact time I had been given to arrive but the other students had arrived at 9am. After knocking, when I opened the door the teacher came towards me. At one glance I saw that sitting in front of class was another rather plump 'NAKED' older lady and the rest of the room was full of young men. Never having been to a life drawing class before at age just sixteen (I was quite naïve) I had not realised that it would be a naked person we would draw rather than a bowl of fruit. I found myself going beetroot red. Because I was the only female wanting to do art relating to printing I had been tagged on to this all male class. Although life drawing was included, the other lessons were more technical drawing and learning the type faces. Talking to one lad I found these students were in their second year of a full time course. They were two years older than me!

For the next few months I would try to focus on the classes. I had overheard some of the conversations between the lads about the life models. These conversations were very derogatory about the physique of the women who sat for us. I was extremely uncomfortable and it added to my dislike of some of the young men of my generation. Wanting to continue the course I had to try to fit in with these rude males in my class but did not go with them at break or lunch. Not wishing to brand all the lads with a tag of disrespect for women, I tried to find a place to sit near two of the less vocal young men.

Because they attended collage full time they had no income and I did, the lads would often ask to borrow a tube of paint or other equipment from me. Apart from this I had as little to do with them as possible. Outside College I had several boyfriends that year but have to say some male students did nothing to improve my opinion of men in general.

During my College time there were still some strange noises in the night and my dreams were becoming more and more vivid. Often things I had dreamed of would link to family or world events that were out of the ordinary. My brother and I would still play games that involved intuition. When events happened that I had foreseen in a dream I would often put it down to coincidence. As more and more tea leaf patterns pointed to specific events that took place later, eventually my belief in some sort of cosmic plan began to grow. Could in some way the future of each human life have a plan, an individual pattern?

Although patterns left in the tea leaves would tell me a lot about what the person would be doing in the near future, I began to get other information through a voice in my ear. Always in my left ear and quite clear, yet seemed as if the voice was talking to me from a distance. It was a male voice and the tone was calm and sort of intermittent as if from a radio that was not quite tuned in properly.

The voice in my ear only ever came whilst I was with a person whom had asked for a reading. The voice would say a sentence but I could only hear parts of it. It was to some extent like a piece of detective work when interpreting for the person requesting the reading. If you have ever been listening to a radio and the signal is intermittent with crackling and gaps, then this is how I would describe what I was hearing. Because I never wanted to presume the voice to be always correct with the information it was giving me, I would tell the enquirer that I could not be 100 % with this verbal link. It was as if the voice talking to me was listening in to my 'reading' the leaves, then chipping in with a bit more information relating to it.

Years later at the Spiritual Church I got chance to talk to others that had similar experiences with a 'voice' in their ear. I came to think of the voice as a person in spirit that was prompting me in some way. The only way I could know that this guidance was honest and giving me correct messages was from the reaction of the people sitting for the readings. This sometimes happened right away as the person would confirm some of the information was accurate. They told me it linked to their lives. Other times the person would not know what the voice was telling me. On those occasions I would mentally ask the voice to confirm the information again. The voice may add 'clue' words, as if to help me. 'Was this my spirit guide' I asked myself?

Over the following years, persons having a reading from me would often come back or contact me to say the information I had been given from the voice had by then proved correct. There were also things I saw in the pattern of the leaves that could later be linked to a place they would go to. There would sometimes be a map in the pattern the leaves made, with streets and roads as if looking at landscape from above. Often with these 'maps' there was a number and a letter of the alphabet. Many people came back to tell me they went to the place like 'my map' and the road name was the initial and door number indicated the house they had visited. These 'maps' would often have other 'clue' symbols near them that had a link to the town, for example a tower may be in the cup next to a 'B' and it would indicate Blackpool.

For me the reading of the leaves is always interesting as I never know what I would 'see' with each sitting. There was always a kind of 'zoning out' for me as I concentrated. Time would fly and many readings became so much more in depth that I would speak for an hour. Sometimes I would draw a diagram of what I could see and give it to the person to take with them. It was interesting as it gave me more and more insight into different lives of others. Over the years it seems now that I have 'looked' at most situations life can throw up.

Reader... If you have the restriction of caring for someone with a disability, then perhaps you have been chosen to carry this restriction because you have a good soul. The power of the positive central cosmic energy, the 'God' power has deemed you the right person for the job of care and protection of this other soul. You have in some way been the chosen 'caretaker' whilst you and they are in the material world. This may not be forever on this plane of existence but your souls for now are entwined.

13/ Tarot lesson, The HANGING MAN

Card No 12...The thirteenth lesson of the Tarot... Halt...Destiny...Delay Song...'Let it be!'...Band...Version...The Beatles.

The Hanging Man seems to show us almost the same lessons as the Temperance card, this is the need we will all face at some point, to be patient. The card represents discipline. There are restrictions we might experience with the expansion life takes on as we leave childhood and go forth into the adult world of work, college or training. Whilst in the later school years the issues of growing and development during puberty can be painful in many ways and often make a young person feel isolated. The lesson of the Hang Man is showing us to become wise to our inner self. Learn about ourselves first to achieve and progress in this life. Sometimes against the odds, we can apply our effort to achieve our goal. When we have gained some knowledge of what we want and who we are, then we must wait, take stock to seek our future place in the world. Perhaps the Hanging Man can show us that there are times when inaction or hiatus can be useful for our development. If presented reversed in a spread, the card could tell us, an atonement may be needed, or a new perspective must be found.

At first glance this card may look ominous. A figure is shown hanging upside down from a tree. His hands are tied behind his back so he is unable to do anything. We may use the phrase 'hands tied' when this card shows up for divination. We may remember the story of Odin the Norse God. As he was said to be stranded, tied, hung upside down, unable to move. He could still think. In his thinking, according to Norse legend, for the many years whilst hanging, in his mind he 'saw' the symbols (RUNES) of what was the beginnings of the first alphabet his people had known. This is said to have morphed later into the Latin alphabet.

We cannot be sure if all this is true, but the story demonstrates that when we cannot do anything physically to alter a situation we can still think and review memories. If we find ourselves impotent in a situation, then we must wait. Some things are said to be 'in the lap of the Gods' and we have to accept when it is not in our power to hurry things along. Bide time may be the message we could give ourselves. After all, we can see the man is hanging by his feet, not his neck. It is possible that he may be cut down from the tree at any moment, by another person. There are times one might feel captive by events out of our control, then it is a time to just BE! Accept that many things are 'In the hand of fate'!

Waiting, during the years 1965 - 1966 would now seem to encapsulate the meaning of the Hang Man of the Tarot for me, desperate to leave school and
be earning, desperate to be free of the school rules and the bully of a prefect, waiting for LIFE, and for romance. What would my next chapter bring?

Reader... If or when you feel captive by events; remember a restriction is given as a 'gift' for the purpose of teaching us patience and to know how it is to just live in the moment. Delay can give us a valuable rest or time to take stock.

Remember the origin of this card where we are told the story of Odin. Whilst you are forced to wait for something another quite unrelated event or idea may take you to unexpected rich experiences.

Chapter 14

1960's continued.

By the mid 1960's my gran, in her effort to come to terms with the loss of Ted and her beloved daughter, Joan, had returned to work at the 'Raincoat Factory'. To me her house still felt strange.

Within a few weeks after the night I saw the spirit of Ted, gran announced she had taken in a lodger. It was not the first time, as during the great depression she had taken in an old man, to save him from the dreaded 'Workhouse'.

Mum and dad had been worried about gran being on her own, especially after Mum and I heard the spooky crashing and banging when we were in the house together one Saturday afternoon. It was when we had arrived before grandma was home. Mum hated to talk about 'spooks', as she felt that talking about a poltergeist may encourage it to return.

Over the years I have thought a lot about those strange happenings and I am of the mind that the spirit of Ted, my lovely grandad, was not at rest for some time after he passed over. I came to the conclusion that the reason for this was that as he departed this world, his daughter Joan, was in the process of a painful divorce. How long will he linger in a transitional phase, going from this life into the next? Was it to help Joan in some way? At the Spiritualist Church, the Medium once told me that sometimes a spirit lingers in the material world for a time after the body has left. Eventually the soul energy of the individual comes to a realisation, or their guiding Angel guides them to the higher realms, where one would hope they find peace.

Auntie Joan had come back to live with her parents a few months before grandad was poorly. It had been obvious for some time that Joan's marriage to uncle Len was over and Len was never going to change his womanising ways. When my dad was in Cyprus with the 'police', mum, John and I were staying with them, poor Joan had arrived at grandma's with the side of her face covered in black bruising. Joan was distraught as she told mum that Len had hit her with a bag of cash. It was the end of her marriage and some would say it had the further impact that later ended her life. Perhaps someone can die of a broken heart.

Now that I was working there had been a gradual lifting of restrictions for me at home. The unspoken rules that my parents had set were largely forgotten. I could stay out later and make my own plans with friends for the weekends as long as dad was told where I was going and that I would be back on the last bus at 11.30pm, if he or another dad couldn't pick us up. Now with the small income I received I could go dancing or to watch a band with a friend. Once a month Mum, Dad, John and I went to Manchester, to stay with Gran. On these weekends my Saturday nights were spent with my cousin Maggie.

The music scene in Manchester was always one step ahead of Preston and we saw many bands at the local Church halls that would go on to be in the music charts within the next few weeks. We saw The Foremost, The Big Three, and many other groups at a local church hall Saturday dance. We saw Tom Jones just before he hit the big time! Maggie was a bit more of a rebel than me at this time. She liked the Rolling Stones and the 'bad boy' image of Jagger and a few others appealed to her.

Mag was definitely more a Mod rather than a Rocker in her taste of clothes and hair styles. My gran would say she was 'Up to the minute'! She had a boyfriend that was definitely not the kind of lad her mum wanted her to mix with. She continued to see the lad even when she had decided for herself he was bad news, just to flout the rules.

Mag and I, and occasionally her friend Linda would go to a 'forbidden' club in town, 'The Twisted Wheel'. This was quite an eye opener for me as it was frequented by some 'way out' people. It was dark inside and one could just about make out the Andy Warhol style paintings on the wall. We would be trying to look trendy and older than our age (the minimum age to enter was eighteen) sauntering in, a black cheroot each between our fingers, I started to cough. There was a whisper going round the club that someone was selling 'purple heart' pills. We never saw any, and getting in whilst under age was enough daring for me. I lived just to dance in those days!

My teenage years in the early sixties had been a shedding of old known beliefs acquired mostly from Sunday school as well as shedding off the 'school girl me' to enter the world of work.

Like many young people I questioned everything. The change in me was perhaps apparent to anyone in my circle and I am sure that some friends and relatives may have noticed me becoming a bit quieter and more reflective at times. Though chatty when in my own social circle, at home I would often privately question the meaning of life, thinking more and more about my 'ghosts'.

The voice in my ear never tried to guide me in my own life decisions, in fact the voice only ever comes to me as I concentrate on the person I am reading for. It is as if there is a kind of rule as to what we humans might know, might be given in advance, and what we must find out by ourselves. A kind of trial and error for situations where there is a choice to be made. For many years this has puzzled me, and over time I have come to the conclusion that there are many things we humans are meant to experience to bring us spiritual progress. Yes, there are signs we may follow just for the issues we are able to learn from. Perhaps our lives are partly mapped out with things we are meant to go through. These we may not be able to change, then there are some matters that we are given the thing we call 'free will'. Perhaps we can avoid making the same mistakes over again when our soul lesson has been learned.

Many spiritual theories exist on the subject of past lives and on returning again and again, in order to become more and more enlightened in each incarnation. With my own experience of looking at the signs for so many years I feel now, that each of us has a potential to follow our true purpose. We may have to come back again if we do not find that true purpose during this life time. The purpose may be different for each of us but the goal could be the same. That end goal is to reach the highest spiritual awareness that could bring us closer to the 'God energy'. The energy responsible for, and that governs our universe. Perhaps we can each help others to reach a higher awareness of that energy only when we can believe it to exist within ourselves.

From the Sunday school scriptures growing up, I see there is much good guidance but like all written words each person may see a different meaning in the same text. In other words, we all have our own individual link to 'God energy' or if you prefer to the way of 'seeking enlightenment'. Although my childhood friend had spoken about his 'past life' my first full awareness of the concept of reincarnation came at the time I started work.

Whilst on the subject of enlightenment we may consider the possibility that if we are able to return to another life on the physical (Earthly) plane then no experience is wasted. Good or bad events may help lead us forward. The lessons in our early years can stay within our memory to help us guide the next generation if they choose to listen to the voice of experience from elders. We do see some children wise or talented beyond normal, from birth. Perhaps they have lived many lives before!

Day to day life during the 1960's was fairly smooth running for us Smiths apart from the sadness of loss. Looking back now I see that it was a good life lesson in many ways that Grandad Ted appeared to me as he did. It taught me to never disbelieve anything without looking at all the possibilities, even the strange or supernatural. I made it a rule then to listen more to my intuitions and never to presume what the reaction of others will be towards what you tell them.

The example set by my Gran in the way she coped with the loss of her husband and daughter was nothing short of heroic. Outwardly she seemed calm and often jovial. She carried on working far after the age most people were retired. She was, to all intents and purpose still her old self. If she had any taste of the house being haunted she kept it to herself. Mum and I knew what we had experienced and so whenever we stayed over, after my seeing the spirit of Ted, we shared the same room. This was more because of mum with the fear she had of the poltergeist activity being repeated. I must confess however that number 167 never seemed to be the cosy safe haven for me that it had during childhood. In my dreams it had taken on a kind of Gothic strangeness that was hard to understand. Aware the spirit body of Ted may be still present did worry me; even long after the night he had visited me. Was he not at peace? Would he find his way to heaven or whatever place souls go to after life in the material world has ended? These questions went round in my mind, forcing me to look at all belief systems in the world and try to quantify them.

Only a few months after Auntie Joan passed away Gran introduced us to her new lodger. We were glad that gran would not be in the house alone as much and although she did not warm to the first lodger we could see it was helping her. The trauma of the two losses seemed to be starting to heal and we could talk about all the good times we had together as a family. Gran would love to regale us with her funny memories of Edwardian life. She could make us laugh at her tales and even the hardships seemed to give her joy in the telling. Comedy was and perhaps always will be the only way to endure such poverty.

The adventures of youth against the backdrop of the historical events such as the sinking of the Titanic and the onset of the first world war would seem an unlikely tale of comfort to anyone, though for gran the telling of the tales certainly was! Her father and younger brother had both perished at sea in the conflict. Healing from the pain of loss is a personal matter and each must try to find comfort in any way that helps, regardless of what others might find inappropriate. This lesson has stayed with me up to the time of writing when we have lost so many more relatives and friends. Each person in grieving, has coped in differing ways, and that is how it must be.

Having now lost my parents, several relations, my dear cousin Maggie plus my close friend Raela, I find myself in quiet moments more and more sure that they are able in very subtle ways to still have communication with me. Of course it is not the same as normal face to face chat and there are those that will dismiss these communications as a figment of my mind. To me however there are too many 'signs' that are sent at random throughout each day, to be just coincidence.

In a daydream whilst dusting or washing up a tune will pop into my head that reminds me of Maggie, then on turning on the radio that tune will be playing. At other times I will be thinking of a place we went to and later that day the place will be mentioned on television or I will see it in a magazine together with the name Margaret.

With my friend Raela the communication is always a colour, a recipe or piece of art that crops up in a paper or book, together with a saying, a word, that I know could only have come from her.

These communications are a comfort but we must still feel the loss of the hug that is now missing. So whenever that pang of loss comes upon me, I try to send out a warm glow (like the rainbow reflections from the sunlight on a piece of crystal) to the mind image of my departed loved ones. Then it reminds me to hug those dear to us that we still have with us.

Reader... We must all experience the loss of a loved one at some point in life. If you are feeling sad or heartbroken, remember you are not alone. There will be someone, somewhere that is experiencing the terrible pang of loss just as deeply as you do. This may not be a comfort to you initially, you may not be able to think that way, but as time passes that thought may give you strength.

In deep despair we must live on to continue the life force that the loved one cannot. This will honour their memory and help you find some purpose for your future. As time passes give yourself a goal that you know would have made your loved one smile. The goal may not need be enormous, you do not need to clime the highest mountain, just a little goal that can be viewed as a tiny positive. The motto is then, 'day by day, one step at a time. Then don't forget to be proud of yourself. Your loved one will be proud of you!

Reader... This is the RUNE Dagaz
The Rune Dagaz is thought to be inked to light,
out of the darkness into the light, transition!

14/ Tarot lesson, TRANSITION/ DEATH

Card No. 13...Lesson fourteen of the Tarot...Transition. Endings. Death.
Song... 'Tambourine Man'...Singer...Bob Dillon...1965

The image on this card may look ominous as on many packs the design is a human skeleton riding a White horse. He carries a banner with a white rose design on a black background. He wears a black cape and on some packs he carries a scythe. In front or under the feet of his horse we see people rising from their graves or prone before him.

Traditionally this card represents a spiritual or physical change. Endings or the finality of something is indicated. Shedding of an outer illusion or the end of an era is one possible meaning. Transition! Like the caterpillar's chrysalis being cast off. We humans in the material world have a will to survive. From the time of early man there were the physical challenges of survival. In the world of the 21st century we as a species may try to survive on this planet by looking to the dangers we face with global warming, polluted atmosphere, starvation, diseases and the threat of nuclear disaster from wars or such mistakes as Chernobyl. As individuals we can only rely on those in power.

In the universal idea of the transforming principal, card number 13 is linked to card 18, The Moon...Number 13 + number 18 = 31...The one and the three exchanged, mirror image! TRANSFORMED! There is a saying that resonates with the meaning of this card 'all things must pass.' The divination meaning of the Death card does not always mean an ending to a life on earth, but as in physical death the card can be to shed off our outer layer (preconceived notions) to transform. If presenting reversed, we might assume there will be a lack of transformation. Perhaps our quest is never ending; perhaps at each twist of fate there is a new adventure to *pursue. Ending job or tie. When there is an end, there needs to be a period of adjustment, transition!*

A transition started for me adjusting to a new persona in working life. The advent of 'Flower Power' marked my transition. From 'tom boy' encased in drab crystallise, (school uniform) into a Butterfly, but mostly on a Wednesday!

Reader... There is no permanent state of being. All chapters in life are transitional. History shows we are capable of adjustment, adapting to change. The saying that comes to mind is... 'As one door closes, another door opens!'

Chapter 15

1960's continued.

As Auntie Joan became more poorly she took great comfort from listening to music. My grandparent's home was always full of music and they were the first people I knew to have radio and a record player as well as a television. It was a strange collection of records as there were comedy recordings such as 'My old man's a dustman' by Lonny Donegan and Charlie Drake singing 'Please mister Custer', as well as all the crooners of the day such as David Whitefield and Mario Lanza, but the most emotional record was 'Are You Lonesome Tonight?'. Hearing Elvis singing this, still to this day brings a tear to my eye as Joan would play this over and over again as she was trying to recover from the breakdown of her marriage.

During those years my mind often turned to pondering the biggest question of all. What is this life all about and is there, at the end of it all some other sort of existence? The poltergeist activity had already started before we lost my Aunt but at that time we, mum and I, thought it a 'peculiarity' of our own house (the police house) in Preston.

It was not until the mid 1960's that I began to fully realise the connection with spirit activity, strong premonitions and my mind set when tea cup reading. I was finding at that time I could often control my dreams. There were some dreams that were so vivid that I later came to think they were 'out of body' experiences. Much later, after marriage I did have quite definite and fully remembered 'out of body' experiences.

There was a vivid reoccurring dream that came every two or three months during my teenage years. When I first had this dream I would find myself looking out of my bedroom window. It was dusk but I could make out the road and the field across from our house. I could even see the sheep. As I watched there was a rushing sound and I started to notice the roadway was flooding. In the dream I was thinking where the water could be coming from. Very quickly the water level was rising and I could hear something coming from the direction of the stairs. I left the window to look what was making the noise inside the house. Coming up the stirs were lots of creatures from the woods. I realised they were running upstairs to escape the flood. I saw rabbits, some rats, a fox and even a hedgehog. I sensed they were terrified as I now saw the water was half way up the stairs. Feeling the fear of the animals I fled back into my room and shut the door quickly.

At the window in this dream, again I saw the water level had risen to be lapping at the window ledge. A thought came that I must escape through the window. Not having learned to swim the stairway was not an option. Looking round I pulled the bottom draw out of my dressing table and decided it might just about hold me. As I opened the window and started to climb into my 'raft' the dream started to fade. Once awake the realness of the dream made my heart pound. The next time that dream came to me it played out as before except it started as the water was up to the window ledge, the creatures were scrambling at my door! The dream came many times for the next few years. Later, living a couple of miles down the road from my parents the dream would be in the setting of my new surroundings.

The dream now started with me walking over a nearby bridge. I could hear a loud roaring sound and looking over the wall of the bridge, the railway had become a gushing river. I crossed over the road to the far side of the bridge and in the distance there was a huge wave on the horizon. At the time of this dream I had no idea what a Tsunami looked like, in fact I don't think I had ever heard of the word. During the dream, realisation came to me that I would possibly drown as the wave reached me, but just as the wave loomed over me the dream ended. Waking just in time a moment before the wave covered me, my heart was again thumping with the seeming reality of it all.

The dream came again a couple of years after my first child was born. This time the dream started with me pushing the baby buggy up the bridge. Fear gripped me as the danger was that both myself and my baby would likely drown. Once again I awoke just in time. When we moved to our next home the dream changed again and I was walking down the main

Liverpool road and looking towards the horizon as the Tsunami was visible coming from the direction of Southport to the west.

We later moved to the outskirts of Southport and the dream changed again. By then we shared a big house with my parents and grandma. Our flat was upstairs and in the dream I would be at the bedroom window looking towards the sea. The Tsunami was visible as a massive wave but my mind was calmer this time. Thinking of the size of the house and the fact that there were so many buildings between us and the sea, the wave may be broken by the time it reached us. The dream came again several times in that way but each time I would feel we would be saved. The dream changed again when I worked in my Predictions shop closer to the sea. This time the dream started as I was outside my shop when the enormous wave was towering right above my head and my last thought was, DOOM!

Later the dream would start as I was floating, as if above the house, looking down over the landscape. When the wave came, the whole of the area became an ocean, all that was visible were a few high buildings and the top half of Blackpool Tower in the distance. Twenty years after the move to Southport, just two weeks after my dad passed away, we watched the news of the 'boxing day Tsunami'. In my grief I had a fancy that dad had been called to help those souls drowned. In his time in the Merchant Navy his ship got torpedoed and later life he would relive the horror of watching as his crew members drowning in the oil coated sea.

After this, the real Tsunami, the dream never came to me again. Was this dream a premonition? Hard to say! Later when global warming is a news feature I pray that my dream of Lancashire and the flat lands from Liverpool to Lancaster being under water, will never become any kind of reality. All we can do is ask protection from our Temperance Angel and be as 'green' as we can in our own habits.

Going back to the years of my early teens I now wonder if my Temperance Angel saved me from a few nasty scrapes. Some of the young men I had liked proved to be less than mannerly. At that time, with the advent of 'the pill' there was a culture amongst some of the male species that seemed to say 'Now we can bed them and don't have, to wed them!' Before the pill, there was pressure within the working class areas for a shotgun wedding to take place if a girl got pregnant. In more well off areas it had now started to be quite trendy to just live together before marriage. In Preston, on a Police estate it would have been unthinkable to ask the family doctor to give you a contraceptive tablet. Now that a pill had been invented, to many young men, all girls had become fair game. It was the norm for them to assume a girl would be 'on the pill' and ask if she may be willing! There is no doubt that this attitude can be perpetuated and at this time of writing we see women making a stand for more respect from men. The film 'Alfie' demonstrated the attitude lots of young men had in the early 1960's towards women and girls. It seemed to me at the time that a girl turning down sexual advances might be valued more. I wanted to be courted in a romantic way just as I had read about in books, and like the women in the 1950's films.

By about 1967 I had begun to think there were few young men of the type I wanted, a man willing to tap into a sensitive, caring energy. The era where 'Flower Power' became the mantra of the younger generation did seem to bring about a sea change, but would this 'Love is all you need' be lasting and was my 'White Knight' out there?

There were times where I shut out my inner voices and paid no regard to my intuitions because the lad chatting me up at first seemed respectful. As my Gran used to say there are a few rotten apples in every barrel! In truth I can't say all the lads were the same. It was a few weeks after starting work when I was getting over my romantic disappointment with Mike (a bit of an Alfie!) when, whilst out with my friend Val, I met Patrick. Things seemed to be looking up and Patrick was very well mannered.

When Patrick came round to my house, he would bring books he wished me to read. This continued for several months until it was time for him to pack for University. It was time to kiss and say, goodbye! Patrick had enhanced my world from his love of books so I thank him for introducing me to the writer H. G. Wells, amongst other great writers, and for showing me respect. I then consoled myself with the fact that I always had Elvis!

Elvis was still my favourite of all the pop stars of all time, and as I had been bought a fab record player for my 16th birthday I could listen to him all evening long! My first single was Cliff Richards singing 'Living Doll' but my heart belonged to Elvis. As soon as I had some wages I bought an L P. 'Elvis Golden Greats'. There was a little self-wallowing when listening to 'Heartbreak Hotel' but the deep strong voice of 'the King' would always sooth my mood. There would be a string of 'might have been' romances before I met my Mr Right, but I had too much pride to pine very long over any lad.

Just before the 1966 World cup a possible contender for equalling Elvis in making my heart flutter, came on the scene. A handsome German sailor, Hans Peter. There was a little sparkle between us, though I'm not sure the chemistry would have matured to love had Hans Peter remained in my life but as it turned out the romance was soon doomed, not by the call of the sea but by the hand of fate.

The spiritual questions remained with me during these fledgling relationships. On nights when the vivid dreams became more and more 'real' it made me feel on waking that I had been to real places and spoken to real people and yet these were never any places or people that I knew. My brother John and I still played intuition games and I had found out that in the right mood I could pick out a winner when shown the racing page of a newspaper. Never a betting family apart from my grandad, and he was never very lucky, I had been told that betting was a mugs game.

It was a lad that used to walk home from work with me that brought this 'gift' to my attention. Sam was an orphan and lived with foster parents.
He had asked me out, but my feelings towards him were just friendship. Sam would bring the racing page and ask me to pick out a winner for the next day's races. He knew I read the tea leaves and so I think he was testing out my potential to pick him a winner. The trouble was the experiment worked and he was there again the next day showing me his winnings.

Sam wanted me to come to the pictures with him to spend his winnings. I agreed to go but only in a group of friends as I was still writing to Hans

Peter. The next Friday as I left work Sam was waiting for me. 'Please pick another winner for me Jen.' He begged. Not wanting him to get into the habit of betting as I knew it could lead to heartache I resisted his plea. He kept on coming to meet me and after a while of him pleading with me to pick a winner I said okay, but this will be the one and only time and I would never do it again no matter what.

Sam asked me to pick three horses one in each of three different races. Eyes closed I ran my finger over the page and stopped when I felt a kind of warmth from the name. Sam noted down the names and we said goodnight. The next day was Saturday and when work finished at noon Sam was waiting for me, beside himself with delight. He told me he had come up on an accumulator. Not knowing what that was I was shocked to hear he had won over three month's wages. Sam wanted to give me some then save the rest. Not wanting to pick any more horses for him I refused the offer. The next Monday Sam's foster mother came to my work to ask me to visit him in hospital. He had been rushed in with a burst appendix.

Remembering my Uncle Jack, after winning the pools and not getting to live to spend them, I feared the fickle laws of the universe. Had LUCK to be paid for in some way? Is luck given us with one hand and taken with the other? Had negative forces made Sam pay? I made my mind up never to use my third eye to bet or to help him bet. After visiting Sam in hospital our paths never crossed again. I had applied and got a new job, still in Art and had never given Sam my address.

My romance with Hans Peter was still on and he would send me a telegram whenever his boat was due to dock in Preston. He would also write me very romantic letters from the West Indies. At the age of seventeen, the kind of broken English he used seemed to me so exciting. Each month when his boat arrived he would come to our house to pick me up. Dad had very different views on the situation than myself. He would frown and mutter something under his breath when Hans Peter called in.
Not forgetting this was just twenty years after the war and some older people found it hard to accept that the German enemy was now a European friend.

During the 1950's and 60's there were many people of Polish and Jewish backgrounds that had suffered heart breaking losses during the war. Although many young people were all about the peace and love with the mood of the 'Flower Power' era of the mid 60's, there were still many to frown on the nationality of my new boyfriend. My attitude at the time was that it was my own business whom I chose to mix with and anyway the German lads I met with Hans Peter all seemed to have nice manners. They were not to blame for the sins of their country. By this age I was all for peace and love. Mum always gave a warm welcome to my friends and remarked what a polite young man Hans Peter was, though dad was quiet on the subject.

After a few months when Hans Peter was in port my Dad softened towards him a little as he made conversation as best he could about the ship and how he liked the life at sea. The verbal communication between myself and Hans was getting slightly better as Dad had given me a German/English dictionary and I was trying to learn a few words of German. I think it helped that my Uncle Stephen had brought home his German speaking wife after serving in Germany just after the war. Mother's side of the family had become fond of her when she told of her wartime ordeals trying to cross from where they had lived on the Polish border. The Nazis had thrown many families off their lands; Ursula's family being one of them. At work I was the only female and did not tell any of the men about Hans Peter.

One other female worked at my new firm's head office in town. She would only come with any paperwork for my boss once a week. The firm did photography and printing for a number of businesses including furniture and clothing for several big name catalogues. The only other girls I saw were one or two of the models from Lucy Clayton agency in Manchester. Several of them told me I should go into modelling as at five foot nine my height and long black hair would get me in.

The thought of taking some of my clothes off in front of men as I had seen they were required to do when modelling underwear, put me off. Although I don't consider myself shy it had been instilled in me at home that a girl must have some modesty. Perhaps this was a narrow minded attitude but at the time I was still rather body conscious.

Each time Hans Peter came to Preston on three days leave it was like starting over again getting to know him. In person the language barrier made chit-chat a tad difficult. I thought it wonderful to get his telegrams and he seemed able to express himself more easily in letters. When we went out for a meal he held the chair back for me and took my coat. I was a little self-conscious eating with him as I had never had a meal out on a date before. We talked as best we could. He seemed amused about the recent World Cup and the fact England had won against the German team. The date went as well if not better than any previous dates I had been on. To my mind he was just as nice as the English lads I knew, and was more respectful to me than some of the local lads.

The fourth time we met up together, Hans Peter came into port a day earlier than he had said in his last telegram. It would turn out to be our last meeting! He knocked on the front door one afternoon as I was painting a large butterfly wall mural in our front room. Covered in paint and upset that he should see me in my scruff I ran upstairs to change. Sitting with a cup of tea later I noticed that he seemed a bit fidgety. He kept adjusting his trousers as if uncomfortable in the chair. It then came into my mind that he was not well. Pushing the thought away I agreed to go with him to the Cinema.

The film showing was 'The Family Way' starring John Mills and his daughter Haley. The film was about a young couple getting married and though they had been very much in love they had wanted to wait to have sex until after the wedding. The young husband was unable at first to consummate the marriage but things turned out right in the end. On our way out Hans Peter asked me what it was all about as his English was not good enough to follow the complicated plot. I was too embarrassed to describe the film but I think he understood that the couple were both virgins on their wedding day. As we walked to the bus stop Hans Peter stopped at a Jewellers shop window and seemed to be a little sad as he looked at rings in the window. He turned to me with a serious look on his face. He asked if I wanted a 'white' wedding. I had not ever thought of marriage or what kind of wedding I wanted. Quite fazed I gulped. Is he trying to propose? My second thought, is he asking if I was a virgin? Not being exactly sure of what he was getting at with his broken English I just said 'yes I would like a white wedding'.

Hans looked crestfallen, then with a tear in his eye he said he must tell me something important and serious. He told me that when he first joined the ship his shipmates had teased him about his lack of experience with the ladies. He said they kept on telling him he must become a man. Not really understanding, I just listened as he went on to say he was very sad as he could never have a white wedding. What the heck could he mean? I was not quite sure where the conversation was going. From what I could gather, when the ship had docked in Barbados, Hans had been more or less dragged to see a 'naughty lady!' A tear dropped onto his cheek as he went on with his story. He told me he was very frightened and was now VERY sick. Hans told me he was very worried about his condition. He said he had caught a disease from the 'Lady' and that it would mean that we had to part. We could not marry. Mixed up in my mind about the conversation, Hans said he had to go home to tell his parents, (both doctors) and they would be very angry. feeling a bit sorry for myself and him, I wished him luck and hoped he would recover. As I boarded the bus my own tears started to fall. Was sex so important for men to think it a test of manhood, to drag someone to a brothel to end their virginity? Could there be any honourable men out there?

The romance of receiving telegrams and letters from so far away was an exciting experience along the path of my life. Looking back now I could see that even if he had not got sick there was never the right vibe between us. Sometimes when young, we let our true instincts be lost in a fairy story we have invented. We forget to tune into our inner self. Even if we had spoken the same language Hans Peter was not 'The One!'

After this experience perhaps some of the lesson of the Temperance card had dawned on me. My inner voice told me that my silver cup of love had spilled its contents in order to make way for a golden cup of romantic nectar in the shape of the kind, handsome, sensitive and romantic man of my dream.

At work there was a young man, Gordon, that had a bit of a twinkle in his eye and I got the feeling he liked me. The rest of the male staff were pleasant enough but my inner voice warned me not to get too friendly with any of them. Was this feeling an intuition or was the Temperance Angel trying to warn me what was to come?

Reader... When the universe refuses to give us what we wish for, perhaps the Temperance Angel knows better than we know ourselves what will be beneficial to the progress of our soul. We might mourn the end of a romance or relationship but we have to realise that close unity into a lasting partnership can only work if there is mutual respect, love and, or desire.

15/ Tarot lesson, TEMPERANCE

Card. 14...Lesson fifteen of the Tarot...Initiative, Changes of life...Aquarius Song...'Are You Lonesome Tonight!'...Singer...Version... Elvis

The Angel on this card is holding a Silver Goblet or Chalice in his left hand and liquid is flowing from it into a Golden Chalice that he holds in his right hand. We might assume the liquid to be the 'Nectar of the Gods' as Angels in many different religions are said to have a link with God. They are purported to be the messengers from God.

Thinking of what this image is trying to tell us we might assume the Silver Chalice to be the situation that we are in now, the position, knowledge we have already gained in this life, and the Golden Chalice is to show the blessings and spiritual growth we might yet find in the future. Not perhaps material gain but a joy we can find in giving out love and using what is best within us. The liquid represents the flow of life force, within the universe and in us. We need to be adaptable and sometimes be ready to compromise, to have patience and seek harmony both within ourselves and in our daily dealings with others. We need also to look to our higher self to do what is right, to be in control. If we see a purpose in this life we have been given, then surely it must be for us to progress even if things go wrong in our lives. Card number 14 in the universal transforming principal links with card 17, The Star... 14 + 17 = 31 again mirror image of 13 = Transformation!

For many this card will spell out protection from our own Guardian Angel as from the biblical teachings. Whether we believe in Angels or not this card definitely speaks to us of nectar from the 'Gods'. There is also the blending of the two forces of nature to be considered. Ying/yang, positive/negative, summer/winter, male/female or is it just showing us light and shade, plus adaptation, needed for life on Earth to survive. As cool night is replaced by warmer Sun energy bringing us from sleep to wakefulness each day. Life on Earth depends on both. In reverse the meaning is lack of moderation, loss of control, believing no possibility of change.

On this card the nectar of life is poured from ethereal feminine moon 'Goddess' silver container, into the waiting golden cup of the male 'God', showing a natural flow of energies from one to another.

At this point in my life my gran and our family would soon have to adapt to the change fate would deal, so would I.

Reader... Often, in life we must adapt to the lives of others. Meditation can help restore inner harmony when the flow of life requires give and take.

Chapter 16

World Cup Year, 1966 onwards...

After the last two doomed romances I wondered if there was a kind and respectful man out there in the big wide world that would love and cherish me. After finding out that Hans Peter and I had only been 'ships that passed in the night' pardon the pun, I remembered the dream I had two years ago when Val and I put wedding cake under our pillows to see if we might 'see in a dream' the man we would marry. Going to bed one night in the late summer of 1966 I noticed the full moon in the clear star studied sky. Thinking of the dream I had of the man in the navy donkey jacket taking me into his arms, **I gazed at a large star close to the moon.** Mentally I addressed the star as my **Angel,** and pleaded that it would not be too long before the Angel, of fate would bring that dream man into my life. I '**Angel ordered'** to ask her to make him hurry.

Throughout the following winter there were many other things to think about rather than Angels and wishes. Much of my leisure time was spent painting and my brother was thrilled with the larger than life World Cup Willy I had painted last Summer. Perhaps it had brought our English team a bit of extra luck. Mum was pleased with Johns mural and the one on the chimney breast that I had made on the day my romance with Hans Peter came to an end. Later I would do one for Gran in her council house in Manchester.

As Christmas was approaching I cheered myself by making some large brightly coloured paper flowers and painting miniature scenes onto the cleaned out, blown goose shells my dad had brought home from his friend's farm.

I was particularly proud of the painted egg shells. The scenes were of Japanese ladies in oriental gardens and some of the details were painted with just a single hair on the brush. These were to be given for Christmas gifts to family.

Saturday evenings would still find me with Val at the dance, either at Grasshoppers rugby club or in town. By this time the 'hippy era' was dictating some of the fashions we wore. The mini skirt was getting ever shorter but the Beatles trip to India had also set a trend for long Kaftan style dresses. We were nothing if not colourful as we danced around our handbags.

Between Hans Peter leaving and Christmas we met a few lads at the dances but none that really lit any spark within my heart. There was Arthur in a band (The Condors) from Liverpool, nice but off touring so after a few letters being exchanged that fledgling romance fizzled out. There was John from Chorley who kept turning up at my door. Dad remarked that John was one of those types that would try to wear a girl down. After the let down with Hans Peter it had been tempting to let John take me here and there on nights out. Dads remark made me realise that I was being mean to John, keeping him dangling, so before Christmas I would tell him that he was not the one for me and not to call again.

Val was going to visit relatives over Christmas and as I had no boyfriend the dancefloor was not looking too promising. At work a meal at a posh place was being arranged, over near Longridge. The executives and their wives would be at the meal as well as all staff and partners. When Gordon whom worked in the darkroom asked if we might sit together, I agreed.

Before the Christmas dinner a new chap, Andrew had started working in the art room, his dad was also a police man on our estate. Andrew had been one of the nicer lads in my class at Art College and was now fully qualified in Graphic art. I had left before completing the course in order to take up the job I was now in. Soon I would have cause to regret that decision as it would give my boss the excuse to sack me. This however would not be for another few weeks and in the meantime there was something I was about to discover. A secret, linking to the boss and the firms rather flirty secretary, Caroline.

A day before the dinner I was eating a sandwich lunch at my work desk, all the male workers were out at a pub lunch. I heard a noise coming from the office next to my work room. Thinking the building to be deserted apart from me, I started to listen carefully. There were groans and shuffling noises and then the sound of a female voice. Realising the boss must still be in his office I kept quiet. After a while the door opened and Caroline came out smoothing down her skirt, the boss came out following her and my door being ajar, I saw them kiss. As Caroline left by the outer door the boss turned to enter my room, he could not disguise his obvious surprise as he saw me. He must have thought the place was deserted. I'm not sure who was most embarrassed, he or myself. He had not seemed to be the kind of man that would so easily give in to the temptations of the flesh. Nothing was said but I was quite upset and my opinion about the boss and his character did take a dive. How could he behave like that when he had a pretty young wife and two gorgeous toddlers at home?

The Christmas meal was perfect but I did not much enjoy it. There was some tension in the air when my boss introduced everyone. Caroline was sat with a chap I had not seen before, Gordon said was her husband. The boss was sat next to his lovely wife. He gave me a sly look as we sat down. He knew that I now knew his dirty little secret.

Gordon was a perfect gentleman as we chatted at the table. We drank a glass of wine together whilst waiting for the starters to arrive. We did a bit of flirting but talked mostly of work and his love of photography and my love of art. At the end of the evening Gordon gave me a lift home and we had one kiss but then, looking sheepish, he mentioned his wife. The little flame between was quickly extinguished. My thoughts for the next few days were preoccupied with the boss, Caroline, plus the interaction with Gordon after the Christmas dinner, so my intuition was not 'with it' on the last day before the Christmas holiday. It turned out to be a day I shall never forget!

The night before, after the kiss with Gordon I had a strange dream that someone was lurking in the woods to harm me. Thinking the dream negativity had been due to the wine and the guilt of the kiss, I shrugged off the shivers. That day there was an unpleasant incident for me during the lunch break.

Once again I was left alone in the art room as all the men were going to the pub for lunch. My boss asked me to wait in as there was a big client due in to collect his Christmas gifts from the firm. He pointed out the two large bottles of Brandy on the shelf near the wall phone. He instructed me to be nice and friendly as Mr 'P' (the expected client) was a very important man who was the owner of a chain of shops and the catalogue firm we relied on for our big contracts.

After lunch I got on with some work spotting flaws from negatives. Concentrating on the task I was startled as a large man stumbled noisily into the doorway of the room. He was a rotund elderly man and quite an imposing figure in his expensive black overcoat as he filled the doorway. He started smirking in a lurid sort of way saying what a pretty girl I was. Something told me I had been set up! After a moment, my thoughts racing, feeling compromised, I had to get out of the place regardless of what the boss would say when he came back. Getting up I went towards the shelf next to the door telling the visitor that these bottles were for him. He tried to grab me, his arms out towards me, there was no option for me but front it out with him. He was still blocking the doorway so I picked up the two bottles and pushed them into his outstretched hands. As he grasped them I pushed past and he fell to one side knocking the phone off the wall. Not wanting to stay around to see what he would do next I legged it out of the building and waited round the corner until I saw the others coming out of the pub. By the time we all went into the building there was no sign of Mr 'P'. To avoid questions, I went straight to the powder room. Returning to the Art room I saw the phone was now on the shelf. It was obvious the phone had been pulled off the wall, but going by the old saying 'least said, soonest mended' I said nothing.

In my mind Mr 'P'. had deserved all he got and I never told any of the lads about what had happened. After Christmas no one asked about the phone so I thought the incident was over. Before long I had the nasty shock of my employment being terminated. It was the day after my 18th birthday, Jan 8th. The Owner of the firm called me into the office. He looked embarrassed and stutteringly he told me he was sorry but the firm was not able to keep me on because I had not got my qualification from College. Asking me to leave, he said not to come back into work after lunch.

No proper explanation was given and very puzzled as to why the firm had taken me on in the first place I walked out that day in tears! In those days I thought it was a terrible thing to have had my job terminated in such a way. Feeling humiliated and shamed I was sure it was because I had not come up to scratch in my abilities. It did not occur to me at that point that my sacking may be a result of my rejecting advances of a silly old man. Or the dirty little secret of the boss and Caroline.

Thinking dad would be angry with me I was surprised when he calmly asked me what had happened at work in the run up to the sacking. Dad sat patiently as I went tearfully through all the story about the boss and his girlfriend and the horrid Mr 'P', ending with what the boss had said. Dad told me to dry my eyes and not to worry.

The day after, at tea time I learned that dad had been in to see the owner of the firm that sacked me and had given him the sharp end of his tongue. Dad left him in no doubt as to the reason he thought I had been dismissed. 'This is not a workplace, it's a Knocking shop!' he said. He came home with two weeks, wages for me. It was heartening that dad was completely on my side.

A week or so later I bumped into Andrew, my workmate. He looked a bit embarrassed and told me he was sorry if he had been the cause of my being sacked. Reassuring him that it was in no way to do with him I wished him well. On reflection I started to think that the boss had taken Andrew on so that later he had reason to tell the owner of the firm that they no longer needed me. The real reason perhaps was the fact he was uncomfortable my knowing about his secret affair or was it my shoving Mr 'P'?

Linking this situation to lessons of Temperance as well as 'The Devil', as I write it comes to me that the Temperance card tells us that the very thing we think is the desired 'Chalice' of delight sometimes turns out to be just a step to another direction, with another valuable life lesson. A handsome boyfriend, a job in a swish prestigious photographic firm seemed like 'golden cups' but were definitely not all they were cracked up to be! Lucky for me that any romance with Gordon had not quite got into the area of temptation and at least he had the honesty to tell me he was spoken for. Now I must wait to find another job and a fresh romance.

Reader... Remember that temptation comes in many forms. Booze, drugs, cigarettes, junk food, theft or abuse from or to other, are just a few that could spoil our life and impact on our loved ones. We might say that if we indulge in any of these we will be our own (Devil) worse enemy. Less obvious temptations are when we put work as top of our agenda, or when we over magnify a worry. In many cases a trouble shared is a trouble halved. None of us are perfect and all we can do if we feel we have been our own worst enemy is to forgive ourselves. If another person is the 'thorn' in your life, then perhaps you might make a change to gently distance yourself from them.

Reader... This is the RUNE of Odin.
This RUNE is left blank.

There are infinite interpretations possible with this Rune. For me it shows that we are all born as if the blank sheet of paper and our life and death are in the hands of God. The power of our inner self can find a way to tune into the 'God' energy in prayer or meditation.

16/ Tarot lesson, THE DEVIL / ADVERSARY

Card 15...Lesson sixteen of the Tarot, Temptations/ Restrictions /Adversary
Song...'Get Off of my Cloud'...Version...Band...The Rolling Stones.

The image on this card looks rather ominous, we see the Horned beast looming over two human figures, a man and a woman with chains weighing them down. Flames are licking the human figures. On some card designs, flames are seen behind the people. The Devil appears to be in control. The Devil or as he is sometimes known, 'the Adversary', indicates more difficult situations we might encounter along the complicated path of life. Interpretation for this card would amount to a restriction to the progress of the enquirer. This may come in the guise of a person, or an event from fate, or just from an inner fear. Card 15 in the universal transforming principal links to card 16, The Tower of destruction...15 + 16 = 31...(look back to Temperance, card 14, and Transition, card 13 to see the link) ??? 15 + 16 = 31... Transformation!

Temptation is after all, the Devils weapon! If this card is cast in an Astrology Tarot circle layout we might link it to a situation where the enquirer is his or her own worst enemy by not hearing his own doubts! Fear is often the enemy of our earthly progress as it can pull us back from following our true instincts. Conversely if we rush into something knowing it may harm or causes complications in our lives we may say it was the temptation of the Devil. We have all heard the saying 'The Devil makes work for idle hands' referring to wrong doing, thus reminding us that it would be better if we stay on the straight and narrow, rather than giving way to our base instincts. It may not be easy but then life can throw us a hurdle that will in *the long run make us more determined to achieve our goals. Sometimes others will try to play the 'Devil's Advocate' by imposing their will upon us. This may be by pushing us into something we do not want to do, or by stopping us from what we do want to do. Presented in reverse this could show the enquirer to fall to a temptation. Sometimes recovery after addiction, rehabilitation.*

Linking the lesson of this card to my life at age 17 when there were several temptations around, yes, I was sometimes my own worst enemy. Observing others at that time it began to strike me just how hard it might be to avoid.

Reader... In life there is often a dilemma about love or relationships. Shall I stand up to someone or let them control me against my own inclinations? Our willpower comes into play. If the 'Devil' lurks within us (temptation) we might look at this lesson to find self-control. We will be our own worst enemy if we allow others to control us, or if we fall to temptation.

Chapter 17

1967-1968

For the next ten weeks I was on the dole. Oh! the shame of it all! Not able to ask for my old job back with my first employer, (would have been too much like egg on the face) I scoured the newspaper for a new job. There was little work available in anything arty, but one evening I spotted something in the paper. It was an advertisement for a Lithographic Printer at County offices for Local Government.

Dad told me I should apply. I had my doubts as I had only worked a Lithographic printer for a couple of times in my first job. Also, remember, it was dad that had told me to apply for that last job and look how that turned out to be!

Not wishing to be on the dole much longer I did apply to the job at County offices. When I arrived, there were thirty girls waiting to be interviewed but to my shock it was me whom landed the job. It would turn out to be another sharp learning curve when it came to the proclivities of other people.

The other girl I worked next to in a small room, Anna, was friendly. There were five women in the three small rooms of the Print Unit when I started the job. Mr 'B' the department boss shared an office with heads of other departments. Myself and Anna worked in a tiny room on two small Lithograph printing machines.

Head of the Print unit was a woman in her mid-forties, Angela. An older lady, Jean, manned the office when Angela was in the Dark Room with Mr B, making plates needed for the printers. There was one other girl working the brand new photocopy machine plus a sweet man, Wilfred who worked in the big paper store room where he cut the paper with a massive guillotine.

After my first couple of weeks a reorganisation was to take place. Three girls were to be working alongside Wilf and his guillotine. We were to have a pay rise if we would take on larger machines. I readily agreed but as Anna was leaving to be married, two new girls would later be joining me. The 'big room' was in the cellar and had one massive old Victorian work bench in the middle. It was dark, dingy, and rather spooky even if the light was on. We would find out just how spooky within a few days!

From the start of my working in the 'big room' all the female staff would eat lunch together around the Victorian bench. Angela was a little bossy, but then
she was supposed to be in charge. As I was the youngest on the team she nominated me to go on the butty run at lunch time. I did not mind much as it gave me a breath of fresh air.

After a while talking about all manner of things round the table the conversation got around to the antiquity of the Victorian table. At this point the other five knew nothing about all my poltergeist activity and tea cup reading. During the conversation Angela said it would be fun to hold a séance at the table. The room was dark enough and the table being a relic of bygone days could hold some vibration from the people who may have used it in the dim and distant past.

Being aware of what my Spiritualist friends in my first job had told me about spirit communications, when sometimes false or mischievous spirits may try to enter, I was a bit wary of getting into a séance especially as I did not really know everyone. The next day Angela brought a pack of cards that had all the letters of the alphabet and a card with 'YES' and one with 'NO'. She was so determined that we were all more or less forced to join in! Only ever having seen a séance on television before, we did not know quite what to expect.

The mood was set by turning off the lights and as the windows were partly obscured by all the stacks of paper and rarely cleaned, the atmosphere was appropriately murky and dark.

Angela told us to be quiet, then said a short prayer. Jean sat at the ready with pen and paper to make a written record of any communications that may come through from the spirit world. I had my doubts, thinking someone may push the upturned glass to spell out any old mumbo jumbo just to spook the rest of us. Angela spoke words one may expect at such a moment...'Is there anybody there?' We were all focusing on the glass as the six of us held our forefingers on it. A small movement from side to side came at first, then the glass went round in a circle. Angela repeated the words 'Is there anybody there?' All at once from small circles the glass made a bigger circle and then moved towards the word YES. One of the girls gasped, we all waited with bated breath. 'Who are you?' Angela whispered. The glass went round at a furious speed. 'It's going too fast.' whispered Jean trying to write down each letter the glass went to.

The glass sped across the old wooden surface of the table. We continued for a while longer and then as we would soon have to get back to work Andrea said 'Thank you.' to the invisible guest and the lights were switched back on. We all had a look at the notes Jean had recorded and we were able to make out the name Thomas and a few words here and there. It looked as if there was coherent thought behind the message as there was a name and what looked like a note someone may write to remind themselves of an appointment. After the name Thomas there were a couple of names of people and a date plus a road name that did exist in our town close by. Nothing dramatic but perhaps the sort of things someone may have had in mind whilst he carried out some day to day task. Because we had to get back to work we left any discussion about the whole thing until later. Work in a print unit is quite noisy and so afternoon break was the next time we could talk. We all agreed it would be interesting if we could find out more about our 'spirit' communicator. During the next few weeks we held these 'spook' meetings at least twice a week. Each sitting a different person was nominated to take the notes. The glass seemed to move more quickly when I entered into things than when I took the notes.

There were some days when the words were indecipherable and other times when we could make out quite a lot about whom ever it was that was directing us. My opinion, by then, was that there had been a possible link to spirits of the dead but I had yet to be fully convinced. Also in my mind was the possibility that one of the others may be pushing the glass. I knew that it was not me, unless in a subconscious way. Because of previous experiences, seeing the spirit of grandad Ted, I was curious to see if we may be able to contact a person in spirit that was known to one of us.

The next day I decided to test the spirit communicator by asking a question about something none of the other girls could know about. I wanted to ensure nobody was subconsciously pushing the glass. It was decided that we should each ask to communicate with a departed relative. Angela said I should go first after her saying the usual prayer. By now we would address the spirit by the name Thomas as the name had been given us many times when we asked who was there. I began by asking the usual question 'Is there anybody there?' Right away the glass sped round and stopped at the word YES. 'Greetings Thomas' I said. 'would it be possible for me to speak to one of my own family that passed away a short time ago?'

The glass spun round again and the glass spun to 'Yes, but only through me!' The other girls looked at me as I pondered on the last words. 'Will you tell my Aunt that I would like to speak to her?' I asked. The glass went round in furious motion for a while and I wondered what was going to happen. I had not given the name of my Aunt and so was amazed when at last the glass spelled out the word 'J-O-A-N.' The glass then went crazy around and around in a zig zag fashion.

A bit shocked that my Aunt's name had been given I decided to ask a question only I could know the answers to. 'Please ask Joan if she knows the names of any children born into our family in the last five years. The glass spelled out MARK and CATHY. All the hairs on my head were on end, how was this possible? My cousin Cathy had only been born after Joan had passed away. Once I had gathered my wits together I asked Joan to describe what it was like in the place she was in.

The glass went to each letter very slowly. This time as it spelled out these words...'IN THE PINK.' After this the glass just spun round in a frenzy and we had to stop. Now I knew the others at the table could not have pushed the glass as they did not know the three names linking to my family, also I had not had my finger on the glass after the name JOAN was given. I could only surmise that we had truly been in touch with the spirits. This improvised séance had shaken me and the next time it was suggested we sit in the circle I said no, I would just take the notes. The others were cross as they said the whole thing worked better when I joined in.

Still in a state of wondering, when I told Wilf about our lunch time dabbling, he warned me to be careful as he thought it a danger in some way. It later came to me that there needs to be harmony within the circle for a spiritual link to be strong and true, though I did believe the contact with Joan was true. Spring that year was to give me much more to think about than spirits. The machine I worked on had become so temperamental that the repair man had to be called in on several occasions.

Angela was often cross with me as she thought I should be able to make up the time lost by working faster rather than putting the truth on my time sheet saying the machine was stopped for repair. She was a bit sulky with me for not wanting to 'play' séance any more. Looking back now it seems to me that the whole work atmosphere had changed, and not for the better. Could it be the spirit of Thomas was feeling neglected and causing havoc with things?

The new lady, Ann had lost both her parents. One day I politely asked her if she was okay as she was giving me what could only be described as 'the evil eye' stare. 'Nothing!' she answered. At lunch time I went round to take the orders for the sandwiches run. My money was in my purse for my own order. After making the list and collecting the money from the others (without counting it because I thought I could trust them all) I got to the shop, put in the order, only to find when it came to payment the money was short. At the sandwich shop I left out my own order. The girls were sat waiting for their lunch when I got back, I said cheerfully, 'Someone forgot to pay.'

Earlier when the Ann started to act strangely I had made allowances and now she answered, 'It wasn't me!' The look on her face was slightly defiant. A voice in my ear told me she had done this deliberately. As they all said they had paid I had to forego my own lunch. That was not the last strange trick she would play on me, there was far more sinister moves to come.

During the first quarter of 1977 the only highlight was the weekend dance night with my friend Val. We loved to get dolled up and go to the Top Rank. There was a cinema on the ground floor, below that was a dance hall. There was always the expectation that we may meet some nice lad but after 'know all' Patrick then good looking Hans Peter my mind was made up that I would be a very choosy when it came to handsome. After all, 'handsome is as handsome does!' my Gran would say!

Between January and April that year Val and I went dancing most Saturdays. Once or twice my friend Pat would get the bus from where she now lived but she could only stay the afternoon, so she had not yet met Val. In the first week of March a letter came from Pat asking if she could visit and stay overnight. She was keen on a lad she had seen months earlier at a Town Hall dance and hoped to see him if we went dancing. She said he was a dead ringer for Dave Clark from the famous group. Val was away that week so it was to be Pat and I and another friend, Deb, going to the dance.

The Town Hall had a larger dance room than the Top Rank but was not as posh. As we arrived the Dave Clark look alike was in the entrance hall with a group of his friends. Pat was annoyed when she saw him wink at me. And even more annoyed later when he came and asked me to dance. Not wanting to upset Pat but quite liking the looks of this lad and always thinking it rude to say no to a dance, I nodded. I tried not to scrutinise 'Dave Clark', or George, (his real name) as we danced. After that one dance with George, Pat came over and asked him if he would have a dance with her. They danced one dance together, then he walked off the dance floor and Pat told me he had gone off to find his friends.

Later on my way to the powder room George was waiting for me and asked if we could meet up the following Saturday outside Timpson's shoe shop at seven o-clock. 'Okay but please don't upset Pat' I told him. Pat then spotted us and asked George for a lift in his little two seater sports car. He agreed but looked quite flustered. Deb and I got the bus home together. When I got in Pat was in raptures about how good looking, how clever, how good mannered George was. 'He said he will give me a lift to the station tomorrow.' She boasted. In confusion I wondered what George could be playing at, agreeing to take Pat home after asking me for a date. 'How can you be sure he will turn up, and will he be in time for you to get the train?' I asked. 'No worries because I got his wallet.' She grinned as she produced a wallet from her bag.

Excited, Pat rushed off to meet George before I had finished breakfast. All the following week I dithered knowing it must have looked strange my pressing him to be friendly with Pat after accepting a date from him. Should I give George a chance? Dithering, the following Friday I talked with Norma, a friend who saw me dance with George. 'I can give George a message when I meet Paul on Saturday on that corner.' she said. Her date was 7.30 pm, just half an hour after I was due to meet George. I decided not to go on the date. 'If he is still waiting by you get there, tell him Jenny is sorry she is not coming.

The next Monday on the bus I asked Norma how things went on Saturday. 'Sorry Jen, George was still there, but as I was plucking up courage to tell him you would not meet him, Paul arrived. I couldn't go over to George.' So he had waited for me. I felt bad! 'Oh well!' I sighed. George would never get to explain and neither would I. Dave Clark poster came down from my wall! Other pop posters, torn from the magazine 'Boyfriend' would adorn my bedroom wall for a little longer, despite mum complaining the sticky tape was ruining the wall paper. So far the year 1977 had been one disappointment after another and it was only the start of Spring. Perhaps this was the lesson of the Falling Tower. Deflated, that night, pondering the twist and turns of fate, 'would I find my own Rowdy Yeats (Clint

Eastwood)? Looking from my bedroom window I saw a bright star. Speaking to the Star again as if it were my Angel, I asked for a tall, kind man with good heart that would love only me. A few weeks later events would prove to me the Angel did listen...

Reader... If plans collapse, think of it as a helpful nudge from your Angel. There may yet be a golden chalice in your future. Assess and decide if you need to pour your energy into a new more enjoyable direction. Try not to think that this or that will never be. All things in the universe, all things in life are a matter of divine timing. Replace a 'never', with maybe or one day.

17/ Tarot lesson, The FALLING TOWER

Card 16...The Seventeenth Lesson of the Tarot, Turmoil.
Song... 'Bits and Pieces.' by Dave Clark Five.

The Falling Tower, sometimes known as the 'Mad House' is possibly the most shocking image of all the Tarot card pack. It shows a scene of destruction as lightning strikes the top of a medieval building. At the foot of the Tower we see people fleeing as part of the building is falling away. Flames leap from the top of the Tower. One figure is jumping from a window. There is a large bird flying away from the flames.

The meaning of the card is often thought to be catastrophic events that we humans cannot control. We know that sometimes in life there are terrible events that can cause loss of stability and rock the foundations of society. That would be the **extreme** *interpretation. On a more every day level the meaning would simply be the warning of an unexpected upheaval that disturbs our routine. A setback out of the blue that may cause a shock of some kind. In its extreme this card can foretell of earthquakes or other so called 'acts of God'. Mostly the event will just be an unexpected setback.*

During the many years I have been reading the cards for people from all walks of life I have known this card to be the most traumatic event though, often it has proved to be a small incident that can feel like a downfall at the time. Everything from someone falling off a ladder, to a person becoming bankrupt. Reversed this card may indicate a situation that had already caused upset, starting again from the aftermath of a disturbance to life, such as need for complete resettlement.

The Tower is the UNKNOWABLE! The unexpected! Sometimes after a downfall we are able to pick ourselves up and learn from negatives as much as the positive things that befall us! A bird flying away from the falling tower is a reference to the legendary Phoenix, and on the card he DOES rise from the ashes. The message is clear...Good can come out of a bad situation even when we, being human, cannot see it. Let the dust settle before we assess the consequences. Often a disruption proves a blessing in disguise! Had my 'Falling Tower' lesson been learned by the crashing out of a job that had looked so promising, or was there another fall to come?

Reader... Think about your own life, has there been an upset out of the blue? Did you rebuild in some way? Are you stronger from this? We may face more than one 'tower' event but there is a resilience to be had even in dire circumstances, as it is within our human nature to survive if we so wish.

Chapter 18

1967, The first Summer of love.

The first few days of April were blustery but not too cold, as yet there was no sign that snow was on its way. After one of my more interesting dreams where I was floating over the wood and the fields near our home, once again thoughts of what happens to us after death came into my mind. And if we **do** go to the place described to me as 'In the pink' by the spirit of my poor Auntie Joan. Deep in thought I went down to Sunday breakfast. Mum was frying bacon and as I was telling her about my dream she suddenly remembered that a letter had come for me the day before. The letter was from Pat asking if she could come for a sleepover next Saturday. Mum said Pat could stay, so after breakfast I wrote a quick letter to tell her to come. It would be interesting to find out if she had been on another date with George.

Val and I had got tickets for a big concert in Blackpool from another friend Debby but that was two weeks away yet on Saturday 15th April. Val had never met Pat but agreed to Pat joining us for the dance next Saturday, the 8th of April. Not now working on Saturdays I was busy curling my hair with my new Carmen Rollers when Pat arrived. She told me she had not seen George and she was not bothered as she was dating another lad from where she lived. So! I thought, that is why she sulked when George had danced with me. Oh well, spilt milk and all that!!!

We were in good spirits as we made our way to the bus stop at the other side of the dual carriageway. The air was still and there was a lovely feeling of quiet, the kind of quiet that sometimes feels like Christmas Eve. The sky was still a little pink from the setting sun. There were some thin clouds in the crisp, clear evening air. Waiting for the bus the strangest feeling came over me!

Pat and Val were talking about past outings with me. Pat said I had not to look at any lads tonight. Thinking back to the last time we were out together at the Town Hall I thought she must be referring to that dance.

As if she had read my mind she began telling Val about George and painting me as a flirt. As they chatted my mind wandered, feeling mesmerised with the strange beauty of the evening.

The bus was late and I remarked on how eerily quiet the road had become. Hardly any cars had passed us and the air was somehow charged and atmospheric. All these years later I can still remember saying 'There is going to be something special happening tonight.' Val and Pat gawped at me oblivious of the vibe, so I told them to look at the sky over the tops of the trees above the woods across the road. The trees had an aura of pink light shining over them. As we gazed out the first flakes of snow started to fall. Large heavy flakes came down and yet the sky still held a little of the pink of sunset. 'Can you feel it? I asked. The two of them seemed amused, but something special was about to happen. I could feel it! This strange atmosphere, a hush in time!

By the time the bus came the snow was a few inches deep. We laughed and chattered all the way to town. Going into the Top Rank we went down the stairway to the dance hall. The Ladies cloak room was our first port of call, wanting to look our best before we went to dance. The music had already started as Pat fluffed up her hair with the back comb, still favouring a big hair look. Val and I now had longer hair, mine influenced by Cher. The fashion in those days was to look as if you had a tan, so a dark foundation cream had to be smoothed in, so no streaks! Black eye liner (Dusty Springfield trend) to show off our pale lipstick, I preferred a peachy pink at the time. We always wore our newest clothes for the dance. That day I had bought a navy mini skirt and matching sleeveless blouse with a frill from the neck to the waist. The outfit was completed with a pair of navy 'shadow' tights and navy strappy stiletto sandals.

Once we had paid the cloakroom attendant we were ready for the music. The big band had just finished their first set and the D.J. was starting the Disco music. We made our way to the side of the stage where there was space for the three of us dancing in a circle round our hand bags. We had only been dancing for a few moments when I had a tingling feeling, someone was watching me. Looking round I saw two young men standing near the steps. The tall one in a dark brown corduroy jacket was looking at me. My heart did a flip! Recognising him, but at first not sure where from, I thought how handsome he was but then quickly looked away. I had sort of promised Pat and Val that I would stay with them. Determined not to let 'Mr Corduroy' see me interested I danced with my back turned towards him.

Several moments later it was as if a magnet pulled my head round for another quick look. His dark eyes were still looking my way. What was he still looking at me for if he wasn't going to ask me to dance? Wishing he would stop looking or else come over, for the next few moments I feigned indifference. Feeling a tap on my shoulder I turned. 'Mr Corduroy' at last came to ask me to dance. The Troggs sounded out 'Wild Thing, you make my heart sing'.

After two more records (Pat frowning at me over his shoulder) 'I know you, don't I?' we both said at the same time, then laughed. We had been to the same senior school but never spoken to each other as he was in an older year group. Our eyes had not even made contact with each other back then. The D.J. announced a slow number. 'Strangers in the Night,' rang out as I was swept into his arms. The attraction between us was immediate and it felt right somehow when he drew me to him for a gentle kiss. There was no cheeky chat up or furtiveness in his eyes, just him looking into mine. Instinct told me I knew this man's nature and knew he was special. Could he be the 'ONE'?

As the Disco music finished I let him lead me to a quiet bar behind the stage. We could now exchange names. 'Roy Pearce' asked me if I would like a Bacardi and Coke. We found a table next to the curtains. Through a gap the snow was still falling yet there were a million stars visible. 'Have you ever wondered if someone up there is looking down towards us at just the moment we are looking towards them?' he mused. Wow! This man was quite different to any others I had known.

Roy told me he had wanted to ask me to dance right away but he did not want to leave one girl out if both he and his friend came over. He said that in the end he just had to come over alone. The evening went by in what felt like a flash, then it was time to catch the last bus home. Roy walked with my friends and I to the bus stop and asked if he could meet me next Saturday. Because my friends and I had tickets for a show at Blackpool I suggested we meet up on the Saturday after. As the bus pulled up he kissed me and told me he would be waiting on a bench by the cross roads, close to our old school. 'See you in two weeks' he called as the bus pulled away. In those days few people had home telephones so we could not speak to each other again before the date.

All the following week my mind was full of my mystery man, Roy, but in the cold light of day I was trying not to get carried away on a romantic wave. There had been too many disappointments for me in the past where men were concerned. Two weeks was such a long time and Roy may go off the idea of meeting up with me. Thinking of what to wear going to the show the week after took my mind of the date. Mum had bought me a gorgeous white blouse with silver threaded through a lace edging on the tie front and at the edge of the 'bell' sleeves.

Many famous bands were performing at the show, plus some solo singers. Jimmy Hendrix and his band were the first act. The Walker Brothers next, then topping the bill was Engelbert Humperdinck, whom I thought was gorgeous! The 'Heathcliff' type with his long sideburns and dark eyes, just like Roy, the man I met last week. Imagine my surprise when Engelbert came down into the audience and sang his 'Spanish Eyes' directly into mine. It was quite a moment, but if I compared the eye contact then, with the eyes that had been looking deeply into mine just one week earlier, there was no contest. It would seem Roy, my dark haired man had captured my heart. The image of him in my mind was intoxicating. I longed for the week to fly.

When we hear people talk of love at first sight it is easy to dismiss it as romantic clap trap. Perhaps I would think that way if it were not for the fact that there is no other way to describe what happened to me that night in 67. If I were to describe the feeling in any other way, then it would be a kind of **recognition** from somewhere deep within me. Since then there have been many 'links', within friendships, that lead me to think we humans do have **'soul recognition'**. Perhaps from within ourselves or perhaps from other lives we have lived in the past.

Whatever it was that passed between us on that night it has now (as I write) lasted over 50 years. On our first date Roy confessed his first name was actually David but he thought his middle name more 'cool'. After two dates you can imagine my surprise when he arrived outside the back door of the Print Unit and I saw he was wearing the same coat as the man in my 'wedding cake' dream, **a navy 'Donkey' jacket**. If truth were told I knew then for sure that this was the man for me.

On our third date my new love arrived on his motorbike and dad made his usual frown over the top of the newspaper. Mum made up for this by saying 'sit down and have a cup of tea'. Dad was making a Giro copter in his spare time and perhaps for a little 'test' dad asked if Dave knew anything about Gimbal Heads. Not only did Dave know what this was, he offered to make the required part on a Lathe at work. That seemed to be the 'pass' mark to show dad that Dave was no feather head. I was still not allowed to ride pillion, so we walked home after the dance each Saturday night and to avoid noise for the neighbours Dave would push his motor bike past all the houses before starting the engine up to go home. Dad said the noise will wake the whole estate, especially as by now it took us longer and longer to kiss goodnight.

During the 'Summer of Love', 1967, before meeting my new man, I had booked with my friend Val to go on holiday to Douglas. By then Dave and I had spent every moment we could together, going for walks each evening and on Saturdays dancing at the Top Rank or at a disco in Chorley called 'The Hot Spot.' One evening we were doing a Twist at the disco when we noticed people being tapped on the shoulder by the DJ, then leaving the dance floor. We carried on Twisting and after a while there was just us and another couple left dancing. The music stopped and it was announced that we had won a Twist competition. The night before this I had a dream that we were running up a hill together towards a large circle of stones. In the middle of the circle was a cup, like a Chalice and as I went to pick it up a spotty dog came up to me and began licking my toes, this woke me up.

This was just another one of my prophesy dreams. One can see the symbolic meaning of the cup was the winning and the spotty dog was the symbolic pointer to the Disco place 'The Hot Spot!' It's hard to explain but these little events seemed to confirm in my mind that we had the beginning of a very special bond, a bond that felt as if we had known each other for ever! Dave was the first male of my generation I had met that I felt relaxed with in a companionship way as well as physical attraction.

Before my forthcoming holiday we went to Southport for the day. 1967 was a hot summer and that day was hotter than ever. We walked along the beach, sunbathed in the dunes then later walking by the lake we talked about our feelings, something I had never done before with anyone.

Sitting by the lake side I was taken aback when Dave went down on one knee and proposed. We thought our parents may not be too happy if we got engaged, as after all we were only eighteen and nineteen at that time. That evening after Dave asked dad if he could marry me, dad asked me 'Is this the man you want to marry?' 'Yes!' I answered firmly. After buying a ring, my parents asked us to wait to make a formal announcement in the newspaper. They said 'Wait two years!' before committing to marriage. Our engagement was announced in the paper on November 5th 1967, just seven months after we first met.

Shortly after our engagement was in the paper I was on the bus home from work when who should come and sit in the seat beside me but my old school 'nemesis'. Remember her? It was our 'not so nice' school prefect, Natalie 'Nag Bag'. She began chatting away in an over friendly sort of way. Wondering why on earth she had suddenly decided to act as if she were my best pal, flabbergasted, I let her do all the talking, (unusual for me I know!) telling me all about her office job at Police headquarters. She went on to say she had been a former close friend of Wendy, sister of Dave's best pal Mike. Then she said she had dated my Dave! That absolutely took the biscuit for me! She smiled, enjoying the revelation, whilst I tried to calm my thoughts. How could Dave like someone who acted in such a horrid manner, bossing younger children at school?

When I got home mum could see something was wrong. 'Hello love, what made your face look like a wet weekend?' she joked. When I told her about Nataly, she said she knew all about her as the grapevine on the estate had been in gossip mode. Mum told me that 'Nag Bag' had been apparently fawning over, first one Bobby, then another, and then, after a torrid affair with an Inspector, by all accounts throwing herself at him, going round and telling his poor wife all about it. 'Your dad can't stand her being in the office after she tried to come on to him.' Mum revealed. It would seem that all the decent chaps tried to avoid her brand of poison. The green eyed monster in me still had to ask Dave about his connection with obnoxious Nataly, but it was not the big issue it might have been if mum had not told me the gossip. My lucky **Star** had brought me the most wonderful man on the planet on that special evening, **man of my dream**. Nataly was not going to spoil it with her poison.

Dave told me he had never been on a date with Nataly and had only seen her when dancing at his friend's birthday parties. It was all in her head and her motive in telling me all this must have been her way of punishing me for all the times Pat and I had gotten away 'Scot Free' with our flouting of her precious school rules.

Dave and I were happy in our twosome. True, there are people whom live happy and fulfilled lives in the single state, but for me being married would give me a different kind of freedom. Free of some of the fear I used to have alone at night, not wanting to see any spirits. Fear when, now and again the negative forces are close to our world from the other dimension. Because out there in the great beyond I **now know** there is the most wonderful sea of souls making their way towards the ultimate glow of great goodness, the energy we call God, but I also know there are some lost souls drifting in and out of our realm at certain times.

Reader... Will your Star of hope set you on a new path? Have you learned the lesson of being positive, following your instincts and going along with the tide of life? If not, then try to be at the centre of your own star and let light shine from you and beam out into the world. The positive belief you will radiate can bring rewards far beyond whatever you might imagine.

Reader... This is the RUNE Laguz

The Rune Laguz is thought to represent water, fluid and the ebb and flow of the tide, thus has connection to the Moon and our ebb and flow of life.

18/ Tarot lesson, THE STAR.

Card 17. The Eighteenth Lesson of the Tarot...Hope
Song...'Strangers in the Night'...Version...singer...Frank Sinatra.

The Star, sometimes known as 'The Star of Hope' is one of the more positive Images of the Tarot. A beautiful woman (sometimes depicted as an Angel) is pouring shimmering liquid onto the Earth from a silver jug in her left hand and from a gold jug in her right hand. There are seven stars in the night sky and the brightest eight pointed star of Heaven is on her head. There is a small bird preparing for flight on a tree to her left. On some ancient Tarot designs the Hebrew letter 'phe' (mouth) indicating 'WORD' is seen. The impression is one of refreshment, purpose, HOPE.

The card holds a note of Fate, as if the Star is guiding the woman. She is replenishing the Earth and it is almost as if she is pouring down the magic of the Star. One analogy might be that she is 'going with the flow of life, adding her energy to the flow of energy from the God or Gods via the Star of Hope, the Star of Destiny.'

If looking for guidance from the Tarot we may interpret this card as a help from above. Right time, right place to be if we are willing to add our own energy to life. Kind of 'TAP IN' and 'GIVE OUT' then all will flow. To me the card indicates there are always situations and people flowing in and out of our lives as we navigate our way. Some people enhance our lives in the experience we share with them, if only for a short time. Others will flow along with us for years or throughout our whole lives.

We must let our own light, our own talents and personality shine forth in order to make the most of whatever the tide of life should bring us. The *positive message when we draw this card is to live, love and be aware that we can only receive as we are willing to give. Tune into our own instincts and remember that the well of hope is the well of love, for others, for ourselves and for the world. In reverse this card would remind us to be of hope, even in our darkest hour. Linking this card to this part of my life was natural as fate was to bring me what I had hoped for, the most amazing partner.*

Reader... My God may differ from your God but let love flow to make this world a better place. Work from the heart as you follow your own star. Let yourself be intrepid sometimes, use your talents, listen to your intuitions. Let your aura colours show. Be a radiator of light energy.

Chapter 19

1967-1968

Mum had been working part time in the sweet kiosk at the new Cinema. She only worked afternoons but it was great as she got a free pass for the family each week to use in the afternoon or week nights. One afternoon I took John and his friends to see Dr Zhivago. Some history for them and my favourite film of the 1960's, and to my mind, still up there with 'Gone with the Wind' and 'Wuthering Heights'. Guess I'm a sucker for the weepy heartbreaker scenes, the beautiful pale tragic heroine, and the handsome hero, especially the hero with the dark, smouldering eyes like my new man.

In childhood I had encountered a poor lady that lived close to my Grandparent's and was cruelly taunted by some people. She was said to be 'Moon Mad' because of her behaviour around the time of the full moon, but she reminded me of the tragic heroines we had seen at the cinema. We do know the moon has an effect on the tide and it seemed to cause this lady to run wild, thrashing her umbrella around as if swishing out at an invisible attacker. She would swear and curse and act as if the Devil were after her. At

other times of the month this same lady would behave in a perfectly normal way, she would smile at us and say hello, and because of this we did believe the strangeness to be caused by the Moon's influence. The Moon has a cycle that makes women ovulate and fertility is dependant in part to this, many women do still call their menstruation a curse, but we may say that, to a woman wishing for a child the Moon could be a blessing. The poor lady we thought 'Moon Mad' had most likely some imbalance within her, and soon I would encounter another woman who displayed similar tendencies in her behaviour.

During the time of our engagement there were many psychic experiences for and around me. Also the situation at my workplace would become quite toxic in the most bizarre way. The problem was perhaps exacerbated by my being too open at times. Going back to work after my holiday with

Val I was eager to share the news of my engagement with the girls in my department. Thinking they would all be happy for me as I was for others when they were celebrating anything, I was taken aback when one of the girls, Ann just shrugged and said 'Better be careful as things could go wrong!'

Feeling a little sorry for her as she had lost both parents, I let her negative remark go. From that day onward my dreams became more bizarre, as did Ann's behaviour.

Earlier when the issue of the missing lunch money was apparent I confess I had thought Ann may be the culprit. My psychic antenna was twitching even before Ann started to throw spanners at me whilst I worked. Yes, **spanners**! The first time I thought the spanner must have been thrown by accident, but couldn't think how. The second time I felt the spanner whiz past my ear it was a bit too close for comfort and I asked Ann, 'What the Dickens', she was thinking about. She feigned surprise and shrugged, saying the spirit Thomas was the culprit. After the incident at home when the heavy photo frame had flown across the room I half thought that this may be true.

Pondering at length after the second 'spanner' throwing a month later, and as the spanner event was in broad daylight and my poltergeist activity had mostly been at night, and had now quietened down, I thought it unlikely to have been caused by any spirit.

The third time the spanner was thrown it skimmed my hair. There was no option but to inform the boss, after all she may yet injure me or someone else. He looked disbelieving and from his expression seemed to think I was imagining things or it was some freak accident. After I left work he would have cause to think again. Ann eventually had to be restrained by medics and sadly put into a straight-jacket. She had put printing ink inside the pockets of the overcoat belonging to Wilf and when questioned went into a screaming frenzy. With medication we all hoped she could get over the sad losses in her life and would fully recover.

Over the years I have often wondered if the lunch time dabble with the spirits could have somehow drawn an unwanted entity into Ann. Was it possible to become possessed? Many religions teach that we mortals should beware of calling the dead to return to us out of morbid curiosity. For this reason, I have always fought within myself on the ethics of conducting a séance. It is my humble opinion that the spirit of a loved one will make himself or herself known if and when they are needed or ready to communicate, like grandad Ted. To me, the construction of an Astrology chart, the consulting of a Tarot card spread, or looking at the signs in a pattern of the leaves is not going to draw the spirits to me; unless the spirit has something to say.

By now, Dad, not wanting me to go on the motor bike had looked round for a cheap car for Dave. He found one that had been declared a 'Right off' by the insurance company because it had been left on Southport beach and covered by the tide. Dad had a lot of friends in the garage business in those days and somehow managed to get what we thought was a wonderful vehicle, a Vauxhall Victor! It would need a lot of work. The next few weeks Dave spent every spare moment stripping down the engine and cleaning the rust away from the underside of the car. Eventually it looked amazing and we thought ourselves very posh riding around in such a 'new' car!

We decided to go on holiday together if my parents would let us. It's hard to imagine these days that a person of eighteen would ask rather than tell their parents they were holidaying together before tying the knot. In 1978 it would have been unthinkable for a girl in my circle to go on holiday with a man without asking fathers permission first.

It came as quite a surprise when dad was okay about the planned holiday. It occurs to me now that he thought it good for us to 'see' if we were ready to be together as a couple before tying the knot. Dave had quite a few moments together with Dad when they were looking at the Gyrocopter project and so it may be that Dad had laid some ground rules out to him in private, before we set off.

Whilst doing the Vauxhall repairs Dave was round at our house each evening and at weekends. It was during this time that another upset would occur. Dad and mum had gone to Grans and taken John. I was busy making lunch when two boys, friends of John came to the back door to ask if they might take Johns doggy for a walk. 'Okay, but don't let him off the lead.' I said feeling reluctant. Later I would beat myself up thinking I should have also told them to come back to bring the dog into the house. The boys for some reason thought it right to just leave the dog in the yard where Dave was under the car. The worst happened, the dog wandered off through the gate that the boys had foolishly left open, and was run over by a red sports car on the main road close by. The driver, quite shaken, had come to the house with our lifeless pet, found Dave and told him what had happened. The next I knew about it was when I went to call Dave for his tea. He was holding the limp dog and looked stricken as he saw my ashen face. We were heartbroken and the worst was we had to break the news to John.

That night the whole family went to bed very tearful. The next morning before fully awake there was a small 'Woof.' And the dog jumped onto my bed just as he had done every morning. At first, in the twilight state between slumber and awake, I had forgotten what happened the day before. This would not to be the last sign for me from a pet and from beyond the veil of death. All the family cried for the next week or so and were especially sad for John.

A few weeks later a neighbour brought John three Guinea Pigs. They would not take the place of his pup but he loved them. Dad made a pen in the garden and for that summer we watched as three became six and six became ten and then something must be done. The pen could not house them all. Several children on our estate were soon the happy recipients of a small pet.

Off to Wales, Dave and I stopped close to a lake for a picnic, then, quite tired after a long walk around the lake we decided to find a place to stay. All the Hotels and Boarding houses in Wales had signs up in the windows 'NO VACANCIES'. It was starting to get dark when, after walking the length of the town we saw a B & B that had a sign saying 'VACANCIES'. Dave knocked and a frosty looking woman of about 60 years old came to the door. He asked if there were two rooms available. You may be thinking why would we want two rooms, but contrary to the 'free love' notions of the time, we had decided to make things special, we would wait for the complete intimacy part until our Wedding night.

The woman said she had one double room left available. Dave looked at me and I could tell he was waiting for me to decide if to share. I was so tired that I gave a nod. 'Can we take it then please?' The woman looked at my hand and saw the engagement ring, (no wedding band), and growled 'This is not that kind of establishment, get away with you!' We felt like a pair of criminals, but that left us no option but to cuddle up to sleep in the car. Lucky then that it had a long front 'Bench' seat, we found a quiet lane and we had Mr Moonlight to set the scene. The next day we drove around the coast and came to a Fairy Castle high up on the Cliff top. The sight of it delighted me.

We drove up the steep hill into the little town and along the main high street. Many houses we passed had No Vacancy signs in front until, close to the end of the town we came to a lovely old Cottage style single story house that had a more modern extension built onto it. The sign outside read 'B & B'. We tentatively knocked on the door and a friendly looking lady opened it. We were delighted when we found she had two rooms, one small box room and one double room. Dave asked if we might take them for the whole week. The Lady explained that she did not let out the small room normally, but as her son was away at University we were in luck if we did not mind that it was full of his African treasures. We readily agreed to take both rooms. It was suggested that Dave, being tall could take the larger room. We were shown to the hallway and the Lady pointed to the two doors and said she had to get to the kitchen as she had left something in the oven. She told us to make ourselves at home and come into the kitchen after unpacking so that she could give us a front door key. We looked into the what would be my room with a single bed. It was a bit daunting when I saw the African masks. There were six in all, their blank eyes making me nervous. Still it was clean and comfortable and as the B &

B was perched on top of the Cliffs it had a view of the sea. This part of the home was quite old and had small wooden doors, the bottom edges of which had clearly been eaten away by mice over the past two centuries. As the house was built in the 1700's it was not surprising that later, during the night I would feel a ghostly vibe. What was surprising, was sensing and hearing, the whispering voice of a child.

The first day was bliss as we explored the town and the beach in the hot sunshine. Relived that we had, that afternoon found and booked B & B. We stayed on the beach until dusk and then went to a newly opened restaurant called 'The Rum Hole.' It very much appealed to us as it was quite arty and very 'Hippy' in its interior. There was a feeling of going into an Arabian tent as the waiting area was festooned with silk wall hangings and there were only massive brightly coloured tapestry floor cushions to sit on. The rustic wooden tables had multi coloured candles dripping wax down the side of wine bottles. The food was scrumptious as most things on offer were doused in rum. The dessert was called 'A Rum Hole Special' and was a warm battered fried banana split on a long dish with three scoops of ice cream, trickled over with rum and syrup with fresh cherries on top. Food for lovers!

During the night I became aware that someone was in the small room with me. First it was the noise of footsteps as if someone was creeping about just outside the room. Then a creaking of the door as if it was being pushed. Rustling noises started as if from the small chest of draws at the end of the bed. Although I tried to tell myself it was just the old house settling I could hear a feint whisper and just knew that a small girl was in the room with me. In the light of day when I told Dave that my room was haunted he said it was probably a breeze or just the sound of the sea.

Almost convinced the sounds were in my imagination, the next night, not wanting to 'see' any spirits I asked in prayer that nothing would appear to me. This was not the first time I had asked not to 'see' spirits. During the poltergeist activity after seeing grandad Ted I had sent out the same prayer.

Determined not to let the nocturnal activity spoil what was otherwise a brilliant place to stay I asked Dave to give me the torch from the car and told myself that there was nothing to fear from someone without solid form. Before the holiday was over we planned to go to Shell Island to hunt for cowry shells for some artwork I had in mind. The lady of the house told us to be careful on the Island as there were strong tidal waves along that beach. She went on to say that a child, staying in the house with her parents, a little girl, had drowned there a few years ago. Though she did not say what room the child was in I was sure it was the 'African' mask room. Not only because of the noises in the night but because it was the only single room in the house.

Despite the 'visit' from the spirit child, the whole week was magical and on the way home we stopped at Lake Bala for tea and some Welsh cake. Walking round the quaint old town we saw a Welsh wool shop with a bright red cape in the window. Dave insisted we go into the shop and with the last of his holiday money he bought it for me along with some black high heeled patent leather shoes and a black pencil slim skirt. I felt like Queen Cleopatra. What a great way to end our first golden holiday together.

Back to work after our holiday it was truly down to earth with a bang! The old printing machine I worked on was breaking down for longer periods each week and required the mechanic to visit. The boss kept complaining that his budget was tight and expected me to catch up with the work by the end of the following week. It was impossible!

In desperation I asked Davie to come in one night as he called to take me home. He managed to fix the old printer but as we were looking at it, Ann had come back in for her bag. She saw me standing by whilst Dave had his head under the machine, she gave me a quite spiteful look. The next day Ann told me a long story about her friend passing away just before she was due to marry. All this happened just before the 'spanner' incident. At the time I could not have known she was so poorly. My stress level was already high as we were trying to make all the wedding arrangements. About a month before the wedding, I became unwell with an allergic reaction to strawberries and my arms, face and legs were covered in red blotches from hives. Then another kind of health issue presented itself.

After seeing the lovely female family doctor, I had started taking the contraceptive pill in readiness for the big event. Everyone was talking about how liberating the pill had made life for young women. Then...WHAM! Just a few days after starting the pill I was having another allergic reaction, a scary blackout whilst at work. This, plus trying to avoid the flying spanner, was the last straw. I gave in my notice. My mind was made up, any job with or without an arty link would do. As soon as the honeymoon was over I could take my time and look for a shop job whilst we lodged with mum and dad.

At home there was the task of finding material for the bridesmaid dresses and sorting out shoes that would be comfortable and go nicely with the dresses. A few months before when out with Jan, the other girl in the print unit, to pick up her wedding dress, not thinking about my own dress that day, there in the window was the dress I had imagined for myself. A silky fitted full length under a white lace overdress with a high Mandarin neckline, embellished with tiny pearl buttons from the neck to the waist. It was just too perfect not to purchase then and there. To my delight it was the cheapest dress in the shop at just £14.99. All the big crinoline dresses like the one Jan chose, and those on display were over £25.00 plus they were not what I wanted anyway.

More and more I was drawn to Oriental designs and patterns; this was apparent to anyone looking at the wall murals I had done in our front room, and now also in two other houses. Gran had been delighted with the Oriental blossom tree stretching around her chimney breast and her neighbour was thrilled with the flowering willow design in her sitting room. My designs mostly had a tree as the focal point then colourful butterfly and 'other worldly' blossoms giving a 'flower power' vibe.

Mum had shown a photograph of my paintings to her friends and as she came in one day about two months before my wedding she said her new boss, Mr Manning wanted to see me about doing a mural. Mum was now

working full time for Mr 'M' at what can only be described as his clothing emporium. It was a shop that had a selection of clothes for the more traditional lady. Mr 'M's idea was for part of the shop to become more modern and sell clothes that were trendy in the city. He wanted a small Boutique area within the store.
There were three large windows fronting the shop and I was asked to do large, eye catching Oriental trees with massive butterfly in zingy psychedelic colours as backdrop for the mannequins.

Mr 'M' explained that he could not afford to pay me very much in money, but if I was agreeable he would be able to let me have the pick of the best of his trendy new stock that were to grace the boutique. Of course I readily agreed to this proposition thinking of attire for my honeymoon. After the whole weekend painting I came home with three fabulous designer dresses. There was a cream dress with bell sleeves, a lacy bolero top and full skirt. A peach coloured, shot silk dress, with long flared sleeves, trimmed with diamante, and a smart multi coloured silk shift dress. The barter system was great! Strange how in the space of just one month I was to have two polar opposite attitudes shown me. The negative 'moon influence' from Ann, then a positive aspect of the 'moon influence' from my 'Rag Trade Angel'.

During our courtship, (a strange word in the world of today) Dave and I had been house hunting. We were of the same mind in so far as we did not think it wise to saddle ourselves with a massive mortgage. We would look for a small house in an area between both our parent's homes. Dave had a good deposit of £700. This was thanks to his mum, as each time he had given her 'housekeeping' from his wage packet she had kindly put part of it into a savings bond.

Most of the houses we looked at were above £2.000 and none were in the right area. We were turned down by the mortgage company on one property that we thought would have been perfect for us and was just £700. The property was a small corner shop and had been empty for a few months. We planned to sell small electrical goods, the idea being that I could man the shop and Dave might eventually be able to become self-employed doing electrical work around the village. It was a disappointment as we were running out of time to be in our own place by our August wedding.

Issues with Ann made a problem when it came to invitations. A card with a trail of silver daisy along one edge had been chosen. Dad asked for a list of who I wanted to invite as he sat down to write the names on each card. It would be rude to invite the girls from work but not Ann, so though it upset me I decided not to invite any of them. The most important thing was that my two cousins, Maggie, and Lynn were to be bridesmaids along with friend Pat and Jean from next door. In keeping with my Daisy theme I chose buttercup yellow for their dresses and a chain of Daisies on the edge of bell sleeves and around their hair.

Excitement was mounting in our house, not just for my wedding but also the first moon landing that was to take place in July. The first man setting foot on the surface of the moon! It was going to be broadcast all around the world live as it was taking place. John, now age nine could not contain himself. We could hardly believe our eyes as we watched it all unfold. There was great relief all round when the men came back down to Earth seemingly unscathed. All the talk about space had taken some of the tension from wedding preparations.

The summer months in 1969 were even hotter than last year and by the 9th of August the weather turned out to be cracking the pavement flags. Dave and I had not found a home of our own so we would be staying with my parents until we did. This was a bit of a disappointment but the plus side was that we would be able to save a little more for a deposit. Meantime we had our honeymoon in the Isle of Man to look forward to. Dave had booked an apartment that was recommended by the Manx Tourist Board in their guide book. We could not wait to be together on our own. The time did fly by as I had to find shoes, a headdress and get a dressmaker for bridesmaid dresses.

Dad had booked our wedding reception at a place near Southport belonging to Jack Pass, his close friend. The food was to be a sumptuous

Buffet by three very talented young Chefs from a private hospital. They were working alternative weekends for Mr Pass at his caravan park, The Riverside. The site had a large building in two rooms. The front room had a stage for cabaret, plus a disco floor. The back room was a cocktail lounge, come ballroom. Our reception would take place in the back room where in the evening there would be a dance band. There was to be full salmon, turkey, beef, plus chicken with all the trimmings and large bowls of hot chips. At the centre, a three tiered wedding cake, gifted to us by Alice, a kind Lady on our estate.

Thursday 7th August was the last evening I would see Dave before our big day. We were to go to St John's Church that evening with our parents and Dave's brother Stan to have a 'rehearsal'. On 8th I went back to the Church to arrange flowers for the alter. Flowers for my bouquet were yellow roses, freesia, daisy and gypsophila and were being done professionally. The whole event was now becoming REAL!

When Maggie arrived the night before the wedding I was rather taken aback as she had changed her hair style. The long tresses that had been similar to mine were gone and in place there was a new style, short cropped at one side and longer at the other, (A-symmetric) that had recently become a big fashion trend because model Twiggy had the same cut from Vidal Sassoon. 'Don't worry' Mag said as she saw my surprised look, I have brought this'. She pulled a long dark wig from her bag. It was on a band that she could fasten the daisy headdress to.

The day was blisteringly hot but thankfully our house being next to the woods was fairly cool. Although mum had to get John dressed in his first grown up suit with smart jacket and long trousers, she insisted I have breakfast in bed. Mag would help the two younger bridesmaids to get ready, whilst I bathed then curled my long hair into ringlets and put on my make-up. Going for a natural look I opted to leave out the 'Dusty Springfield' eye's but by the time I was ready everyone, bar dad had gone in the first wedding car. Dad and I had a few moments before our car would arrive.

Dad looked emotional as he asked if I was ready. Looking down at my shoes after assuring dad that I was fine, I began to worry that my shoes were all wrong. They were my 'something old', the something new was my dress, my something borrowed was a small handkerchief, a something blue were the Sapphires in my engagement ring. It was too late to change shoes as the second car was now outside. Several ladies from our estate were at the front of the house and I felt a little flushed when dad refused to let us to get into the car. No white ribbon attached to the bonnet as was customary for a car carrying a bride. The driver was flustered as dad insisted on him going back to his base to get white ribbon. 'No dad!' I protested. 'We will be late!'

By the time the driver had debated with dad on the time problems of going back to base, I was starting to stress. It was already 2.15 pm and we should be at Church by 2.30 pm. Eventually after the driver had found some artificial flowers in the car boot and set them into the back window and put a tiny thin cream ribbon round the silver lady on the car's bonnet, dad reluctantly agreed to set off. Looking at my watch as we turned from the Lane into the main road I saw it was now 2.20 pm. We had several miles to travel and would be very late! Just then a small fleet of police motor cycles passing us, formed a 'squad' escort in front of our car all the way into town, sounding police sirens to clear the route. Dad had not known his team had arranged an escort for us! What a relief, it helped get us to the Church, if not on time, then at least not too late!

The day went off well but later when we were on the plane Dave told me he had been getting worried when it got passed 2.45pm. By then, dad and I were outside Church with the bridesmaids, having photographs taken. We got to the altar at 2.55pm.

After our Wedding Breakfast, we went back to my home for me to change. My 'going away' outfit was the latest fashion trend, a matching dress and coat in Union Jack pattern teamed with a red bag and strappy sandals, plus a large brimmed 'floppy' hat. We went back to the reception to say our farewells then had to leave to catch a flight from Blackpool at 7pm. We would miss the dancing but we were Mr and Mrs and the only other company we needed was Mr Moonlight.

The plane had been in use during the second World War and by the standards of today would defiantly be classed as needing to be retired from service. It was an hour late setting off so when we landed in the Isle of Man it was 10.30pm. By taxi it would take half an hour to our resort in Douglas. It was a very dark night with just a sliver of moonlight. On arrival we saw a six foot locked gate bearing a sign reading 'Closed from 11pm until 8am'. The booking office is closed until morning.' Our spirits took a dive as we looked up at the words. How could the gate be locked when we should have been expected? Feeling a bit put out we decided to trot over to the Inn across the road. Asking about at the bar about our booking, the Landlord pointed us to a young man sitting at the door. He was the key holder to the holiday complex. We got a meek apology as he opened the gate. This was a new resort that was, (in the advertisement in the Lancashire Evening Post) recommended by the Manx government. Security seemed more of a concern than a honeymoon couple arriving after hours. Never mind, we were here and now had two whole weeks to relax and to explore the island.

From 1967 to 1969 I had now experienced both the negative and positive aspects of the moons influence on our lives and perhaps we should all remember that life goes in phases just like the moon. When we are in a dark place we have to know that all things shall pass. We can only look for that glimmer of light, sometimes within, for ourselves. Sometimes by showing love to ourselves or to others when they need a helping hand of empathy or kindness. It is only by experiencing emotional pain that we can know the pain of others. As individuals we cannot fix the whole world, we can only try to make a difference in our own small way wherever, whenever possible. Love given is never wasted!

Reader... Have you ever been mesmerized by the moon or felt you were able to tap into its feminine energy? When next you see the full moon, have a look at the timeless face and bathe in the silvery magic as it casts light upon you. Feel the wonder of the miracle that rules the tide, let yourself be positive in that special moment.

Reader... This is the RUNE Sowelu

The Rune Sowelu represents the Sun and Life force. Energy that brings forth all things creative including life on Earth. Spiritual wholeness is another meaning as we might find the light within us by tuning into the light of God.

19/ Tarot lesson, THE MOON

Card 18... The Nineteenth Lesson of the Tarot...Mystery/ Boundaries/ Phases. Song...'Dedicated to the One I Love'...Band...Version...Mama's and Papa's...1967

The image on this card shows the closest solid sphere to our own Earth, the Moon. Two dogs are howling at the moon from the far side of a pool of water. The dogs are in front of two Tower structures. The Moon lights up a pathway leading between and beyond the structures away into the distance. A Crab or Scorpion guards the pool.

In Astrology the Moon is said to have a strong effect on our emotions as well as on the tides of our planet. The traditional interpretation is Fluctuation and the things that are hidden. The **deep**, or the things of, or that stir our imagination. The Towers on the card represent the boundaries, of life, or of the human mind. Reversed the meaning is deception or madness. To me this card is says that we must be aware of obstacles, we may not know everything but must try not to look on the dark side. My belief is that in adversity we must look to the light. In reverse the card would remind us of this fact.

The image of the moon conjures up a feeling of mystery. Twilight and evening mist and the aura that often can be seen around our moon makes me think of the wonders of the universe. There are many things that remain a mystery to us even in these days of science and exploration. There are so many questions about who we are and where we came from and what does it all mean. Is there a purpose or is it all random? The part of our mind that looks for provable definite answers will always fight with the part of our mind that explores the inner self, the imagination, our intuition.

The female cycle is ruled by the Moon just like the tide. The Moon gives out a feminine aspect but the face of the Moon is more like Old Father time, and is often referred to as Mr Moonlight. Where would we humans be without a sprinkle of moon magic? It can ignite a romance or enhance awareness of nature. The Sun and Moon are both givers of light, and so give us the balance. The feminine 'Moon Goddess' is linked to the metal **Silver** in many cultures and the masculine 'Sun God' links to **Gold**. A partnership that provides light.

Think of the face to be seen on the moon. Is it there as a reminder of the all seeing eye? A 'God energy', as it looks down on the lives of us tiny humans! I linked this card to the next phase of my life because events would illustrate the romance of the moon within a courtship, and with a few darker clouds that came my way at work, plus this was the era where we would see the actual Moon landing. For our small time on Earth we have no option but to try and balance the light and shade in our lives. Sometimes making allowances for what may appear to us to be the disruptive actions or madness of others. We must try to overcome, rise above the Chaos. The feminine energy, the gentle touch can often bring the silver lining.

Reader... Have you felt hemmed in by a situation? How did you deal with it? Did you learn that stress adds to any problem? The lesson of the 'Moon'; all clouds must pass!

Chapter 20

August 10th 1969 – Christmas

Out and about around the Island on a hired motor scooter we went visiting little villages and had picnics on the beach. On the fourth day we were on our way to Castletown (stopping at the little bridge to say the customary greeting to the Fairy folk) when we saw a young woman pushing a baby carriage across the road. Dave waved at the girl and when she came over he explained she was his cousin, Mary.

On Mary's invitation, we went to visit her parents and were made very welcome by them. Then later by all the young people of the town at the new Friday night disco Mary had started in a local Church hall. She explained that the Manx authorities were trying to close all the discos on the Island and young people would have nowhere to go to meet or dance. It was quite a campaign she and her friends were undertaking at that time. 'Will you join us when we go as a group into the Manx Summer Festival?' She asked us. It sounded like good fun and so we agreed.

We continued our days out on the scooter despite the weather turning a little cooler. One glorious day we went to Peel Castle where we ate fish and chips on the sea front. Mooching round the shops Dave bought me a chain belt and matching bracelet in a Celtic design. That evening we rode up to the top of Douglas Head where we had seen the lights of a Fairground from the distance. It was another of those special moments where I felt a kind of pull towards the place. As we entered we saw that there were tents and stalls with an old fashioned Carnival atmosphere. Right by the entrance, outside a large, tent there was a sign… 'Authentic Romany Gypsy FORTUNE TELLER. 2/ 6 d'. This was of course pre decimalisation - Half a Crown as we used to call this sum of money - just 12.5 pence in the coinage of today. It felt as if I were destined to go inside. Although I had given many readings from the pattern of the tea leaves, nobody had ever read them for me. To be honest I had never been curious about the future for myself. May be it was the naivety of youth but I always had a notion that my future would unfold well.

As I drew back the curtain entrance to the large tent I saw there was a rag rug on the floor and just a glimmer of light from two old lamps on a stand behind a table where sat, a small wizened old woman. My first thought was that she looked like a little walnut wrapped in a shawl that went round her head and was fastened under her chin. Her face reminded me of the lady who came to me in spirit when I was a child. On the table was a dark green velvet cloth. She motioned for me to sit opposite her and asked me to cross her palm with silver. As my coin went into her left hand she tucked it under her shawl, and at the same time reached for my hand with her right hand. She turned my hand palm upwards and held it cupped in hers. She did not appear to look at lines on my hand but proceeded to talk quite fast in a broad Irish accent. It was as if she were in a trance as she came out with a stream of information.

This is what the old Gypsy lady told me...

"You are just Wed... You will move to your first home right on Christmas... You will live there for a couple of years, then move again... Your husband will be unemployed for a short time, then he will work for himself... When self-employed he will do many jobs for a man with the initial 'J'. After some years he will go back working for a firm for fourteen years... Then he will work for himself again... You will have two children, seven to ten years apart, one of each, like your mother before you... You will move again and then work very hard, harder than ever before when self-employed during your thirties. You will be famous by age forty through 'word of mouth.'... You will live happily together into a ripe old age... You will end your days in a Bungalow next to a park."

Right away after leaving the tent of the old gypsy lady, so as to help me remember her words, I recounted the information to Dave, asking 'How could anyone become famous through word of mouth?' Puzzled I went over and over her words. What could possibly make me famous? Could it be my artwork? Could it be writing a book? If it was from working for myself, as the gypsy had said, then what could I work at that people would want to pass on by word? Well we would just have to wait and see. We did hope the bit about us being in our own home by Christmas would prove true.

We were invited to go out on a small boat with Mary's father during our second week on the Island, then afterwards, despite my sea sickness, we went to supper with Mary, her hubby and their friends to make our costumes for the Carnival. It was to take place on our last day on the Island.

We all sat in Mary's sitting room making grass skirts out of palm leaves gathered from the local park. The girls were to dress up in Hula - Hula garments of grass skirts with bikini tops, flowers behind our ears and garlands round our necks. The lads were to wear flower patterned shirts tied at the waist and shorts or rolled up trousers. It was planned that we would all sing 'Give Peace a Chance.' Whilst marching down Douglas prom, then half way we were to sing loudly as we passed the group of Councillors, changing the words to 'Give Disco a Chance.'

Mary and her gang certainly made our last day memorable. As we all marched along there were photographers from the local Newspaper snapping away. We joked with the Bobbies lining the route and ended up throwing our garlands round their necks. The lads had fashioned spears from long sticks and as we came to the droppings from the police horses they did a dance around the little piles, singing and laughing.

The next day we were on our way home but with great memories, and for me lots to think about from what the gypsy had told me. At home the Summer weather had gone and it rained a lot as we searched for a home each weekend. Driving round, we came across an old cottage in Hutton. We could see that it was empty by the dirty windows, overgrown garden and ivy climbing up the walls. There was no 'For Sale' sign outside but we knocked at the house next door to get information as to the situation.

The lady next door to the cottage told us that the previous owner had passed away some years ago. From what she gathered the solicitor could not find their relatives. She gave us a phone number for the Solicitor. We found it could take years before the house could be sold, but strangely this would not be our last link with the Cottage.

After our Honeymoon I got work in a fashion store in town. Dave had finished his apprenticeship and we were eager to find a home. In September we came across an end terrace. The price was £1.700, so within our budget. After viewing it we knew there was a lot of work to be done, but it was not overlooked at the back or front. We moved in on December 23rd. Right on Christmas just as the gypsy told me we would!

The Manageress, Mrs P, of the clothing shop where I worked had put me in charge of the boutique. I was in my element at first as there was a commission on each sale and it was a job that required me to dress the shop window each week and decorate the back wall with a theme. The shop owner was pleased with my efforts on his weekly visit, and when Mrs 'P' was off work with a virus he asked me to open the shop each morning. This was okay with me, but when Mrs 'P' returned to work, although fully fit, she only came into the shop at noon, then left at 3pm to get her train home. She asked me to cash up the money from the tills and take it to the bank. This was a big responsibility and yet no extra reward in my pay packet. After a while the fact that the firm was essentially using me as Manageress, but only giving me basic pay, started to bug me. The last straw was when Mrs 'P' went on holiday and I would be responsible for the whole shop for two weeks. On her return I used my lunch hour to get a new job in the china and glass department store, 'O & O' with promise of becoming Manageress of an 'in store' Boutique, due to open soon.

Whilst on china and glass I was able to purchase a few items we would need for the home we would soon have. By December we could measure up for the carpet my parents had promised as a wedding, come joint 21st birthday gift. They gave us a bedroom suite and a white portable T.V. In a second hand furniture shop we bought four spindle chairs and a drop leaf table to paint bright blue. Dave's parents bought us a radiogram. We bought two new swivelling barrel chairs in a flower pattern of bright colours. We were all set for when we could move in as soon as the conveyancing was completed.

By 20th of December we had been given the key to our new home despite the fact that the papers would not be signed until after Christmas. The carpet was laid on the 22nd and a phone cable put in place. As there was a cooker (left by the previous owner) we had invited Dave's parents to have Christmas dinner with us as a chance for them to see the house. Whilst I worked on Christmas eve, Dave was arranging the furniture and cleaning the oven ready for me to cook the Turkey. Working until 5 o-clock on Christmas Eve would not leave me much time to put up decorations, but at lunch hour I did manage to purchase a Christmas tree, lights, tinsel, gold baubles, a Santa and an Angel.

We spent the whole of Christmas Eve making the house look as if we had always been there. Just after midnight we dropped exhausted into bed for the first night in our own home. On Christmas morning I discovered that the oven was not big enough to house the turkey. Determined to get ready for lunch, we managed to squeeze it into the oven but the door kept coming open. Dave tied a piece of cable right around the oven and we crossed our fingers it would be cooked in time for our guests. It was! We were so happy and so proud to show off our home making skills. By the looks of delight on the faces of Roy and Lucy we did a good job.

We enjoyed a golden Christmas together but would soon face the reality of being home owners. There would be a few hurdles as the world moved into the new decade. The 1970's proved challenging to us in many ways but nothing has sullied the golden memories of the early days of our marriage.

Reader... Be a light in this world, for if we can all add a small sparkle of light we can illuminate the whole world to greater harmony and enlightenment. Enjoy your life as a brief moment in the sun, a moment in this world, a time so precious for you to shine your unique light, all the good and creative and positive energy that is you, within you!

20/ Tarot lesson, THE SUN

Card 19...The twentieth Lesson...The Sun Card
Song...'Here Comes the Sun'...Band...Version...The Beatles.

The image on the card is of our Sun, blazing down in all its glory upon two child friends standing in a fortified place on golden sand. In ancient times our Sun was thought of as the Creator of human kind, lighting our world, lighting up civilisation. The Hebrew symbol of 'koph' is shown on traditional and more ancient Tarot packs. This denotes the axe, defence, effort and the material existence.

The Sun has long been worshiped by many civilisations from the Incas to the Egyptians. The evidence of this has been found on walls of caves and from artefacts found by archaeologists. It is not hard to see why, as our Sun is the centre of our solar system, without which life on earth would not have been possible. Because we know this we may then understand the Sun Tarot card to be the instigator, the dawning of life, or new insight and warmth radiating from an event or a person or a place we travel to.

Just as the Moon lights up our darkest hours, the Sun lights up our lives in the daytime hours. It is traditionally thought to represent joy in awakening. The brightness brought into our lives, seen by most Tarot students as indicating happiness. An event that brings light or we awaken to a new dawn in our own life path. If showing up in an Astrological layout the Sun card is thought to be a good omen. Unless reversed the message must always be one of events that bring light to the life of the enquirer. We may see this in a new chapter to their life, one that brings brighter aspects, or clarity. In reverse this would show the enquirer to be under a cloud. Downcast, outcast or confused.

*In Egyptian mythology the Sun God 'Ra' is seen as the Father of creation. The metal **Gold** is much sought after in our world as the closest thing on Earth to the golden rays of our Sun. Thus gold is the metal of masculinity, the male Sun 'God', strong, just as 'Silver' is feminine, mysterious, attributes of the 'Moon' Goddess. In tradition, the magic of wearing Gold could bring us strength, wearing Silver is said to bring us intuition. Light comes from both the Moon (feminine) aspect of ourselves and the (male) Sun aspect, we are all born of father and mother and so can nurture our dynamic and strong self, as well as the intuitive and artistic self, within us all.*

Reader... Stop and take a moment. Close your eyes and think of a golden sunflower. Absorb the golden light, feel the healing warmth within your body. Let yourself enjoy and absorb the strength from this image. The 'Sun' card says we must enjoy the golden moments of our lives to the full.

Chapter 21
1970-1976

During January 1970 we celebrated my 21st birthday with a night out with my parents and grandma at 'The Riverside', where we had our wedding reception. It was an evening with entertainers and a competition called 'Lady of Style.' I entered wearing a dress made by my gran. It was a knitted 'Sweater Dress' in a cornflour blue shade with a matching beret. Gran was thrilled that I wore the dress, though I did not win.

We had a great evening and got to know more about the Riverside. Dad's friend, Jack Pass and his wife had started the campsite after the war. Jack, a master craftsman had done the work on the interior himself. It was a grand achievement. Some of the decor was obtained from a London auction house and came from the Houses of Parliament.

Although money was a bit tight, whilst trying to decorate our new home and pay for a new bathroom suite, we often had a kind of working night out with my parents. Mum had been doing her 'Hobby job' of catering for Christmas parties for the Police crowd and local Bowls club, so we went along to help her, and then get to join in for the dancing. Life ran along quite well until Dave was made redundant from work. We were lucky in so far as we only had a small mortgage, and we had my job, but we were going to have to tighten our purse strings quite a lot whilst Dave found work. It was his aim to set up working for himself doing electrical fitting but he would need a bit of part time work until he got known in our new area. He tried doing a morning milk round but after being up at 3am. and only finishing at one 1pm. there was not much time or energy to do anything in the afternoon. Dad's friend Jack Pass came to the rescue when he sent word that he needed a re-wire of the ballroom at his Caravan Club at the end of the summer season, also before then, he required staff for Friday evening and weekend events at the club.

We both went to see Mr Pass and it was arranged that I would be behind the Cocktail bar, Dave would be on the door, by the side of an older man, Mr Grimes, (an ex-boxer) who was the bouncer.

There was a String Quartet playing in the dance area of the Cocktail Lounge on Friday, Saturday and Sunday evenings. This was mostly frequented by an older age group as they enjoyed the ballroom dancing. On Saturday there was a cabaret act on followed by 'Disco' in the front room, more frequented by the under thirty age group. The whole place was buzzing with action. Mr Pass had catered for all ages and each Saturday night there was a set plated buffet of chicken, pork pie, crisps and a sprig of salad served on paper plates. At the end of the shift when the 'punters' had left, all the staff could sit down with a drink and enjoy a supper. It was Heaven sent for us as when I finished work on Friday and Saturday evenings Dave would pick me up and by six thirty we would be all 'dolled up' and on our way to a fun working night out.

During this time, we were earning more during the weekends than I was paid for working all week. Also good tips were given me from the drinkers in the bar, which I would count on our way home. Each time I counted another £1.00 from the many small coins given me I would hoop with delight and Dave, driving, had to stop me from grabbing his arm. On New Year's Eve 1971 my tips alone came to ten whole pounds. Because we were young and now slightly more solvent we were able to improve the house and enjoy ourselves into the bargain, but life was about to change again. Just before Christmas 1971, whilst at work one Saturday I started to miscarry. It was only about five weeks into the pregnancy but still a painful experience and it made me quite emotional. Luckily working in the shop during the week and at the Riverside each weekend gave me other things to focus on.

During 1971 my dad retired from work just a few months after mum opened a café in Chorley. On his retirement dad found his 'house fund' was not quite what he had hoped and soon they would have to vacate the Police house. Where will they find a house within their budget? This was on all our minds.

Whilst we were all talking about the lack of affordable houses in our area, suddenly a voice in my head said 'What about the old cottage that you looked at?' Quite honestly this voice had literally popped in from nowhere.

Could it be that the solicitor had now found the person to inherited the old place? After telling dad and mum about this it was decided that we all go round to look at the outside. The cottage was still empty but Dave thought he could do some of the work needed and that the cottage could be transformed. Dad was confident about Dave's ability in renovation as by now he had done a great job of fitting out the Café for mum. After contacting the Solicitor, it was soon all systems GO! Stryands, close to the police estate became their home for the next six years, and soon, for just a short time it would became ours too.

Though we were loving working at the Riverside, listening to the music of the 70's as we worked, I became slightly unsettled in our home, and soon the two of us would become three. The first three months of my pregnancy I was overtaken by unduly harsh morning, well actually, 'all day' sickness. The house started to feel quite claustrophobic. The front door opened onto the steep stairs, and there would be little room for all the child equipment we would need. This was a consideration for moving, as well as the rather nosy lady next door. Whenever I was in the garden she would make critical remarks about my washing and say she thought we were staying in bed too late on Sundays. There were no other young people in the road and when, as my confinement got nearer, after giving up the shop work, I felt isolated. Not wanting to face lonely days at home when my baby came we decided to move to an estate nearer to my parents, where there were other young families. Fate, however had other ideas in mind for us!

During Summer we had our offer accepted on a bungalow on a new estate and had found a buyer for our house. All seemed to be going well and we hoped to be in our new home by the time our baby was due. Then I had another one of my Tsunami dreams where I was pushing a baby in his pushchair up a hill near our house when I saw the wave of water, we would be safe if I could get to the top of the hill. In the dream I knew the baby was a boy and I awoke as I got to the top of the hill. This dream made me want to move more than ever. We would be sad to leave our modern decor and orange coloured bench seat Dave had made as a day bed. Also the big butterfly mural I had painted on the wall behind it, but we had a feeling it was the right thing for us to do.

To our utter dismay, reliant on a firm hand shake from the owner of a desirable bungalow, we got, what was now called 'gazumped'. Only four months to go until baby day and we were frantically looking for somewhere to live. In that era the house prices started to zoom in an upward direction.

The mysterious hand of fate was in action and we would just have to go with the flow! It was decided we would store our furniture in the small garage at the Cottage, pack stuff into one of the three bedrooms and move in once again, temporarily with my parents and John. We soon found another house but the price was much higher than we expected and it needed massive renovation as an old man had lived there on his own since before the war.

Dave was still working at the Riverside at weekends as well as during the week doing work on the house in preparation for us to move into after baby arrived. My brother John kindly moved into the box room of the cottage so that we could cram as many of our household goods into his room as possible. We had about four inches between the side of our bed and the baby cot we had bought, but we would have to make do for a few weeks.

Christmas was looming once again and our baby was due on December 24th 1972. We could not spend much time together because Dave was working all hours on our new home plus weekend, at the Riverside. Mum and dad were out all day and I was getting bigger by the minute. By the 24th of December there had been no sign for arrival of baby Pearce, so Dave went off to work that evening as usual. By midnight I was beginning to worry about him as he was usually home. He had stayed after closing to have a chat with his friend. I wasn't best pleased when he came in but could not stay cross with him for long as next day was Christmas, and after all he had been working hard to make things perfect for our move. Because the weather was so cold and freezing and the house had been empty so long, we feared the baby catching cold so we decided to wait to move in when we saw the first sign of spring.

Christmas day came and went without any sign of baby. Mum had bought me a gorgeous dressing gown in red velvet with caftan sleeves and high Indian styled neckline piped with a gold edging. It hid my enormous baby bump and though very tired, it made me feel quite the glamorous house guest.

The days dragged on after Christmas and there were plenty of jokes about phantom pregnancy as we approached New Year. On the morning of 30th December I started to get a few twinges. At 2pm the ambulance was called and mum came in it with me. Dave was at our new house working on the heating system. In the ambulance my contractions were coming every five minutes.

On admission my contractions had abated. A nurse took me to a ward and brought me a tablet and water telling me to press a button if things started up again. Whatever I had been given seemed to send me off into a deep sleep. The morning of 31st December a contraction woke me up at six o-clock. Labour was slow, but by 2.30pm in the afternoon I was taken to a delivery room and examined by a Doctor. He assured me after a minor procedure that my baby would soon be in my arms. Soon would prove to be another long 24 hours. Still lying on the delivery bed at midnight, I could hear singing of 'Auld Lang Syne' from the nurses, in their quarters below. After another tablet the pains eased a little, feeling a bit sorry for myself I tried to sleep.

Whatever drug I had been given had worn off by the early hours and I had a desperate thirst. When I reached out (still on the delivery bed) to pour water from the jug my balance faltered and the jug fell from my hands, smashing into a thousand pieces. The Nurse came in just as I was bending to try and pick up the glass. Berated, she helped me back onto the delivery bed where I spent the rest of an uncomfortable night.

Our son, Matthew was born on 2nd January 1972 just missing out on a silver spoon from the Lord Mayor (always given to the first baby to arrive after the stroke of midnight in a Preston Guild year) but strong and healthy. My first thought on looking at him when he was placed next to me was how old and wrinkly he looked. As that thought came he gave me a lob sided smile and raised his left eyebrow, looking just like my dad but so cute. I was relieved, though exhausted and wondering where the blazes Dave had got to. He had been waiting in the corridor! He had asked to be there for the birth but a Nurse had told him to wait until he was called. In those days there were still some medical people that did not approve of the husband being present at a birth and we were too young and inexperienced to push for what we wanted.

My hospital stay was six days and on the third day when the Doctor did his rounds he said he could tell my son was very overdue by the fact he was quite red and his skin was peeling, he was over ripe! I would spend my 23rd birthday in the ward. Mum delighted everyone by bringing in a large birthday cake to share with all the other new mothers. She also brought me a bottle of Guinness to put back what the experience had taken out of me. Dave's parents bought me a massive basket of blue and purple flowers and a gift set of 'Heaven Scent' perfumed toiletries. I felt so very pampered.

Because the weather was very cold, despite being in the cramped bedroom, we stayed at Stryands for the next few weeks. Dave would put the finishing touches on our new home. He was working so hard doing our renovations, so was very tired and in a deep sleep at night. I had felt a strong presence in the room each time I came awake to give Matthew his 1 o-clock feed. It felt as if someone sat down on my side of the bed next to my feet. At first I tried to reason with myself that there was nothing and nobody there. Telling myself not to start imagining things and thinking It was just tiredness, but there had been several other signs that the house was inhabited by someone in spirit. Each night the presence felt stronger, I could see the indentation on the bed.

Since my parents had moved into the cottage they had been hearing noises coming from upstairs when they were downstairs and the phone would tinkle as if about to ring. When the receiver was picked up there was a sound of breathing. It was as if a person was on the upstairs phone trying to ring to downstairs. This would happen during the day as well as in the evening; everyone apart from myself and baby were out all day, when the phone would do a lot of this tinkling, not wishing to see the spirit, I would put Matthew into the pram and go off for long walks.

All the family' at one point or another; had gone to the phone when it rang to hear this 'Shhhhush', like a person sucking in a deep breath. Dad said it was a loose connection but that did not account for the fact we had all been in the living room when we could hear footsteps upstairs. Dad tried to laugh it off, saying it was the warming or cooling of the wall bricks but mum and I knew better after our previous bout of spirit activity in the Police house. The more the situation continued, the presence in our bedroom became stronger.

In the night I wanted Dave to see the indentation on top of the bed covers. It was real, there was someone with me in spirit. Too many signs had been given to believe it was just imagination. There was no feeling of danger or dread when the presence came at night and after a while my inner voice told me the spirit person was just curious and liked to see the baby feeding. Several times I would nudge Dave in the middle of the night, he was so tired that he just grunted and rolled over. Eventually Dave sat up one night as I told him I could feel the indentation and the weight of someone sitting there, and he said he could see it. We would soon be moving and I wondered if the spirit would be sad to see us go. Would she (sure now that the presence was female) eventually move on, or move with us, or were they somehow attached to the Cottage and earthbound?

After our move to Penwortham we made friends with two young couples. Lynn and Tom across the road had a little boy the same age as Matthew and a couple from next door but two, Paula and Mark had a boy at infant school and younger girl age three, about to start nursery. We all socialised together but it was just us girls that decided to sign up for a night class at the Secondary School I had previously attended. We joined a class for basket weave the first year, later we would go on to do a class in needlework, making soft toys.

One tea break time at the class I noticed some leaves at the bottom of Paula's cup and told them about my reading of tea leaves. After reading these leaves for her, Paula suggested we might all go to the Spiritual church. In discussion, because Lynn and I had small children we were both tied up during the day and were too tired at night, the idea was shelved.

As Dave was finding it hard to get payment from some people he had done wiring jobs for I sat making toy Wombles to sell hoping to make ends meet. Mum was a bit of a life saver during these lean years as she paid me for baking three pies each day to be served the next day in her Café. She would bring us any food that was unused on her day off. By the time Matthew was sitting up in his high chair I would keep him quiet whilst baking by putting several chocolate buttons on the tray. He was covered in chocolate by the time the pies were in the oven. When older he would play with some pastry, making a nice, if a somewhat mucky pie for daddy.

On mum's day off I would sometimes walk the three miles to Stryands with Matt in his push chair. On these visits she would tell me about the continuation of the paranormal activities that were still going on in the Cottage. There was one time when she was particularly het up about what John had told her. Apparently he had been woken during the night to see all his fifty or so table tennis balls (ping pong type) fly out of a box he kept them in and bounce hither and thither all about the room. It was not hard for me to believe what John said; he had once again taken up residence back in his old room, the same one where I had felt someone sitting on my side of the bed. Not wanting to scare him we never told John about the 'spirit' in that room.
On another occasion visiting mum, she said she had, had the fright of her life that morning, she told me she had been fast asleep when a sound had

wakened her. She opened her eyes to see a small old lady floating into the bedroom. She squeezed her eyes in a tight blink, thinking she was dreaming and when she opened them the woman's face was about six inches from her face. 'What did she look like?' I enquired. 'She was quite small, very brown and wrinkly, like a witch, very old with white hair at the front. She wore a brimmed hat with some sort of scarf tied round it under her chin and her clothes were drab. Oh! and she was carrying a basket.' She recalled. I asked what happened next. She said that as she started to scream the old woman just floated right out of the room. Dad had stuck to his usual sceptical line, saying she must have been dreaming. Well it was, from her description of the old lady, the **same apparition** that I had seen all those years ago as a child. I wondered, after mum seeing this spirit, if it was attached to me or our family, maybe a spirit of a relation. Perhaps that would account for her interest in the baby.

One afternoon when Matthew was at a nursery school Paula asked me to go to an 'Open Circle' as it was called. At this circle there was a Medium who led the meeting. Each person gave out any 'message' they may have received by seeing or hearing a spirit. Several persons gave out messages to others in the circle. Nothing was coming to me so I just sat quietly. When there was a pause in the talking the Medium asked me if I had seen anything. 'No, nothing but the cat that ran under your chair.' I replied. One other person said they had seen a cat They described the cat and it was the same one that I had seen. The old lady sat next to the Medium said it was her cat. It had died the day before and she had come with the desire to know if the cat was okay.

After the circle concluded, a professional Medium came to give a demonstration. He asked people in the room to place an item of jewellery, or any small personal object onto a tray that was sent round. I placed my watch on the tray. When the Medium picked up each item he looked towards the person it came from and said a few words. When he came to my watch he put it to his forehead and closing his eyes, he said I was going on a journey, going very high, higher than I thought. 'Whatever could he mean?' I asked myself.

Intrigued by his message we went home to sit in the sunshine in my garden. We were sipping tea, talking about the Medium and I told Paula about all the poltergeist activity of my teenage years. Paula said she was studying Astrology and she would do my chart in exchange for me to 'read' her tea leaves again. School pick up time ended our chat and we made arrangements to meet the next afternoon to see what I could see for her.

The following afternoon after a cup of tea Paula proffered her cup. 'Okay there are plenty of leaves but let me try to read from your watch or ring first.' I offered. Holding her wedding ring to my head with my eyes closed, just as the Medium had done with my watch, I tried to make my mind a blank. After a moment, still eyes closed I could 'see' Paula riding her bike down a lane. 'You are riding down the lane where we walk sometimes with the kids. You are getting off your bike and sitting on the bench. Oh! now a black car has pulled up near you. A man with white hair in a grey suit has got out and is coming towards you. Oh gosh, you are snogging him!' I exclaimed in surprise. Looking up I said 'I'm sorry I must have my wires crossed.' Paula looked aghast. 'No you haven't!' she muttered, 'and you do know him.' She added. It was not what I wanted to hear, or for that matter not what I wanted to know.

Sworn to secrecy by Paula, I felt like I was the one cheating on Mark, especially when I found out Paula was using me as an alibi. In the end the secret weighed so heavily on me that I did tell Dave. We decided it wasn't our place to upset Mark as perhaps the 'fling' would blow over. We could hardly look Mark in the face. When the Insurance man came to collect our monthly payment we did not want to look him in his cheating eyes either. We had decided to just stay out of it and see less of Paula and Mark in the hope they could get their marriage back on track!

As Matthew was growing, money was not getting much better for us, despite any work Dave was getting. There were many who would defer payment for a month after the job was done and one time a local Church made Dave wait for almost three months even though he they had accepted his quote before the work started.

Mum had now sold the Café so I decided to get a part time job. Mum offered to have Matt for a few hours when I got a job in a card shop. After forking out for bus fair, with only a small wage I found the job not worth the time away from motherhood care.

One day a few weeks later Paula came round to say there was a job going in the cake shop where she worked part time, so I began two afternoons a week. The perk was leftover cakes at the end of the day, not too healthy, but surely something with short hours but better earnings would turn up for me soon. Trying to avoid Paula was tricky as she would often be in the shop or come round and just let herself in our back door. We managed to avoid going out with her and Mark by joining my mum and dad at the Police club on a Saturday evening. This was just now and again when Dave's parents could baby sit. At least this did not cost much and we got a dance and to let our hair down.

Fed up, having failed my driving test plus crossing paths with Paula, now wanting to confide her problem love life issues, coming round at the most inconvenient times, I decided to sign up to do a short course on make up with a firm called 'Lady K'. It would require me doing party bookings. It was not ideal as bookings had to be in the evening once Dave arrived home to take over child care. With Dave's meal on the table as he got in, I had to be ready to go out. Matthew ready for sleep would be dressed in pyjamas and coat, so that after dinner Dave could drive me with Matthew along to drop me of at the address for my booking. Later, with Matthew in bed asleep, Lynn from across the road would babysit for the short time it would take for Dave to come back to drive me home. Although I loved doing the facials and make up for the hostess at these party bookings, and I could earn a little extra in the evenings, it wasn't ideal balancing the two jobs and not able to drive.

We did have many happy times whilst living in Penwortham. Mary, Dave's cousin, now back from the Isle of Man, would come round for a visit on her motorbike with the four children in the side car. My school friend, Rose, often called in now that she was home from the West Indies where she had done voluntary work in a school where her brother was teaching. On afternoons when not working at the bakery I would take Matthew for a walk and then our thing was to have something that we called 'snooze coffee'. This was a strong, real coffee for me and a warm milk for him, with a portion of Caramac chocolate bar before an afternoon nap. The coffee helped me keep up with the extra work but along with cakes, it did nothing to improve my waistline.

By 1976 Matthew had started infant school and I had agreed to look after Richard, the son of my uncle during the week (his wife had left him). Richard was ready for school and I would take him with Matthew. It was arranged that his dad would pick him up on Friday afternoon for them to spend the weekend together. My heart went out to Richard as he was missing his mummy and his home life had been so disrupted. His mother only came to visit once during the year he was staying with us. She was busy running her posh clothing shop in Marple, Cheshire.

It was all very sad as she and my uncle had what we might all think was a good life in a pleasant area with no financial worries. They had had a successful joint business and all the trimmings, but from what I could gather she had fallen for a famous football player. It was my grandma Smith that asked me to look after Richard because she had found she could not manage to do so because he was rather hyper active. My uncle had started another shop whilst trying to build up a new life. All this made life for us quite full but I still loved doing the occasional tea cup reading and found time to read many books on esoteric subjects.

Richard had been with us about three months when I had managed to pass my driving test, thanks to Dave putting me in for it without telling me until the evening before it was due. I had no time to get myself into a stress. By now my make-up party bookings were quite lucrative but the rushing about was a bind. This hectic activity could not go on!

One evening, feeling exhausted I asked my Angel to step in and guide me to some work to fit my skills. It had worked before when I asked for a nice man. 'Angel please let me find a job that I am good at and one that is right for me, something to help us with finances.' The Angel did listen but it would take a couple more years for the magic to arrive, and for her to point me in the right direction. Before then we would be on the move again.

Dad, ever the sailor had asked Dave to help him build a small boat to take to his caravan in Anglesey, Wales. After the boat was made we all went to the caravan to cheer at the Maiden voyage. It was great fun to watch, but I knew from the motion sickness I had suffered on busses, in the back of the car, as well as on the short boat ride on our Honeymoon that I would only be able to go across the bay on a calm day. My Tsunami dreams had not happened for a while but deep water still gave me the eebie jeebies!

Often during these days, I would have a sketchy dream about an Imp chasing me around the house. The last time this dream would end with me turning to face the Imp at the foot of the stairs only to find out it was the strange little man from our time in Bolton, the man my gran had bandaged after he had come to our door with a bleeding head. One morning as I woke up he (his ghost) was standing at the foot of our bed and smiling. He said he was sorry he had scared me and then he immediately disappeared. Well I thought, perhaps he had to do this so that his spirit could find some rest. Strange though as shortly after I would hear of another head accident…

A few weeks after our trip with the boat, my brother John had the most shocking accident one night. He had been serving the tables for a special 'Big Wig' dinner at police headquarters as was expected of the cadets. It was a cold and frosty night and the 'big wigs' had gone on revelling until after midnight. John was walking home along the pavement when a car came from out of nowhere and skidded off the road knocking into him, casting him over the bonnet, cracking his head into the windscreen landing him thirty feet behind the car onto the road. This was just around the corner from home. A man living close by, heard the screech of brakes, looking out of the window he saw John laying on the road.

John was unconscious when the man got to him. By then the driver and his wife had got out of the car. The driver, a Doctor, started to tend to

John. Knowing that John lived just around the corner the man from the house ran to fetch my dad. John was lucky in so far as he had been wearing his great coat and police hat. His thick boots had been torn from his feet, but our own Doctor said the uniform had saved his life.

John would go on to make us all proud by passing nine 'A' levels whilst on his Police training, and later winning an award for his bravery by saving a man from a burning building. In time, his injury and others he would suffer in the course of his duties would take its toll on his health. John never complained about his accident and went on to complete all his training. On the day of his 'passing out parade' we were all so happy. All the family plus Kathleen, John's new girlfriend went to watch him being presented with his medal, all of us with beaming smiles.

After John got his first posting, dad announced that he and mum were thinking of a move. We were a bit surprised but perhaps the accident had played a part in their decision. Another consideration was that gran would soon be alone. Her lodger was about to get wed. She had twice been a target of burglars and we were all worried that she would have no help in an attack. They intended on gran being installed with them, but the Cottage was not big enough for gran to have her own space or bits of furniture. John had been posted to Blackpool and was living in 'Digs' so at first the idea was to move in that direction. Mum fancied running a B & B. After a while it was uncertain if John would even stay in Blackpool so the 'moving' net was cast a little further.

Dave and I went with mum and dad to look at a few houses, but there was always a snag. We had decided that if they moved, we might do likewise. Dave had been working for Edna, a lady in her late 80's who had taken a bit of a shine to him. She said how handy it would be for her to have a good workman like him live close by. Dave was close to finishing the re-wire for Edna when she told him she had a piece of land she wanted to sell just opposite her house. She asked if he would be interested in buying the land to build himself a home and said she would not expect to get payment until building plans were granted.

We had often spoken about doing this and it would be great if we could have the project of building our own home joined on to a home for dad, mum and gran. Dave sent off for some house designs to get an idea of what we might need. He had done most of the building and fitting out of a new home for Mr D. Pass, a junior brother of Mr J. Pass, close to the Riverside. From the design, digging foundation footings, wiring, plumbing, woodwork and even the brick work, with help of a young 'Bricky' He thought he would be able to do much the same for ourselves.

We spoke to dad and found he and mum were interested in our idea, especially as it was on the Southport side of Longton, close to the Dual Carriageway. We had often had a day out to the beach and John had loved Peter Pan's Playground on Southport seafront. In fact, Dave and I had looked at some old Victorian houses there before we married. Was Southport even then, somehow calling us again?

For the next few weeks we poured over all the design books, Dave drew many designs himself after viewing the plot of land. We put in for planning permission to the Local Authority. Edna had insisted that we did this before completing the sale. The plot had been an allotment some years before her husband had passed away. The plot was overgrown and at the end of a row of houses, as if the last house had been forgotten. On the other side of the plot was an unmade track edging a field, and beyond this a railway embankment left from before the Tory minister (Mr Beaching) did away with the Preston to Southport Train line.

When the letter came we were so disappointed to read that the council would not grant us the permission to build on that space. The letter said it would be at least ten years before they would even consider another application '**judgment**' as this was a 'green belt' area. It did not make sense to us at the time but later we found out a councillor had bought the plot and within two years had built his own home there. The councillor buying the plot we had been after could not have been coincidence. Some things do make us 'smell a rat'. We would find out that the said councillor owned another property across the field behind the vacant plot. There was nothing we could do but wondered about the ethics, an old boys network was still as alive as ever?

Was this my lesson on matters of judgement. My way of thinking was that despite any underhand sneakiness it was all just the hand of FATE leading us to something else, somewhere we were meant to go!

We had become set on moving for several reasons not connected to mum and dad. For one I wanted to distance myself from the trouble brewing between Paula and Mark. I tried to tell her she was lucky to have a kind, handsome, hard-working husband and that her lies were bound to be discovered soon. The other reason was the Plumber next door. He came round onto our drive, ranting and raving as Dave got home from work one evening. He accused Dave of pinching his customers. His wife then joined him shouting the odds. Dave stood there totally taken aback. It was ridiculous as Dave did electrical work and only touched plumbing if he was installing an electrical boiler. After this he and his wife, Liz would not even nod or reply when I said 'Good morning'. So I had become their enemy too, without ever having said a bad word to them. We felt we were living between a love cheat and a pair of mute Aliens. A year or two later, Liz would cross my path again but her asking for my skill and help!

Whilst still living in Penwortham Dave and I had a wonderful holiday weekend in Paris. Mum was happy to look after Matthew whilst we were away. We intended to go by air but after the Medium at the Spiritualist church saying 'You are going much higher than you think!' the idea of flying was taboo! Did he mean we were going to the 'other side', was he giving me a warning? Just in case, we decided to go by train.

The weekend was memorable and romantic. It was the first holiday we had been on since our Honeymoon. The journey was okay down to Dover. The ferry crossing was not as bad as I had envisaged, luckily no sickly feeling for me. The train journey across France was uncomfortable on wooden bench seats but we were thrilled to be in Paris. We had booked just bedroom at the Hotel and to save money we had taken a Tupperware box full of sandwiches for the journey and to see us through the first day sightseeing. We explored the City on foot, going up Mont Mart through the artist quarter seeing all the art work on display in a little square. Our food now gone we came across a patisserie and bought half a quiche and a bottle of sweet French wine.

We walked up the quaint old steep cobbled street until we came to the Cathedral at the top. Wonderful music sounded from the entrance and as we watched we saw a bride and groom appear followed by their wedding guests. It felt like we were in a fairy-tale! Standing there looking at the wedding and all the fantastic architecture and absorbing the atmosphere we were mesmerised. There were people, like ourselves, just sight-seeing and other local people stopping to look, taking a pause in their own day. As we marvelled at the view the warm spring sunshine gave the morning an unreal glow.

After watching the Wedding group for a while we ambled across to the park. There on the highest level of the Mount we sat to eat lunch and guzzle the wine. We drank straight from the bottle as we had no glass, in the mood of the moment, looking at the panoramic view, manners didn't matter. An elderly scruffy looking gentleman came over to us and wanted us to buy six battered looking scenic post cards. We had no money but gave him the remainder of our wine. He went off looking very happy!

Reader... If a complexity of life is causing you stress think of ways to make life more of a balance. If at a crossroads in life and you have a worry, do not act without first seeking or taking impartial advice.

Reader... This is the RUNE Jera

The Rune Jera represents harvest, one year and outcomes. To me this Rune also represents reward for efforts. The more we put into life, love, work and friendship the more we gain.

21/ Tarot lesson, JUDGEMENT

Card 20...The 21st Lesson of the Tarot...Judgement...Rebirth.
Song....'The Long and Winding Road'... Band...Version ... The Beatles

The Judgement card depicts an Archangel sounding a trumpet whilst hovering over three human figures, a man, woman and child, arising from graves. On some designs the arms of the humans are raised up towards the Archangel on others their hands are together in prayer. It looks like the people are awakening. The Biblical indication from this image is of Judgment Day. The hope of resurrection and eternal life is the promise for those repentant of sin. In reverse, this would be lack of Judgement.

__Awakening, rebirth__ and __surprise__ must be taken into consideration when trying to interpret this card. We might see an actual Judgement being made by the enquirer or by someone of authority, sometimes even a legal Judgement. As death could often be a release from earthly toil, pain or troubles we might also consider the words __relief__ and __release__ when this card is drawn. If someone were trying to follow a very spiritual path when this card is drawn, we might interpret this to be progress in control of the ego, the self that is within us all, and concern with material gains, onward towards being in touch with a higher self that can tune into the 'God' energy.

In everyday situations we are required to make judgements to end some situation so the path is clear to begin a new project. We might interpret this card as a prelude to a new direction. Worth noting, this card is number 20 and is followed by card 21, The World, the shape of a sphere, and so death and resurrection is followed by a beginning, a circle into infinity. Also 1 + 2 = 3 the number of divinity. We shall consider all aspects of The World card in the next chapter but need to mention it here so that we may understand judgment is promise of another incarnation, in this life, or after physical death, on to another life. This card linked easily with the next section of my life as there were many things to weigh up. Restrictions of youth would be replaced by responsibility, nest building/ renovating property and budgeting!

Reader... Do you want to lift restrictions in your work or relationships? Then the Judgment card may hint that change is needed. Think of ways you might be able to 'let go' of past negative experiences that may be holding you back.

Chapter 21

1970's continued.

During the day, whilst Matt and Rick were at school, I had been further studying the meanings of both the Nordic Runes and playing cards in the art of divination. In the Summer months I had been asked to play the role of 'Fortune Teller' at a couple of 'Church Fates' and it would not be possible to read the Tea Leaves. From these events there were a few ladies that came to visit me later at our home for a reading. My payment was often a Box of Chocolates or a small gift, I had no thought to make a charge. The Tea cup method was still my favourite, and so I decided to design a set of modern Runes. Runes that would have symbols on. The symbols being those that were often visible to me when reading the Tea leaves.

On paper I drew thirty symbols. When Dave came in I asked him what material I could use that would be more durable than card. The Nordic Runes I had in my possession were painted on pebbles but I wanted something warmer 'Why not carve the symbols on wood?' Dave answered. It was a bit of a lightbulb moment as the thirty symbols would work out as six on each face, like dice. Dave cut wood into cube shapes and I etched the patterns onto them. From then on I used my own 'Rune' set, for some readings if tea leaves were not available, casting them on a hand painted cloth divided into five sections.

By the time I had designed my modern 'RUNE' set there was news that mum and dad had got a buyer for the Cottage and were starting to wonder where they would go if the sale went through quickly. They were desperate to find somewhere that would become a home for gran as well as themselves. We had talked of getting one big house that could be converted to two flats or divided in some way to give us all our own space. Before Dave and I bought our first house we had looked at a house in Southport but it had been much too big for our needs. Now a house like that would fit the bill if we were joining in with my parents and gran.

We found the perfect house on our first house hunting visit to Southport. Number 223. Adding up to number seven! Magic seven again! It makes me smile now, thinking of that first viewing. Dad, for all his scepticism about psychic matters asked me what my vibes were telling me as soon as we got into the hall. Closing my eyes, I got a strong mental picture of three children in Victorian/ Edwardian clothes. There was a boy in breeches in a tweed sort of coat and cap. My inner eye saw the boy sliding down the wooden banister, he looked about thirteen years old, with two giggling girls running after him. The girls were perhaps 8 and 10 years old. They wore dresses covered with white pinafores and beneath the hem there was an inch or so of petticoat showing and the lace edging of their long bloomers. They both had long hair in ringlets held on top with a bow. One was fair the other had brown hair. 'So you think this is a happy house?' said dad after I told him what I saw.

It was decided that this was the house we were looking for, and what was great, it would be vacant on possession as Mr Hoy, the previous owner had bought a bungalow in Devon and could move right away. Only one snag, much repair was needed.

Once our Penwortham house was on the market we soon got a buyer. Dad and mum had already moved during May and we were packing things up going back and forth to and from Southport taking ornaments, kitchen utensils and bits of furniture. On one visit Mum and I had a trip down Lord Street looking for decor inspiration. In a shop window mum spotted a beautiful crystal ball. She insisted it was meant for me. So this was another item to add to my growing 'psychic kit' tool box.

We eventually moved during early September 1978 as the record 'Greece' topped the charts. It felt that month that the records in the chats were reflecting our life path. As if we had moved from 'Dire Straits' in our 'Walk of Life' with finances before the end of August, like greece lightening to brighter prospects now that we had money left over from the sale of our house in Penwortham.

This was the first house we had lived in where one might expect to find a Ghost and we would not have to wait long before he or she would make themselves felt, but before this we were to have another strange experience. Mum was with us on a journey to the new house from the one we were leaving. It was early evening at the beginning of July when we had sold but not yet signed over our place to the purchaser. The car was packed with small items and we were going to stay with Mum and dad as John was soon to be married and we wanted to make arrangements.

As we travelled down the main road into Southport I spotted a large oval shape in the sky just up ahead of us. People traveling the opposite way to us were stopping their cars to look up at the object. Dave was driving and only glanced at the object as we were in heavy traffic. Mum asked 'Is it a Space Ship?' I shouted 'STOP!' as it was such an unusual spectacle. Dave, trying to keep his eye on the heavy traffic, said 'I can't!' He thought it unwise to stop on a main road in the rush hour traffic. Matthew, in the back seat behind mum, got excited when I agreed with mum that it could be from space. My position in the back behind Dave gave me the best view of the object.

The thing was certainly nothing like anything else we had ever seen. It was about thirty feet above the houses. It was the length of the two semi-detached houses it hovered (absolutely still) over, and about as wide as the houses. It glowed a bright orange / red colour, like fire, but no flame. The speed we were going gave me a good view as we approached the thing. As we passed it, I turned round to see it from the back window of the car. It hovered soundlessly, as if suspended in thin air. Suddenly it zoomed off toward the Ribble estuary, in less than ten seconds it was gone. The sky was clear that day and the whole thing seemed too strange to be true.

'What the heck was that?' I asked Dave. 'Probably a Thunderbolt he said, but then added that, to his knowledge, a Thunderbolt does not just hover. Whatever it was there must have been at least a dozen other people looking up at the thing but we never saw anything in the local paper about it. One thing it taught me, 'Truth is definitely stranger than fiction'. What was it about our family that attracted these strange events? Well, in all the years we would spent at 223, our house was often referred to as 'the centre of weirdness' by the family as we encountered so many inexplicable events.

In August 1978 my brother John got married to Kathleen. Dave and I had not yet moved to Southport, and gran had not yet joined mum and dad, but we had stayed the night to set off to the wedding together from 223. Thankfully the wedding went off without the usual calamity that often occurred around John. Kathleen looked beautiful in a full length lacy white dress and pretty coronet. My gran had bought me a peach pink dress with emerald green trim plus green sandals and bag to match. Matthew wore his first 'grown up' pale blue denim suit. With his fair hair the blue really brought out the colour of his eyes. We all had a lovely memorable day.

Less than a month after the Wedding, in September, we moved, joining Mum and dad at 223. Matthew had been promised a place at the local school, Dave had finished the house re-wire, and we could start to make the upstairs rooms into a self-contained home. Dave was installing a kitchen for us and had to up-grade the bathroom. He had already modernised a kitchen for mum and dad, and was now busy transforming what was once the butler's pantry, into a downstairs bathroom for them.

There were seven beams under the flooring that had to be replaced, and whilst this was within Dave's capability, we had to get in an established firm in order to obtain our smaller Mortgage. At first we were having to walk across planks whilst the under floor work was done. All throughout the house, work had to be done that first year. Dad was able to support us all to some degree whilst Dave did most of the renovation. Dad enjoyed helping wherever he could, but later the large garden became his province, growing much of our fruit, herbs and vegetables, whilst Dave was inside maintenance man! Mum and I were often in the way of the work during September and October that year, so we would go into town and look for soft furnishings.

On one of our trips I got a sudden horrid stabbing pain across my shin. The pain felt as if I had been struck with a wooden club. It only lasted a few seconds but had made me stop in my tracks. 'Are you okay?' mum asked. At that moment a mental image of John popped into my mind and at the same time the name John. 'I hope John hasn't been injured, or broken his leg!' I said. Mum then told me John was playing football for a Police Charity that day. Sure enough when we got home we had the news that John had broken his leg at the shin, just in the same place I had felt a moment of sharp pain earlier.

After a few weeks of home making I decided to look for a job. Before the move I had done well with the make-up firm, they had asked me to be Team leader, and offered me a car. The down side was all the traveling they would expect me to do. The actual demonstrating, facial massage, and application of make-up was enjoyable but leading a team was not for me. Seeing an advert in a department store 'Sales Lady Required for Estee Lauder make-up department.' I decided to apply!

Standing next to the lift there was an attendant (a man in a military style uniform of red jacket with gold braid) to take shoppers to the top floor. In those days high class stores employed a man to assist customers with their bags, into and out of the lift or to a waiting Bentley or Taxi cab. This was a curtesy to encourage the rich and famous to shop with the store again. I knocked at a door marked 'Personnel Officer'. Within twenty minutes I had got myself a full time job for the Christmas period with a view to a permanent position in the New Year. Whilst working in the store I saw quite a few famous faces and the perfume Youth Dew was very popular with many 'posh' Ladies. White Linen was the new scent being launched with a big promotion.

On the first day of my new job I became acquainted with the other girl, Eileen on the counter. Soon we were chatting away like we had known each other for ages. In the conversation I had mentioned my hobby of reading the tea leaves. 'You must do mine sometime.' She said. It would be a while before this could happen as when it was our lunch break one of us had to stay on the shop floor when the other went to the canteen. After a few days, word got round, some of the girls asked me to look in their cup during lunch break. It passed a nice hour for us all.

During my second week in the new job I was a bit late getting up and had to run for the bus. Finding myself panting, and a little out of breath. This had never happened to me before and I told myself to get fit. The next day on the bus I started to feel rather queasy and by the time I got to work I wanted to be sick. Eileen was very good and said she would hold the fort whilst I went to the powder room. After an hour, feeling back to normal, I put it down to a dodgy sandwich, or was it all the 'White Linen', the new perfume we were expected to spray onto each customer through the door? When the same thing happened for the next two mornings it started to dawn on me that I may be pregnant. For the last four years we had wanted a second child, so when our new Doctor confirmed what I suspected, Dave and I were delighted. 'New Home New Baby!' exclaimed Eileen when I gave her the news.

Matthew would be seven in January and though I had suffered with morning sickness when pregnant with him, this time the sickness was off the Richter Scale! A permanent job would not be possible in January if this sickness continued. Eileen was very good by covering for me when, several times each morning I had to dash to the lift and get Mr Williams, the lift attendant, to take me to the top floor, as quickly as possible. My flight to the lift became so regular that 'Mr W' would watch for me leaving my counter and have the lift doors open and ready.

For the next four months I could hardly look at hot food let alone eat it. Mum would often cook me some dinner. She had become worried that I was losing weight, rather than gaining it. It was kind of her, but any sniff of onions cooking made me dash to the toilet. The only food I could eat was a pear drop sweet, or dry bread with a slice of lean dry boiled ham. Any hint of butter or any other meat, fish or vegetables were out of the question.

By Christmas I was glad to be leaving work. Eileen promised to keep in touch and there would be plenty of time now for me to prepare for the new baby, but would the colour of the room be blue, pink or should we settle for a shade of apple green? No longer out at 'Este Lauder' there were a few workmates that came to see me for a cuppa and a reading. They would sometimes phone and ask if I would do a 'reading' for their sister or friend, people I did not know. These ladies would often bring me small gifts, I suppose as a payment, though I never asked for anything and enjoyed passing time in such that way.

Eileen was a regular visitor on her day off and we would enjoy a cuppa and a chat together with me, mum and gran in the 'communal' room of the house, the Sun room Dave and dad had built at the back of the house.

Now feeling a bit less sickly, I had taken over from mum with the school pick up for Matthew. On Thursday 5th April just before Easter, there was a bunch of mothers congregated around the school gate. Not knowing any of them yet I stood a few paces away. One of the mothers turned round. 'Are you free tonight?' she asked. 'Only we are having a 'Fortune Teller' and she only comes if we have ten people or more.' she added. I said I would go and it was agreed I could bring mum too.

Mum and I were the last to arrive at the house for the 'Fortune Teller' as I had put Matthew to bed before we went. On arrival the girl who's house it was (as yet I did not know her name) explained that the other nine girls had all taken their turn. Mum was to go in now and I was to wait in the hall. I was last of the eleven to have my 'reading'. We were told to pay £1.00 directly to the Fortune Teller and then at the end we would all chip in 25 pence for her to pay for a Taxi home.

From my seat in the hall I could not hear anything that was said to mum. After about ten minutes a voice called out 'Come In.' Mum had gone through to another room so I sat down opposite the lady. The first thing she said was formed as a question 'Who is David and who is May?' she asked. Quite impressed, I listened as she went on to say (glancing at my baby bump) she thought I would be having a happy event around October. 'Good grief!' I thought! My due date was late July. She went on to tell me that someone in my family wearing a uniform was going to reach great heights. 'John!' I thought. She told me that one of my children would be very musical and that I had nothing to worry about. She said I must take things easy and enjoy looking forward to all the many good things in store for me in the future. That was about it!

When I entered the room where the others were sitting they all looked quite dejected. Mum was visibly upset and one or two others were too.

After our hostess had seen off the 'Fortune Teller' we started to compare all the information we had been given. Mum spoke first and asked what the lady had told me. I thought she had got some psychic ability but apart from the two correct names there was not a lot to tell. Mum looked upset as she said the lady told her that she would be a widow within a year!!!

Each of the guests recounted the information they had been given, another girl said that she also had been told she was to be a widow too, then another girl said 'Me too!' All, in all there would be five widows amongst this group of eleven and another girl was told she will have some loss in her family, according to the Fortune Teller.

Whilst they were all bemoaning their gloomy predictions, I was thinking the Fortune Teller must have her wires crossed. 'Well I cannot see this being true!' I piped up. They all looked at me. 'Law of averages tells me that you can't all be having bereavements!' I reasoned. 'Get the kettle on and I will cheer you all up with a little look at the tea leaves.' I told them. 'Oh! Do you read the tea leaves?' questioned our hostess. Mum answered for me, saying that I had been reading tea leaves since I was about ten years old and she thought they would be pleased with my kind of reading. As some of the ladies had to go home to get their kiddies to bed it was decided that there would be another little gathering next week, on Thursday 12th April. All were agreeable and eager that I should do them a reading from the tea leaves!

Through the following week my mind was taken up with home events. It would soon be gran's 80th birthday and she had moved into the little bed-sitting room now prepared for her. We were having visitors over Easter as family from Manchester wanted to see the house and visit gran. Dave's parents, Roy and Lucy would also be coming for tea on Easter Saturday. The house would be buzzing with people.

Thursday 24th March came and at 7 o'clock I walked the short way from 223 to the house round the corner where the ten Ladies were waiting for me to do their Tea leaf readings. After greetings were exchanged in the sitting room the hostess showed me into another room where she had set up a table and two chairs ready for me. The time flew past as it always did when I was conducting any readings.

When all nine had been in to see me the hostess came for her reading. After this she thanked me. 'The others have gone now, they asked me to tell you they were very pleased.' She remarked as she held out a ten-pound note. 'Oh no! I did not expect payment.' I said. She insisted on me taking the money, saying 'It's a gift, you deserve it after giving up a whole evening, whilst we sat drinking wine, enjoying ourselves. Thanks so much.'

Bewildered I went home wondering, was it okay to take the money for just doing what I had often done for pleasure? In the end I put it to the back of my mind. The baby would be born in Summer and there was still a lot to organise. Easter came and went as I got bigger and bigger. About three weeks after the tea leaf reading event there was a knock on the front door. Mum had answered and was calling me down. 'This lady wants to know if you will do her a reading.' Said mum, adding 'I can brew a pot of tea if you would like to take her through to the sun room.' The woman told me she had been sent by her daughter as her reading from me had proved accurate. Once again a pound note, was pressed into my hand after I had finished the reading.

From this time there were several visitors that would come knocking to ask for readings. Without any advertising or even without any real intention I had been able to earn a little pin money from my own ability. I thought back to when I had asked my Angel to help me find my work direction, before our move a few months earlier.

In doing so many more readings I had come to think that there were differences in the depth of information I was able to pick up. Could this be that there were some people that were more on my vibration and others that were not? Or was it down to their psychic ability as well as mine? There were so many factors that may be taken into account it just baffled me, but I did, and still do, think that doubting the ability might somehow stop the flow.

As Summer came and the weather got very hot I had to turn down anyone wanting a reading as my due date got nearer. My appetite had returned by then and apart from a very pointed bump restricting me, I felt well and had been sleeping well. My dreams had been 'low key' and hazy, not like the 'film plot' that sometimes had been the case. I tell you this as my next strange event was **NOT** a dream.

In our new bedroom we had placed the bed in the position of feet facing towards North-East, along a wall on the left side. My need to use the bathroom during the pregnancy prompted me to be on the outside right, Dave next to the wall. We had gone to sleep at around 11pm. At around midnight I woke up and found myself floating free of my body, horizontal but directly above it. Fully conscious my first thought was this...'I am having one of those out of body experiences I had read about. Just go with it!' I told myself. As this thought came I found myself slowly floating into an upright position, my feet just a few inches above the bedcover. 'Lucky we have such high ceilings in this house!' I thought.

Without even thinking about movement I floated towards Dave's side of the large open door of the fitted wardrobe he had made. Looking back towards the bed, there in bed, I could see myself (my body) next to Dave. Looking down I saw Dave's work clothes in a little pile on the floor. Oh! He must have been too tired to pick them up, I thought. My next thought then came as to where I would go, now that I was in this strange state. The instant the thought was formed I found myself floating through the clothes hanging in the wardrobe as if they were made of thin air. Then through the outer brick wall in just the same way.

Now outside, level with our upstairs bedroom, I looked down at the roof of the bungalow next door covered with moss. I wondered (just as one might wonder when, (fully awake) if it would need scraping off. Then I noted the light from a lamp post, glistening on the wet roof tiles. My astral body then started to float over the front garden of the bungalow, across the garden on the corner, across a side road then over the next two front gardens. All the houses were in darkness but one or two cars passed along the main road. I wondered if they could see me, or my ghost as I floated along. Until then there was no fear, just a wonderful lightness to my whole being.

Without any conscious thought, my body floated on along towards some spare ground past the houses. It was at this point that FEAR set in to me. 'What If I can't get back to my body?' No sooner had the words came to mind, when a strong force or power of some kind threw, well slammed me, back into my 'Earth' body.

Shocked by the force of coming back, as if on a piece of giant elastic, my body felt heavy and so very tired, although fully aware of what had just happened, my body must sleep. On waking the next morning, I noted the clothes Dave had dropped on the floor and the wardrobe door was open, just as my 'astral' self, had seen it. Going over my nocturnal experience the next day I went out to the front of the house and sure enough the Bungalow next door had got moss growing all over the roof and the street lamp was directly in front which I had never noticed before.

The next night the same thing happened, but this time it was just as I was drifting in the twilight state, before slumber deepens. The sensation of floating came upon me, but now, my astral (spirit) body drifted out from my right side until it was in mid-air, horizontal, as if suspended, right next to the bed. Slowly without any conscious thought of doing so, my astral body started slowly to come to an upright position. My feet were not on the floor but as soon as I became upright, again I started to float towards the front of the open door at Dave's side of the wardrobe. Looking down, there again was a little pile of work clothes on the floor. Without any thought my Astral body moved forward as if I were just a puppet, without any control but able to see and think normally.

This time my travels took me about half a mile past the houses and a large field, level with the top of the street lamps, above the pavement along the main road. Wondering if I might float all the way to Liverpool and wondering what force was at play in these weird night travels, it was only as I came to a big junction that the fear came upon me again...What If I cannot get back! **Thwack**! In the blink of an eye but with a great shocking speed, the force slammed me into my 'Earth' body again.

A few nights after the out of body experience the floating feeling came upon me again, waking me up during the night. Opening my eyes to find the darkness was deep. Not a trace of moonlight, and because of the heavy curtains not even a chink of light from the street lamp. A sensation of someone or something being in the room with us, I tried to move but found myself frozen, rigid, paralysed. There was a sensation of a being/entity, hovering over me. A great dreadful wave of fear gripped my heart, then after a moment an 'inner knowing' came to me.

The fear passed, replaced by a strange inner calm as, within my mind a voice hushed me and said, 'I bring the soul, come to enter your child'. An instinct, or intuition told me this was an old soul, a shaman, or someone wise beyond my understanding. Gradually the frozen, rigid feeling abated and left me with this great elation, a joy! All was as it should be.

On Saturday, August the 4th in Southport hospital, this time with Dave holding my hand, our beautiful, sweet daughter came into the world (now **one of each, as predicted by the Fortune Teller** whilst on Honeymoon) and only a week late. Another Leo personality to keep dad company in our four generation home, along with the five Earth signs.

Before my new arrival, some girl's names had been on our list. Rose was at the top because of the flower, the Rose, is the most perfect flower of all. However, whilst in hospital I had another strange happening. This time it was only a bad dream, or was it? After the nine hours in labour, greatly tired, I fell into a deep sleep. 'My name is Rose and I died in this bed!' the voice said as a face loomed over me. My own scream woke me up and there was a nurse telling me that my baby wanted a feed. That day Dave brought Matthew to meet his little sister. The hospital did not allow children into the ward but Dave, ever the problem solver had gone around the back, into the hospital gardens and found the window next to my bed.

Feeling so lucky that the fates had sent me a wonderful gift, a second child, a pretty little girl, I was first in the queue each morning to go for a pink rose patterned baby gown rather than the plain white ones. Loving all the little garments that were now in fashion for either boy or girl but wanting to make the most of the 'Girly' baby days I would choose red, pink, lemon, lilac or powder blue for my little princess, and silver shoes whenever possible.

On returning home with our new little bundle of joy the family made it a special celebration. We went through to the communal room where mum had prepared a nice tea for us all, then took some lovely photographs with everyone holding baby. We took one of Matthew sitting on the front doorstep, gently cradling his new sister.

We felt so lucky to have a second child after such a long wait. The weather was glorious and the sunshine Angels had brought my little sunny Leo child. Now all we had to do was think of a special name for her. Because I believe in the vibrational power of a name I wanted a name that resonated a warmth.

We had several visitors during the first few days back at home and we still had not found her the special name I wanted. At the back of my mind was the thought of the 'Guide' that had spoken to me of bringing the baby a soul, the name had to fit, and be memorable. The Naming book only made the choice harder with so many names to choose from, so for the next few days we pondered!

One morning my dad quietly asked me to consider using my mother's first name, Edwina. Mum had only used her middle name, May, and dad said that he loved the name Edwina. Mum had been christened after her father

Edward and the more I looked at our baby the more the name seemed to fit. We then added the name Lucy after Dave's mum and gran, and because I also wanted a name of her own we added Roselyn, but at her Christening the Vicar pronounced this Rosalind. Still, a rose by any other name is still my rose!

22/ Tarot lesson, THE WORLD/ THE SPHERE

Card 21...The 22nd. ^(some packs say lesson, 21) Lesson of the Tarot.
Songs...'The Walk of Life'...Band... Version...Dire Straits

The image on the card shows a beautiful, fair, woman. A gossamer sash floats over her shoulder coming down across her lower body. She stands inside a circle of Laurel leaves, like a Crown. The Crown is considered a Kabbalistic symbol. She holds a wand in each hand. Above her, outside the circle, to her left there is an Angel on a Cloud (Water). Above, to her right an Eagle (Air) sits on another cloud. Below her outside the circle is a Bull (Earth) and a Lion/ Sphinx (Fire). The Angel and the creatures show the four elements. The woman is 'Truth', looking, surveying, summing up the whole, World, Cosmos, Life! The card represents instigation, initiation, the meaning is Reward.

In some Tarot packs, when the World card comes after the Fool card, the Fool is considered the last card in the sequence of the Major Arcana. On all the packs that have found me the Fool is 0, or there is no number shown, therefore I see the World card as the first of the major cards, apart from the extra card in my pack, the Comet. Then after the World, we begin the minor Arcana. In the Tarot pack I refer to here, the World is followed by the Comet as we shall see in the next chapter.

We might liken the circle of the crown (Woman inside) to the cosmic womb holding the whole of humanity or the womb that carries the infant after conception until birth. If we consider the circle as having no beginning or end then we may see the World as an indication of everlasting life, reincarnation. Think of the World we live on, our planet, holding humanity inside the circle.

We, the human race, are the infant in times continuum. When we relate the word 'instigation' to the image of the world we can interpret the meaning as the moment of conception, of a child, of the Universe or of a new chapter in the life of the enquirer. At the end of one era a new one begins and so it goes on, and on for as long as we are on the material plane.
The reader must interpret this card together with the other cards drawn at each sitting, for each individual enquirer. The World card speaks to me of wholeness, plenty and abundance.

The World card gives us each an inkling that we are a link to the natural world around us. Our Earth has been abundant in comparison to other planets in our solar system, she has been a fruitful mother, nourishing us all. Our 'green' planet was mother to us for centuries past and it pains me to see her raped of her bounty. How do we repay her for her abundance? We must curb the greed, think of the whole and not just the self. If we starve ourselves from existence, then no doubt the Earth could regenerate. Plants and animals would come to flourish again; maybe without us, or maybe those few of us who survive will have realisation of foolish greed, the cycle of life would begin all over again until we become more enlightened.

Reader... Life has it's seasons just like nature. Enjoy your season, blossom, love, live and grow in knowledge and spirit. Give mother Earth respect and conserve, recycle, plant trees if you can. Be aware of all nature. Take time away from the mechanical and the technology devices of modern life, if only for a few moments each day. Meditation for inner healing is often just the act of closing eyes and allowing your mind to be blank.
Reader... This is the RUNE Berkana

Berkana is the Rune of Growth, rebirth and the symbol is said to come from the Birch tree. We learn if we can and use this knowledge to improve. This is the cycle of life and rebirth!

Chapter 23

Into the 1980's and beyond.

As any new mother will tell you, the first few weeks with your new baby can be draining. Just as I was getting into a routine I swivelled out of bed one morning and something pinged in my back. Mum and gran, being just downstairs, were a boon after this. It turned out, according to our doctor, I had a 'slipped' a disc. Doctor Haddock told me to stay in bed and keep flat without any pillow. This was nigh on impossible as I had to sit up to feed baby. Everyone helped with the chores and shopping and after a few days with rest in between feeds, I felt much better.

One morning as Dave was fitting Kitchen cupboards in the room next to our bedroom, (I was sat up in bed feeding Edwina) a black cat ran from the landing across from the door of the room and darted through a small gap into the wardrobe. I knew that it was not a good idea to have a cat in the house where there was a baby. According to mum, I almost suffocated by a cat sitting on my face whilst in my baby carriage. I shouted Dave. He came to see what I wanted. 'A cat has just run into your side of the wardrobe.' I told him. 'It must still be in there as I have kept my eye on the door and not seen it come out' I said. After going right into our enormous wardrobe Dave came out but no cat was found. He did a search of the whole house. Thinking I must have missed the cat running out, we forgot about the incident, but the next day another event told me the phantom cat was still with us.

A routine call by the Health Visitor, (as was practice in those days) come to see how the baby was thriving and how I was coping. We chatted over a cup of tea and just as the visitor was getting up to leave we both heard a very loud 'MEEYOW!' from behind the sofa. 'You shouldn't have a cat anywhere there is a baby as they can sit on the face if baby is sleeping.' She remarked. 'We don't have a cat!' I replied. She was so sure we had a cat in the room she pulled the sofa out and looked behind it.

We often heard the sound of a cat after this and once or twice I caught sight of our 'friendly fury spirit' cat darting into the wardrobe; in just the same place where I had departed the house on the evenings I had been Astral travelling. Could there be a portal of some kind in that exact spot? We would never know for sure but the puss was not the only spirit to make themselves at home in 223 as we would later find out.

Gran was amazing for someone of eighty, she would love to walk baby in her pram whenever any random caller would want a tea leaf reading from me. Mum was also a great help in playing with Edwina when two or three people might want to visit me for readings. Dave, now working on shifts for the Metal Box company had to work. Our four generation home was ideal in many ways as we were on hand to keep gran company when mum and dad went on holiday, and they were on hand if Dave and I wanted the odd evening out. The arrangement may not work for everyone but it worked well for us. We all had our own private space to retreat to but we had each other when needed.

Gran became friendly and would chat with the couple living next door but one, as she went past with baby each day. They were a lovely old couple, Matilda, (known as Mattie) and Henry, who still lived and kept Chickens in the back yard of a Cottage that once was part of a Farm owned by Mattie's parents. When I went to buy some eggs from them, I had asked about the family that we knew had built and lived in our house in the 1890's. Mattie, born in 1898, remembered them well. She told me the family were quite rich but always made her welcome. She was often invited round when it was a birthday or a special event. 'They had three children, one boy and two younger girls. The father owned a Laundry factory next door.' Mattie told me.

'I was invited to the party for one of the two girls each year.' Matty went on. So after she described them and what they wore I knew my first 'vision' of the spirit children when we had come to view the house was true. The house always had a happy kind of vibe and we had soon accepted there were friendly ghosts/ spirits present in the house, but would dad ever be convinced?

Dave and I had not had a holiday for two years before our move, so we decided to go to dad's Caravan in Rhosnigr. Dave could take his small motor bike to do some scrambling and have some time with our boy. I could enjoy some quiet time with our new baby and we could use the dingy for Dave to 'ferry' Matthew, the beach things plus the baby box, down the shallow river to the bay. The weather that September was perfect for our first 'family of four' holiday.

On that first evening we unpacked the car, put Matt to bed and sat outside the Caravan listening to the car radio, just chilling out, bliss! We settled down early after Edwina had a 10pm feed. The next feed was due between 1-2 am. Tired from the journey we fell into a deep sleep. The next thing I was aware of was the noise of the scrabbling sound of the feet of the seagulls on the roof of the Caravan. At first I wondered where I was as light was streaming in from the sky-light above the bed. Realising it must be daytime now and there had been no 'night feed' baby could surely not be old enough at just four weeks to sleep through and miss a feed.

I sat up on my elbow to look into the carry cot at the foot of the bed. Gaping in shock I saw a figure of someone in a bending forward position, reaching over my part of the bed with his hands on the top of the covers over Dave's shin. I heard myself make a choked sort of screaming sound. The thought came to me that we had an intruder, the figure turned his head towards me and I saw scars of burning on his face. He was as startled as I was! Dave, on hearing my noise tried to rouse himself as I pointed towards the man. The man was wearing what looked like clothes for playing cricket or tennis. A cream coloured knitted jumper with open shirt collar showing in the 'V' and white trousers. He was obviously someone that had been badly injured in fire.

All I could say about the face of the man I saw were the large surprised looking eyes. In that moment I began to realise the man was in spirit form. He was fully visible to me but as Dave sat up he started to just fade out.

Our night visitor worried me all through the next day. After all the ghostly events of my teenage years I had prayed not to see any more. The next evening, we left a bedside light on, thinking that light would put off our 'Ghost'. On the third day when Dave came back from scrambling on the bike he was injured just below the Knee. He had tumbled off the bike and the exhaust had burned his leg in the exact place I had seen the spirit touching. Was the man a guide of Dave? Was he just a warning? Why else would the apparition have come to us? There were more questions than answers, but eventually I would find out more clues about our night intruder!

As the house was now more adapted to the needs of the whole family Dave went to work in the Southport branch of the Metal Box Company. Dad found work as an advisor in a Security innovation for the local authority. Dad had also taken up playing the organ-keyboard. Whilst he was playing, mum and I would sometimes go into the living room and have a little dance. One day we could hear him playing as we were in the communal room with Gran. 'Let's go and give him a clap!' said mum. As we went towards the room dad had stopped playing. He was wiping his glasses and looked a little startled. 'I have just seen the ghost of Mr Hoy!' dad stated. 'Whilst I was playing I had the feeling that someone had entered the room and when I looked round, there he was just leaning on the fireplace smoking his pipe just listening to me play!' We had had news a few months earlier that Mr Hoy (the previous house owner) had passed away. At last dad could put aside his sceptical views!

When Edwina was about three or four months old, my friend Eileen came to visit along with another girl I had worked with. After they had admired baby we had all had tea. They asked me to read the leaves (we always used loose tea in those days). In both the tea cups I could see patterns of joined rings and thought this was saying that very soon they would both meet men they would end up married to within a short space of time. We laughed as I said it was what all gypsy fortune tellers might say.

Later both the reading for Eileen and the other girl did come true; though at the time I was doubting myself, or should I say doubting that fate had already set a future path for them both. Hoping that I had got it right, interpreting the patterns that to them looked just random.

This thing of 'FATE versus FREE WILL' had puzzled me since many things that the gypsy had told me on Honeymoon, had already come true. It has been my own motto not to set out to give anyone the impression that I can always 'see' everything that lies ahead for them, I don't / can't! No Tarot reader, gypsy or psychic can see ALL that fate has in store for the sitter. The person 'reading' the signs cannot know all, and anyone curious about their future should realise this. After looking at the signs for hundreds of people over the past forty years, I think that only the energy we call God can see the whole pattern. Many things in life happen by the hand of 'FATE', things we do not decide, but we are able to direct our own actions on some matters. Choice, is where our own intuition comes in handy!

In Eileen's cup there were many pictures formed by the leaves. I could see the word LOVE, also the word CASTLE, and two people standing side by side, near two rings joined like a chain. One of the people looked much taller than the other. I though Eileen would soon meet a very tall man. There were some shapes looking like furniture in a room, a chair fashioned like a deck-chair, a large box with the lid propped open with a stick. These were quite unusual items of furniture. Further down the cup I saw a pattern, a map of a large continent and letter 'A'. Eileen said this would be Australia, but the map looked like North America to me. Telling her it looked as if she would go right across America (a dotted line marked a route) she said it was more likely Australia as her brothers lived there. Well, only time would tell!

By the time Edwina was three years old Eileen had met the very tall man and was shortly to be married to him. Mum and gran were looking after Edwina as Dave and I were invited to the wedding. Edwina was brought in her push chair to wave to the happy couple. Eileen looked fab in her long Edwardian style dress and big floppy hat. She reminded me of the film, 'Gone with the Wind'! She resembled the heroin, Scarlett O'harea. Soon, strangely, she would be riding across the whole of America on an adventure style Honeymoon.
Later I would hear about the trip across America and about the items of furniture Eileen saw when she first went into the home of her new love.

Yes, you guessed it, at his house in Castle Street there was a gramophone box with a stick to hold the lid open and an armchair styled on the same principal as a deck-chair. Again, the fact these things were there in a pattern of leaves that are left at the bottom of a cup, just did not make sense to the part of my brain that demanded explanations.

For fifteen years or so I had grappled with this mystical alternative view of the world and found nothing to fully understand how these things were possible. Over time I came to realise that readings are more accurate when the doubts are banished from my mind. To make the most of sixth sense we must just make our mind a blank, then, go with the flow! There is also the fact that some readings are more detailed than others. This may be that my vibrations are more in tune with some 'sitters' than others, or that it is a two-way energy that is at work...If the sitter is unquestioning as to how the 'seeing' is possible then any block is eliminated, whereas if the sitter is questioning or unbelieving then this could blur the vision and block the flow of psychic connection.

There was a small but steady stream of regular clients by the time Edwina was two years old, but up to then these had been only female, then one day there was a phone call where a woman asked if she and her friend could have an appointment each for a reading from tea leaves. When the woman arrived she said she wanted her reading in private so her friend was waiting in the car. After the reading as I was showing her out I told her to send the other person that was with her and as it was windy, closed the front door and waited until the 'friend' knocked. There in the porch as I opened was a rather portly, elderly man wearing a mackintosh and trilby hat. Surprised to see a man was 'the friend' the woman had told me was wanting a reading I exclaimed 'Oh!' in surprise as I opened the door. Gathering myself together, I politely asked him in. Mum had told me to use her sitting room as Gran had a friend in the communal room.

There had been nothing from the first reading that might have prepared me for the vibe I was getting from this elderly man. He reminded me of a picture I had seen of someone, but could not remember who. After asking him to sit down I went to the kitchen to brew a fresh pot of tea.

It was customary for me to stir the pot first, and then as the client was drinking I would try to tune into my higher self. Instead of the man drinking the tea I had handed him, he was staring at me in a way that made me feel unsettled. The next few moments we sat in silence, me wondering if he was ever going to pick up and drink his tea. All of a sudden the man reached into his inside breast pocket and produced a pack of cards. The glazed stare he was giving me was somehow compelling yet quite creepy. 'I do readings too!' he stated and then he put out four cards onto the coffee table, all the while still staring at me. Looking at the clock I said that as time was getting on would he better drink his tea so that I could get on with his reading. Knowing mum and dad were in the house should I need them I tried to shake off the uneasy feeling this man was giving me, after all he was older than my dad and had come along with the nice woman, saying he was her friend.

In the pattern of the tea leaves I could see a post box and a shop front with a letter 'F' plus a star shape. The rest of the reading was a blur as the man kept staring and was leaning forward towards me in a very disconcerting manor.

When I put the cup down and started to rise from my chair he said 'Just wait a moment, you were right I run a shop, a post Office near Formby. The Lady with me is one of my assistants. Now I want to give you a reading.' Not wishing to be rude I sat down again and just said that time was getting on and I must make the dinner. 'Look at me!' he said as he placed the four cards he had previously taken from his pocket into a line. He did not take his eyes from mine and I felt hypnotised by his stare as he told me to pick a card. I tried to look at the door but he again asked me to look at him. 'Point to a card.' He commanded. Glancing at the four cards I tried to point to the Ace of Cups but found my finger inexplicably going towards the card showing a circle, the Ace of Coins.

'You have chosen this card because you know that you are going to be free within one month by the death from a wheel.' He said. My mouth went dry and then he went on 'I see a small child with fair hair named Edwina and there is a name Edward linked with her from someone in spirit'. The fact that he had spoken the names of my family did take me aback and I wanted to get him out of the house but went speechless and felt glued to the spot.

Eventually, though the room had gone very cold, I managed to stand up and walk towards the door. The man followed on, talking all the time as I went to the hallway. 'You and I are soul mates, we have been together in a past life, and you have been meeting me in your Astral travels for some time, that is why you were surprised to see me when you opened the door you remembered me. Within one month a person close to you will die by a wheel, then you will be free'. By the time he was uttering the last sentence, I, speechless, had opened the door. As he went through to the porch he said he would phone me in a month. I gave him no answer and shut the door immediately. Feeling I had escaped some kind of evil spell I told myself that he was just a silly old man, but later, inside, I knew he was dabbling in Occult darkness, led by his ego.

A few weeks before the strange man came for a reading I had met a lady, Winnie from the Spiritualist Church when she and her friend had been to see me. Betty told me that if I ever needed help or advice about Spirit matters I would be welcome to visit her. Winnie was in her late eighties and had been a member of the Church for many years. She had many books that could be of help to me and she had said she would be pleased to lend, or give some to me. After the man giving me the creeps, I was in some dilemma as to what to do if he rang. Also the fact that this man had been able to make me feel mesmerised and had told me about a death had worried me. So I went to visit Winnie to see if she knew about him or his powers.

After telling Winnie the whole experience I said I had thought of asking Dave to answer the phone for the next month and tell the man not to come to our home ever again. 'No!' said Winnie. 'It has to be you that tells this man never to contact you ever again. You must be the one to break the connection. I think I have heard of him and if he is the man I think he is, he runs a group of people, mostly the middle aged Ladies who work for him, that are in his Coven. Three women who work for him are in his thrall.

He is influenced by the debauched 'seer' Allister Crowley who hypnotised many women in his day. You must tell him to back off so as to break any link or spell he may have over you.' It dawned on me then that I had seen a picture of Crowley in a book and that he was the person that I was reminded of when the man came for the reading. It made me shudder at the thought of him and his words.

Because Dave still rode his motorbike each Sunday to go to his bike club I was fearful that somehow the evil man had truly seen an accident from a wheel. Was he in any danger? Trying to put the whole thing to the back of my mind I determined to break the link this creep might think he has over me. The power of the mind can be strong if we set our thoughts the right way. By then I had learned to bring my Aura down like a shield around me before starting any reading and I hoped that doing this had already made a barrier between the 'Crowley' man and myself.

During the next month I had glanced in the tea cup of a visiting relation and seen a pattern of a sea horse in the leaves. Because this relative was in a rush to get home before the evening traffic built up, there was not time for me to study the leaves in any great depth. Later I would be glad that this was the case...

Whilst mum and dad were away on holiday we had some extremely bad news. My Aunt Margaret, mum of Maggie (my bridesmaid) had drowned. It was at 11.50pm on Friday 13th March. This terrible event had been just one month from my visit by the 'Crowley' man. Had the Wheel been the wheel of a boat, or was the connection the fact Margaret had been working for her husband in his tyre company? Did this horrid person truly have a gift, and if so was he using it for evil, twisting what he saw into what he wanted to read into it all? The whole family were quite devastated and all we could think about was the funeral and the inquest that would follow.

My mind was on these family matters as I went round with the Hoover one Sunday morning. Suddenly the face of the 'Crowley' man popped into my mind. The next moment the phone rang and the hairs on my head were standing on end as a shiver went through me. It was him! Steeling myself,

I picked up the phone and after 'Crowley' said Hello, I quickly cut in by telling him that he was never to contact me or even think of me ever again and there was no way I had ever met him, on the Astral plane, or in a past life and my husband was my true soul-mate, the only one I would ever want and the death was nothing to free me and he was crazy if he thought otherwise. Then before he could speak I put the phone down. It worked, he never contacted me again. I HAD MANAGED TO BREAK THE SPELL.

There is an old Gypsy belief that if a person is destined to 'read' the Tarot cards then they will be given, or find a pack when the time is right. For me Tassiology, (tea leaf reading) along with the poltergeist activity during my teen years had been the kick start of my psychic awareness. Designing and using my own Runes, study of playing cards, looking into the crystal ball my mum bought me, plus learning the Zodiac personalities in Astrology, were the tools to further my Esoteric journey. Even seeing the dark (Crowley) side, was a kind of gathering, an apprenticeship time before, and in preparation for the Tarot. The Tarot cards then came to me quite unexpectedly...

Mum and I went to look for a gift for a new baby in the family. At that time there were many small corner shops in our area and one of them was a haberdashery and wool shop selling hand knitted baby coats. We went inside and the shopkeeper was in the act of tidying a rack of Ladies tights on a counter stand. Mum struck up a lengthy conversation with her about the baby clothes. Whilst they were in conversation I could not help but notice the lady going over and over the stand of tights. It was as if she wanted them to be in a perfect line. She worked as if on automatic pilot whilst continuing the conversation. When she and mum paused from talking I just had to ask her this question...'Are you by any chance the zodiac sign of Virgo?' Answering 'Yes, how did you know that?' and at the same time bending down to a shelf below the counter pulling out a small box. 'If you are interested in that sort of thing please take these as I will never use them.' She presented me with my first pack of Tarot.
The Lady told us that a Rep had given them to her when he delivered the tights. The reason I had been able to tell her zodiac sign was because she was so like my own mother (they had connected) and so particular about

getting the counter in order that she must be the same sign. It is often a Virgo trait to like things in order.

We came out of the shop, mum having made a new friend and myself happy to at last been deemed worthy by the Gods (God energy) of my first pack of Tarot. And from a complete stranger! The numerology I had already learned, associated with reading the normal playing cards would be the same meaning, give me a start, in learning the Tarot.

A few weeks after being given the Tarot there were three events that prompted me into a more professional 'Seer' occupation mode. Firstly, my dad said I must get an accountant now that so many people were asking for readings and giving me £1.00 in payment. He suggested I might have to look for premises from which to work from if many more people were traipsing through the house. It had dawned on me that my little hobby job was rather intrusive for gran as her room opened onto the communal room I used to give the readings. She never complained and I think it tickled her to think I was reading the tea leaves just like her sister used to do when they were young.

Then one day as I opened the door to a 'client' I had a feeling she was a reporter for a newspaper. After showing her into our community room, (my part time office) I went off to brew the tea. Whispering to mum that I thought the woman was a reporter, mum asked if she could see the woman by bringing in the tea. The reading revealed to me several things about the woman. The letter 'E' was visible to me three times...'E...E...E' in the area of the cup representing finances and occupational interests. From this I deducted that her job title began with the letter E and the boss she worked for had the same initial as his job title, E, and the firms title was also 'E'. There were several arrows pointing in and out of the work area of the cup towards the travel area that led me to think that her job involved a lot of traveling back and forth. There were several other minor details about her life and people close to her which she acknowledged with a nod of her head.

The number of phone calls asking for appointments with me suddenly doubled and as this coincided with Edwina starting at Nursery School each morning I would be free to earn a little more from my readings. It turned out that the woman with the three E's in her cup was the **E**ditor of the Woman's page in the **E**cho newspaper and above her was the **E**ditor. About three weeks after she had come for the reading, but unknown to me, she did an article that gave points to each of five local Fortune Tellers. The points were from poor to best, given by the number of stars as she valued the accuracy of the reading. Another client told me about the 'judgment' in the article and that I had been awarded the top mark of five stars in the article. It pleased me to know that the reading was accurate and it determined me to rent a place to work full time from.

The third event to steer my work life into yet another new direction was a Sunday walk down the promenade and through a busy avenue that led to Lord Street. There was an empty shop on a corner near all the Café's, Ice cream parlours and buckets / spade Summer shops. Knowing I was now able to pay a year's rent from my own money I went to see the Landlord. My parents were a bit worried that the rent would be too much on my own and suggested I have a partner on going into the project. A week earlier there had been a girl visit me for a Tea cup reading who told me that she read the Tarot cards from her home. After going to see if she was interested in my little venture it was agreed that we would work independently but from the same shop.

Dave helped me by cleaning the shop and fitting two booths plus making a sign 'Predictions' over the front window. The name of Predictions was the name I had used to produce some box sets of my own designed Rune Cubes. I had been to see a Patent Advisor to safeguard my design but had been told that to secure a patent on my Runes it would be £6.000 per side of each Rune. As that would amount to 6 x £6.000 for each of six symbols. 5 in each Rune cube set, totalling £180,000 the cost was out of my reach. The Patent Advisor told me I could protect my idea another way. This would involve getting the story into a newspaper as this could provide a dated proof. As things turned out my Prediction Runes would feature in a newspaper and so the idea was protected, but were only destined to go to around three hundred people as they had to be made by hand, so not financially viable to make in great numbers. Perhaps all methods of aid to psychic intuition, like the Tarot, should 'find' the person the Gods intend to 'read' them and are only destined to be used by some.

The Predictions shop soon became a little hub of interest. We were lucky enough to have some free publicity on our opening day from the local newspaper. Then our story became a full page article in the Lancashire Life magazine where they described myself and my business friend as 'Two smart women about Town rather than the archetype 'Old Crone' fortune tellers of old'. A short time later we were asked onto a radio programme to be interviewed about my Runes and readings. After this there were several newspaper pieces about my Rune invention and the other methods we used. It felt as if the Dawn of Aquarius had begun to kick in, at least in Southport.

My time working from the shop was the busiest time of my life and at first stemming from the **'word of mouth'** recommendations passed on from one sitter to another. This was just as the Fortune Teller predicted for me during my Honeymoon. She truly had an amazing 'gift' and I just hoped I might be half as accurate with my 'gift.' That Summer the shop became so busy we had to purchase more chairs for our waiting area. At first Edwina was not happy being dropped off at Nursery school. At 9am I would take her, then be on my way to start work for 9.30am. After parking my car had under the Pier each morning, I enjoyed walking to work. The bright shops with coloured beach balls, the stall holders with a cheery 'Hello' getting ready for the crowds of holiday makers and day trippers coming from the train station, added to the pleasure of the fresh air and anticipation of each new day.

As Autumn breezed into Winter the demand for readings became greater rather than dwindling as I thought they might. It would mean that the shop stayed open each day unlike the other 'Summer' shops in the avenue. We found most people wanted to book readings for after 10 o-clock during colder months. If someone came without booking by telephone first, we give them a reading if they were prepared to wait. So there was a mixture of those coming on speck and those who booked an appointment.

Reader... Lesson of 'The Spiral' is that we are not in control of the material dimension we are born into and so we must aspire to be part of the universe and not try to always be tied to our mortal plans. The sheer nature of the universe is one of surprise. If we cannot believe in the God of our Sunday school days we must surely need to be open minded about life beyond this one.

23/ Tarot lesson, THE COMET

Card 22...The Comet...The Spiral...Invisible Paths
Song...'Love is all around'... Band... The Trogs.

This card is not present in all packs of Tarot and perhaps it is not meant to be. If you were to find a pack of The Royal Fez Moroccan Tarot you would see that it contains the card named The Comet. The design is said to be derived from a 13th Century pack of Moroccan Fortune Telling Cards. On the front of the box it tells us that there are 22 Grand Arcana and 56 Minor Arcana but within the box there is also the mystery of the extra card...The Comet...El Cometa...Le Comete! The image on the card is of a Cherub like being riding upon a four pointed Star. Within the Star we see a Pentacle bearing a five pointed star. There is a dividing line across the image. On the left of the dividing line we see one half of the star in only black and white. The other, right hand side of the image is in colours. This image says to me that nothing / everything in the universe is not what it may seem.

*The meaning of this card is thought to be...The Unusual, the Strange, the Supernatural. Now, as you will have read, my life up to the end of the 1970's has had its fair share of unusual events. Each pack of cards I had used for purpose of divination from 1981 up to the 1990's would come to me by chance. The Moroccan Fez pack only came into my possession after several years of using the other packs that has all 'found' me! Each design of the six previous packs of Tarot I had used, gave me a small increase in esoteric knowledge. Each of them adding information to use to help my 'sitter' but none of them described what is almost impossible to put into words. A kind of sacred knowledge that has been put into this world for us all to learn from. This is not by way of reading the Tarot, but in **all we***

see and from ***all those whom touch our lives*** and from ***all*** that is available to us from use of our senses. Not just the five senses, taste, touch, sight, sound and smell, but our other invaluable sense, our 6th, INTUITION. The Comet is all about the spiral of our soul on its journey towards the central hub of the 'God' energy.

Reader... If we have an impediment to one of our accepted five senses, another will often work harder, become sharper, in some way compensating. There may be no scientific proof of a sixth sense, but there are stories of intuition playing a part to save life when in danger. Linking the Comet to the remainder of my own story came to me, in meditation, just as I meditated on the card for each preceding chapter. We are all forever part of the father / mother 'GOD' energy from which we are made. We are all part of the ETERNAL SPIRAL of the Universe. No story is ever truly ended! You have the power to progress in this life and beyond it in the eternal journey of your soul.

Chapter 24

The 1980's onwards.

At times life in the shop was hectic and I wondered at the hand of fate that had led me into this strange occupation. Some evenings during the 1980's I would do party bookings, travelling to different houses if I could be guaranteed at least five sitters. Often there were more. Because each reading would take around half an hour I set a limit of eight persons at each party and would only take one party booking each week. At the shop we each took a day off. One on Monday, the other, Tuesday, so there would always be one of us in the shop. On Sunday we were closed. After a while this became exhausting and I remembered the last words the Fortune Teller had said to me about working very hard during my thirties. Hating to rush a reading, I only had time to see eight or at most, ten persons a day.

One day, my business partner wanted me to go to lunch with her at noon to meet a mutual friend. The morning had been busy and I had three telephone bookings to do before then. At around 11 o-clock two women arrived into the shop asking for me. As I still had two readings booked in I asked if they could come on another day or have a reading from my partner. One of the women said she had recommended me to her friend as she had previously seen me. They had come by train from Manchester. The moment I looked at the woman's friend I had a sudden feeling of dread but could hardly refuse. It has always been my policy not to refuse a reading just because I thought there was a negativity in someone's Aura. If refused they might imagine some bad things were to come and become worried.

As the woman entered my booth, sadness swept over me, surely there would be something positive or some help I could give? By now I was 'reading' the Tarot, unless clients particularly asked for a tea cup reading. After I have shuffled the cards and mentally asked my guide to be with me I always cut the pack into three. This is acknowledgment of the power of the Divinity. Then I ask my sitter to shuffle the cards, not wishing, but thinking on all matters that are of importance to them.

In a card spread, the cards are laid out by the 'seer' in the order chosen by a sitter. Three rows of three cards! The first row represents issues from the past still relevant in the sitter's life now. A middle row is laid out to represent the things that have bearing on the immediate future. A third row is laid out to represent the future possibilities that could affect the sitter.

Like any professional person I wanted to reach a high standard of accuracy in my work. After each reading I would judge myself. In my mind I rate my performance as low, average, good or top form. My confidence grew each time someone came on recommendation. The woman from Manchester posed me a problem I had not faced before. Her whole persona shouted desperation and turmoil. Not wanting to flunk the reading I tried to relax, to tune in but the 'dread' would not go away.

The cards went down in the usual manor 3-3-3 as described. There was not one positive aspect in the nine cards in front of me. This fact, coupled with this feeling of dread made me hesitant in what I should say. The first card told me that something most terrible had happened in the past. The second card indicated that a following waiting period had made matters worse. The third card showed great heartache had followed. The cards representing the now and the immediate future showed deep sorrow, anger and some self-recrimination.

All this darkness was upon this poor lady despite the fact that I knew by her aura she had a good heart. The three cards representing the future told me that unless she could find solace within herself she would continue this spiral of torment. It was as if a dark black cloud hung over her through no fault of her own.

Expressing my sadness for her and saying that I thought she had gone through the most hateful, dreadful experience in the past that was preventing her from living a life with any kind of joy from day to day. I told her if she could find a way forward it would be a test of some magnitude but that I believed there were those who loved her that were willing to help. I felt as if someone in spirit was urging her to believe in another life beyond this one.

At this point my work partner knocked to say she had to go as her friend is waiting. Telling her not to wait for me I would follow later, I went on struggling through the reading, thinking 'How can I help this sad lady?'

After the reading I asked if she wanted to talk about her burden. She looked into my eyes and thanked me for trying, but said there was nothing I, or anyone could do or say that would make a difference. Empathy was not enough for me to give for whatever had befallen her! As she got up to leave she said she could never, ever find a way to get over the what had happened, but she could not bring herself to utter the words on what caused this blackness for her.

The rest of the week, my thoughts kept going back to that reading. The sadness in the face of the lady would always stay imprinted on my mind. Whatever had befallen her to cause the darkness was beyond my comprehension.

A week after the 'darkness' reading I was sat thinking in our community room. As dad got up to go out he gave me his newspaper. There in front of me was the face of the woman, the Lady from Manchester, the one who's aura was heavy with heart breaking pain. She was the mother of a murder victim. In the article this Lady said she had seen a psychic in Southport that could tell she had had been through Hell, but could not help her to understand WHY. She could not understand why someone should commit such a heinous crime. I felt somehow I let that woman down. If only the reading had been done in the quiet privacy of the home office I used to work from, then perhaps my tuning in would have worked better. If only word could have come through from the spirit of her poor young daughter.

It was after this reading that I started to feel more and more that my readings would be better in a quieter place, though many readings were full of happy events and more often about 'love life' issues, where guidance could be gained from the signs shown in the cards.

After so many years have passed the readings that stand out in memory are the more unusual stories that came to me. The hardest part of doing a forecast is knowing what to reveal and what NOT to reveal to the sitter. The gypsy superstition, that one should NEVER read for oneself is right because the 'seer' or 'reader' is needed as a filter. Whilst trying to be accurate it is my feeling that a seer must never presume they know more than God when it comes to matters of life and death.

By the time the shop was doing well I felt in some instances it is right for the seer to sensor some of the negative information as perhaps we are not meant to know too much of any black clouds in advance or it may spoil the now.

Maybe we are supposed to live for the joy life can bring and knowing something too bad is ahead, we could not enjoy the moment. That is one good reason why the Tarot should not be read by everyone and why a pack must find its way to the ones that can respect this unwritten rule. Also this is why we must all focus on the good things we have in life at the moment. If there was a situation 'shown' me in advance, then I might give a warning, but it would be wrong to dramatize things.

An example of a client not taking on board what the cards warned was when a group of smartly dressed young men came to see me, all together from the same office in town. The readings were a mix of personal and work situations, but in one of the readings I could 'see' a theft from the back of a van. I knew the theft would have a personal aspect and was imminent. It seemed unlikely that this young man would be in the kind of job requiring a van as he was dressed for office work.

I had learned by now however, never to assume from outer appearance so I told the young man to be sure to lock his van whenever he left it parked up. The next day the young man came in to tell me he had been foolish. Not fully believing in the 'reading' he brushed aside the caution and the consequences were that all the tools of his trade had been stolen that very night. A personal aspect was that some of the tools had belonged to his grandfather and could not be replaced.

An Indian man, a doctor, once told me that by Indian tradition a 'seer' puts himself or herself into this work before coming to their present incarnation. There is some belief that the 'seer' takes on the burden of his enquirer. If this is the case, then the ritual of bringing down the light around the body, protecting the self, before starting to 'read' Tarot is a good idea. I do this by visualising a cloak of shimmering light around myself. As the violet light of the seventh ray in the rainbow has always made me feel calm this is my cloak.

My luck in finding a supportive partner has also helped me to do this work, and to help me shed any negative vibes that would otherwise linger. There have been a few times where I have judged a reading not up to my best standards and felt frustrated. It is then I have wondered if the criticism of others about this work being against the law of God is right, then, on the other hand, I think that any talent or 'gift' should surely be used. One thing I'm sure of, it's not the easiest way to make a living!

Many of my clients would shy away from the Tarot as they had a fear from one or other sections of faith that preached against predicting the future. It was funny but they did not equate the reading of the patterns of leaves in a tea cup as being as 'evil' as the Tarot. To most 'seers' it matters not the method of choice as to whichever method is used, it is focus that counts.

A 'seer' is required to 'tune in' to the part of the 'God energy' or if you prefer, the 'Collective Consciousness' that somehow floats through the universe. To my mind the information is available to us all, but some just find it easier to do the tuning in. We all might tune in whilst asleep and that can produce dreams that come true, just as Joseph, with the coat of many colours, did in ancient Egypt. My own brother has told me of several dreams he had that we later saw a real news events.

On my arrival home from work one afternoon I found mum and Edwina in mum's kitchen, both wearing a pinafore rolling out some pastry. 'Tea in the pot.' Mum pointed out. Standing watching them as I sipped my tea quietly mum asked Edwina (then aged about 4 years old) to pass the rolling pin. Mum and I were astonished to hear Edwina say dreamily, 'My name isn't Edwina, my name is Joan!' Mum spoke a little sharply as she and I looked at each other. 'Your name is Edwina!' mum retorted. 'No it's not, It's Joan!' Edwina repeated. We both thought of Aunt Joan, mum's sister. At the time I wondered if Edwina had been recalling a past life, or was it just that she had used the psychic part of her mind to link to the spirit of Joan. In years gone by it would have been a common sight to see mum and Joan together in the kitchen at their childhood home, baking together.

Remembering, when expecting Edwina, I heard the 'spirit' voice saying they were bringing the soul to my child, I had often played intuition games with her just as I had with my brother John when he was little.

It is my belief that young children can more easily tap into their psychic intuition than most adults because they have no barriers. Not having been told it is wrong, or impossible, they are like the blank canvas where, through their purity of soul images can flow without any preconceived notions.

Wanting to know about all aspects relating to the hidden powers of the mind I had started to read books on past lives, reincarnation. My reading time was late evenings when Dave had to work a night shift. One book led me to yet another peculiar experience, the book 'Life Between Life' by Dr Joel Whitton. There were many accounts of past life recollection from the people Dr Whitton had seen in his long career, treating people with phobia problems through Hypnotism.

At the end of the book there was a meditation to practice if the reader wished to glimpse into his or her past life. One evening when very tired I thought I would try the meditation. Alone in bed I could 'tune in' as Dave was at work and would not be home until early morning. Following the words in the book that were intended to produce a mental state of openness I read the 'instructions' through a couple of times. My eyes began to feel heavy. I remember putting the book down and then going through the meditation in my mind, step by step with the visual images outlined in the book.

Before little time had passed I found myself floating through a mass of coloured orbs. Each orb was like an elongated bubble of colour. There was every shade one can imagine, all floating in and out of each other. Words cannot describe the feelings that came to me other than saying that a great joy, euphoria came upon me as I drifted through this sea of colour.
At first I did not have any notion of where or even what I was. Then a face appeared to me in one of these 'orbs'. The nearest thing to help me explain the state was if you can imagine a balloon like colour but without a defined edge. This colour coming towards me was a glowing iridescent green 'balloon' shaped 'orb' with a face. I saw the face as it came close to my face. Somehow I knew that this was a soul that had a connection to me. The thousands of other 'orbs', souls that were floating wherever this place was, gave off a sound vibration. Not a tune, but a deeper note of elation, surrounded by their own colour. All the colours of the rainbow and yet more beautiful.

Without thinking I looked down and saw that I was just a colour, an 'orb' of light in a shade of blue that was like violet. The green orb that was visible came up to me and floated through my colour as if we were both made of cloud. Another colour then came close to mine and I saw a face within the orb colour of a different blue. This was a face I knew. It was indistinct but it was my grandad Ted. All these colours, 'orbs' were in a sea of souls, drifting through a space in colour and sound of great joy. A feeling of love beyond words washed over me. I did not want to come back to the world, as Dave came in at 6.30 am he woke me up. The time had flashed forward to morning as if in just the blink of my eye. It felt as if I had only been in the sea of colour for just a moment but it had been a whole seven hours. It was the best rest I have ever had from a night's sleep!

The meditation had started with visualisation of a vast building and thinking one's self as going inside and then down into the cellar to find a store of the Archaistic records (said to contain all past and future lives of all humans). Before starting the meditation, I had imagined peeping into one of my past lives. Me as a Victorian lady, or an Egyptian dancer. Never did I think I would see a between-time. Time after passing and being reborn into this present life. Was this heaven?

At the shop one day, on bringing tea for a waiting client, coming back into the seating area I could not help overhearing a conversation. Talking about her holiday in the town of Rhosneigr in Wales, a woman said she and her brother had experienced something very spooky. As dad's caravan was in Rhosneigr, where the spirit of the burn victim appeared to me, my curiosity was pricked. Asking my next client if they minded a short wait, we listened to her story.

The lady recalled that she and her brother were walking across an unmade track that cuts across R.A.F. valley. She was picking wild flowers growing along the fencing on the edge of the air field. Her brother was walking a few steps behind, stopping now and again to look through his binoculars, as his hobby was ornithology and he also liked to watch planes taking off. This was very close to where dad had the caravan we had stayed in. I could easily visualise the lady and her brother meandering along on a summer afternoon hearing only the sound of waves and nothing but the odd calling of a gull. It was always quiet there unless the planes were taking off just twice a day.

The woman said there was no other person to be seen on the open ground, either inside the fenced off R.A.F. area, in the other field or on the track ahead. She suddenly looked up and saw a man was approaching on foot. As he got within a few paces of her she was about to say hello but the man looked straight ahead and walked past without a sound.

Something about the man made her turn to see him walking away. She noted that the man passed within inches of her brother but seemed not to notice her brothers nod of acknowledgment. To their astonishment the man just disappeared before their eyes. It was as if he had not been able to see either of them. If the man had gone along to the end of the track and along the main road they would have had a clear view of him walking away. The spot where the man vanished, was less than ten feet away from a small rise where dad's caravan was situated!

The there was a postscript to their tale... After their evening meal at the Inn where they were staying they asked some of the locals in the bar if there had been any strange events in the area about a ghost. They were told that there was a ghost, a wartime legend... Young R.A.F. trainee pilots were each asked to do a solo flight at the end of their training period. One young man refused to climb into the plane he was designated to fly, saying 'my plane is doomed.

The young man refused orders even at the risk of a 'Court-Marshal'. Nothing could persuade him to take the flight. He said he had a premonition, and insisted there was something at fault with the engine and he would be killed if he went up! The other 'rookies' were beginning to get spooked by the young man's insistence that someone would be killed if they took flight in this particular aircraft. None of them would fly that plane. In exasperation the Flight Lieutenant phoned his Squadron Leader who was off duties, playing cricket at the time. When the word eventually got through to him he quickly drove his motorbike to the airfield.

After unsuccessfully trying to persuade the men that there was nothing amiss with the plane in question, he said he would prove it! Not dressed for flying, being still in cricket whites, he took the plane up. As all the men watched, it climbed. The men watching all gasped in horror to see the plane burst into flame as it went plunging toward the small rise at the far end of the valley. The Squadron Leader sadly died in the flames. My client was convinced she and her brother had seen the ghost of the Squadron

Leader. If this were the 'spirit man' I had encountered in dad's caravan, then was he still bound to the spot where he had perished?

Had the Squadron Leader been warning Dave to take care? Was he able to know that within a couple of days Dave would need salve on a burn from the exhaust of his motorbike? It was also a strange coincidence that this lady was telling this tale in my shop, and that I should overhear her words.

We did go back to the caravan again a couple of times during the early 1980's but there was no other visit from the Squadron Leader so perhaps he had found rest at last. I said a prayer, that he could find his way to the light, the 'God energy' and asked my Angel not to let me see him again. Perhaps the fact we only went together with other family members after that first visit, there were too many mixed vibrations around. Why he should appear to me was a mystery. After this I would hear a spirit voice sometimes, often this was when the person sitting for a reading needed a message. Maybe a spirit only comes when they have something to say or just to revisit a special place.

My intention was never to think of myself as a 'Medium', in fact I have never been minded to call myself a psychic or fortune teller, just to look at the signs that I believe are there for all to see. My belief in my own version of God had been strengthened now because I was now so sure that events of the future could sometimes be predicted. Still, I did not want to see dead people! To a large extent I felt these 'ghosts' could now be blocked.

Whenever the chill of an inner knowing comes about me, when the veil is thin, dividing the every-day material life from the ethereal life of spirit, it is possible to somehow stay or become 'closed' within your own aura. However, that was not the case the next time a spirit appeared to me, this time I did not have time to 'Close off' as it was early morning when I had just emerging from sleep. The next 'spirit' had the effect of confirming for me that the soul does indeed go on!

Mum and I once again went into the wool shop where the lady gave me my first Tarot She had taken on an assistant who asked me to do a small party booking for her and two others at her home as soon as possible. She explained that she wanted me to 'read' the tea cup for her cousin as he was afraid of the Tarot but it had to be in the next week whist he was staying with her. She said he worked in television. 'Don't tell me any more about him as I prefer to work without any information.' I told her.

On arriving I was shown into the kitchen for readings to be conducted in private. The young woman introduced me to her cousin and his partner. The two young men were wearing sports clothes, as if having just arrived from a Squash court. They both looked the picture of health and I had seen them on children's TV. The reading for the men has stuck in my mind because of what would happen about a week later and because a sudden sinking feeling that came over me as I shook hands with one of them. In the cup of the man introduced to me as her cousin there was a pattern of a cross with a number next to it, I thought It was a hospital sign and the number of the appointment date. Below this was a name next to a house and a pen on a dotted line. The word mum had a tear drop next to it and a cloud.

From the pattern of the leaves in his cup, I told the young man that it looked to me as if he and his partner were buying a house but for some reason his mum was upset. The young man said the reading was accurate and the date was important as it was the date he was due to have open heart surgery. He went on to tell me he had no option but to have the surgery as he had only a few months to live if he did not. He then asked me if he should sign to commit to buying a house with his partner. He was due to sign in just two days and was afraid to lumber his partner with a mortgage if he should not pull through. My heart sank when he asked this! 'Well if you truly can't put off the signing of the house purchase until after your operation then if I were you I would sign, because if you do not then you are presuming you will not make a recovery, you will not be giving yourself any promise of a future at all if you tell yourself not to sign.' I told him.

My fear for the young man was great as in truth there was no sign of events such as travel or family matters. These were usually visible far into the long term from the pattern of the leaves in a cup. My hope was that perhaps the enormity of what was happening in the immediate had been more important. Once again my logic was at odds with the inner knowing! Telling myself that the 'God energy' was in charge and not me, I tried to put the fear I had for this young man out of my mind and just hoped things would turn out brighter than they looked for him.

Because of the feeling I had with the reading I had made a mental note of the date of his operation. The date was a 23rd. On the morning of the 24th Dave had gone to work at 6am and left alone in bed I had been in a deep sleep when the bedroom door half opened and a shape appeared. Blinking my eyes open, I saw the young man quite clearly as he peeked round the door. 'Just come to tell you I'm okay now!' he said happily. He then backed out of the room as I gawped, shaking myself, thinking, knowing, that he had now passed away, hoping I was wrong and it had been a dream.

At 11a.m. that morning I received a phone call from his cousin telling me of his death. She told me that his mother was very upset with me because he had gone ahead and signed the house deal with his partner. She said I should have told him not to go ahead with it. Searching my mind, feeling guilt for not having stopped him signing, I came to the conclusion that in future I would try not to tell someone what I would do if it were linked to medical matters.

The young man could have pulled through as the operation had a good survival rate. It is my belief that we will only go to the afterlife when it is our time to go, or if we give up. I prayed that his partner could find a lodger or house share friend to help him pay the mortgage. The spirit of the young man was smiling as he told me he was okay, he looked radiantly happy. Seeing his spirit made me think over what the tea leaves had shown me. I don't know what I could have said differently as a warning would only have made his last days on Earth more fearful than they already were. After all, I can't give advice in a reading, only channel what I see. The powers of fate, or God, may change the outcome at the last moment.

Other events from readings that took place during 1981 and early 1982 sadly came to mind whilst thinking about the symbolic meaning of SWORDS. This was from thinking of things that had shown up in several tea cup readings. In a kind of cluster of readings, I could make out the word WAR in the pattern of leaves. This was shown in several cups, at different times and from different enquirers. Then after the reading these women would tell me they were wed to a soldier. Often there was a symbol of a sword near the word WAR or ARMY and a pattern of a beret with plumb on the left side, as worn by the Lancashire Fusiliers Regiment. Thankfully in these readings there was no ominous feeling and no signs that the husband or son would not return. I know that many people would not give credit to the fact that these patterns can be seen in a cup, but that was what I saw several times within a few months. All this was puzzling until the war in the Falklands broke out in April 1982.

At the Spiritualist Church, a few times my friend and I had come across the psychic link with the universe as demonstrated by a psychic artist. We saw sketches being made that members of the audience claimed as being their loved one from the other side. Because I had begun to worry about 'seeing' the word WAR so often I decided to try to tune into my own guide through psychic art. Holding the pencil loosely, I let my mind drift and started to draw. The results were a surprise to me as the sketches turned out to be of quite swarthy men, sometimes with beards, sometimes with deep set eyes. In one sketch for some reason the man had a cover across his eyes.

Some women that had received the 'WAR' readings came back to say their husband or son had returned. When that war ended on 2nd June, I thought that would be the end of my seeing those kind of images, well I hoped so! However, around 1988, I started to dream that I was in an Eastern City, running away from an enemy. As I ran across flat roofed buildings there was gun fire. My clothing was a rough material in army colour. Dodging bullets skimming past my head I jumped from one rooftop to another and ran along walls in terror of being caught. During the dreams I felt as if I were a soldier in a hopeless fight. In 1990 after the Gulf war had begun, the dreams stopped.

There was no reason that these army images should come to me as nobody in my immediate family was in the army, however my heart goes out to the wounded and their families. My gran used to say 'There are no winners in a war!' and she had lived through two world wars. If only the world could be as one, or at least the leaders of the world could remember that most of their subjects want peace.

Sometimes in a reading a sword card would represent a victory, not from war, but from a person making a good recovery even against the odds. This is why no single card can be read without looking at the cards near it. Understanding the many and various combinations will come only with practice and use of intuition.

One of my enquirers had been having many nightmares and so had come for a reading to clarify if there was anything to come in her future that her dreams were warning her about. The 7 of Swords was followed by the Falling Tower and then the Knight of Cups. The number seven has a link with psychic ability and so this would indicate that her dreams were a warning of some kind. At the time, the Tarot that I had used for her reading had a horse rearing up on its hind legs in front of the image of the Falling Tower. For some reason my eye went more to the image of the horse than the Tower, and the flames on the card also stood out. The Knight holding out the cup looked like some person coming to the rescue in an emergency. In just this reading, the horse, to me looked like a real horse escaping a fire from his stable with the help of the man, the Knight with his cup (water to put out the flames) to the rescue, so this is what I was able to tell the woman.

A week later this lady rang me to say she had avoided loss of seven horses when the stables had caught fire because her stable manager (newly appointed young man) saw flames, opened the stable doors quickly and freed the horses.

The brave young stable hand had then had put a hosepipe onto the fire whilst waiting for the fire engine but this lady's own intuition had played a part. As well as the reading (7 Swords) she had a sudden 'inner' qualm and told the young man to look in at the stables that evening. He had truly become the Knight in shining armour. There was that lucky seven once again!

There is another image of the Sword that might be seen for a military wedding. In readings, this has only come up for my enquirer on one occasion and sure enough, the lady in question married a military hero and had a real Guard of Honour, with arched swords, lined up at the door of the Church.

One lady that came to see me had a pattern of letters in her cup like this... NASA. Then a pattern of a rocket. Further down the cup the same letters appeared again... NASA. Next to these were shortened versions of a man's name. Then in the Tarot cards the 2 of Swords came out. When I had finished the reading I was astounded to hear that this frail, rather shabbily dressed older woman had two sons who both were working for NASA. The swords were the division of distance they lived from her and possibly difference in life style. The names were the names of her two sons. Never judge the book by its cover was the motto for me in future.

In one reading I did for a man in his thirties there were three Sword cards in the hobbies area of the Astrology Tarot layout which was unusual. This would indicate that there were many clashes in his social life or that he had a pastime that involved the use of sharp objects. I said these could even be swords, as in the sport of fencing. Fencing he told me was in fact his main hobby. Sometimes the information for a 'seer' is factual, just say what you see! The Tarot always tells the truth but it is easy to misinterpret cards as we humans often presume the most startling facts cannot be true.

Reader... Have you crossed swords in argument or has someone been cutting to you in word or deed? If so you may have learned the lesson of the Tarot suit of Swords. The lesson being that it is futile to continue to hold your opponent in contempt or hate as this will only serve to hurt yourself. Cut past hurt from your mind in order to be fully free in order to face any future challenges. This will then lift your own spiritual vibrations, enabling you to draw into your life people and situations that are in harmony with you.

24/ Tarot lesson, The Suit of Swords...The Air Element

Representing the Zodiac signs of Gemini, Libra and Aquarius.
For interpretation... Personalities or matters or relating to swiftness, surprise, quick thinking, sharp mind, sharp actions, dreams ideas, innovation and sometimes unpredictable events or actions.
Song... 'We Don't Need Another Hero'... song... version... Tina Turner

KNIGHT of SWORDS.

QUEEN of SWORDS.

KING of SWORDS.

There are fourteen cards in each suit of the Minor Arcana and as with the Major Arcana each card has links to things that can happen to us in life. All that life teaches us, if we are willing to learn. Astrological and numerological sequences are linked to each suit. Many Tarot designs reflect the history of the origins of the cards. Egyptian, Greek, Hebrew symbols show up on many Tarot decks even today. The connection to the Masonic and Kabbalistic knowledge that were the building blocks of our ancient forefathers is also apparent on many designs. Much of this knowledge has been lost to mankind through the problems in language translation, and customs, plus geographical changes in the landscape. The necessary migration of people affected by these changes. What we have with the Tarot is a small window into the wisdom of the advanced, but now lost civilisations. This wisdom was guarded and protected throughout the ages by wise custodians whom we may call Monks, Sages, High Priests or

Wizards. The Early knowledge of faiths such as Zoroastrianism (from this came the word Wizard) and the beginning of life as seen in the Old Testament of the Bible. Stories that are or once were apparent in many faiths such as Judaism, Islam and perhaps even the Cather traditions can all be linked with imagery of the Tarot, often showing Angels that are figures from all of these belief systems.

Linking the SWORD of the Tarot deck to changes in my life and how it illustrates both sides to some of the many emotional 'stories' of the clients I would see as I tried to gain more wisdom in reading the symbols. The 'SWORD' in British symbolism is our 'Excalibur', the power of courage and integrity to seek justice and find our true aim.
In the world of today this may be, winning a trophy, fighting to get the perfect job, battling with chores or through obstacles. Things that we may say are a needing of our determination from the inner self. Innovations that bring joy to the eye or mind, such as writing, painting, the sword to shape our destiny by fulfilling our potential, all link with the suit of swords. Fight the good fight is the message here, even if things get tough, with the emphasis on GOOD!

As we think on the word, good, we can also be reminded of Angel Michael with his sword of karmic justice, then to interpret, think of the laws of the land and the laws of a civilised society.

The sword can often be viewed as the pen, the written word that has been so relevant in the development of mankind. The pen being the tool of the knowledge givers. If we were to put those from history into the SWORD, element, then such people as Shakespeare, Leonardo Da'vinci and Mozart would be some positive examples. The only warning from the SWORD element is to keep control of the inner 'sword', not jump to conclusions or be too swift to make a disagreement into a war. The Sword card can also indicate battling for freedom and cutting off from a person or situation.

Each of the four 'Royal' face cards in each suit serve to represent people... The Queen, an adult woman or mother. The King, an adult man or father. The Knight, a youthful man or boy. The Princess, a maiden, or girl.

*In many packs, as with my Moroccan Fez Tarot there is only a Knight and Page. Then a Page represents the child. Traditionally the Cup and Coin Page represent a maiden. whilst the Sword and Rod / Baton represent a male child. As tradition holds MARS as the planet of war, the male aspect of Knight is apparent as the soldier. A 'Royal' Sword card can represent a person born under a zodiac Air sign, see * below.*

 A Sword card can represent the Army or an actual soldier. More often than not the Sword represents some kind of ideal that the enquirer holds or is fighting.

Authority, law makers, police or governments could be symbolised with the characters depicted by the suit of Swords. The Sword can also show a cutting of ties, such as arguments, rifts, divorce, or battling to forgive.
*The Gemini personality often shows a great deal of mental energy and this may work well with people, born under fire signs, Leo, Sagittarius and Aries.
*The Libra personality do not like risks, they get on well with others if their scales can balance with more daring notions of other zodiac personalities.
*The Aquarius sign has high ideals. As we move more into the Aquarian age these capable, far thinking individuals should come very much into their own.

Reader...The information in this chapter is only a small peek into the meanings of the Sword cards in the Minor Arcana. These are just my own observations and just as we all 'see' things in our own way, we might all have a valid explanation as to what the meaning of a symbol on a card is saying to us.

Chapter 25

1980's – 1990's

Only seven seats in our waiting area, the shop would then become very crowded especially in summer. Many people were still happy to wait. This meant we must put the 'closed' sign up by 3.30pm in order to finish at 5pm. One Saturday as seeing out my seventh client of the day, there in our waiting area was a familiar face. Liz, from next door to where we used to live! I had heard her tell my business partner that she would wait to see me, as I had been recommended by her friend.

When Liz saw my face. 'Oh!' She exclaimed, I had no idea you did readings. Giving my warmest smile I acted as if we had never had problems from her or her hubby. My shop policy was to welcome all who may enter our little sanctuary. Putting my best professional face on I escorted Liz into my booth. To this day my client confidentiality prevents me from giving any personal information out to all and sundry. Let us just say I was pleased that the Tarot came through for me in so far as the big secret she was keeping at that time was revealed in the cards. Liz, quite red faced and hot under the collar had to be reassured of my professional code of conduct before she left. Liz came back twice for an updated reading, was all sweetness and light and quite complimentary about my ability. She liked the Runes as well as the Tarot. In fact, as I remember she even purchased a set of my Prediction Rune Cubes to see if she or her daughter could test their intuition.

In recounting this memory, I do not wish to say that my readings are any more accurate than another psychic would give, only that the 'reader' can be a shoulder to cry on. A filter for any information that may upset the enquirer.

A 'seer' is kind of go-between / interpreter from their 'Guide' to the guide of the enquirer. Any person wishing to become the professional 'seer' needs to realise they have a moral obligation towards their client so as not to build any bad karma for themselves.

Many people still wanted a reading from the Teacup as some feared the Tarot. Even being in the same room as a pack was entertaining evil. This notion had been driven into them by some religions. Nobody from a faith, organisation or a Church ever came to object to what we were doing in the shop. We did have leaflets pushed through the letterbox about... THE WORK OF THE DEVIL! Something along the lines of... BEWARE GOD'S WRATH! Why, if this message was so important to them did they push the leaflets through rather than coming in to speak to us 'face to face'?

Being a girl brought up to 'do only as you wish to be done by' and 'let he who is without sin cast the first stone' I do hold on to FAITH, HOPE and CHARITY in my life. These remarks did upset me at that time. The judgemental notes caused me to question if my 'gift' was a stain on my soul. Thinking the matter through, wondering about the spiritual aspects of my being, I went see Betty, who lived in Bath Street.

Betty had come to me originally for a reading as recommended from persons at the Spiritualist Church. 'If you are doing the work of the Devil, then all I can say is thank God for the Devil!' She remarked.
Betty was in her late eighties and had been a member of the Spiritualist movement for most of her life. She was a family friend of William Roach, the actor from Coronation Street and she kindly invited me to go to see Mr Roach give a speech alongside a demonstration from a renowned gentleman Medium of the time. The Mediumship was amazing and the speech from Mr Roach was extremely enlightening. Betty said that if giving readings was of help to those who came to me and I worked with pure intention then the 'gift' was given me to use. Betty gave me the confidence to carry on with my readings, though I was in a quandary as to the need for a quieter place to do them. At the shop those waiting could sometimes be a distraction if they were chatting in a loud voice.

One day a gentleman of some standing in the police community where I grew up, came into the shop for a reading. At the time I had no idea of his connection with the law, and it was only later when my dad asked me if Mr 'P' had been to see me that I understood some of the gravity of events in his past. This gentleman had been responsible for administering justice to many of those who had committed the most serious of crimes. As he entered the shop I noticed he had a lovely blue aura and from the reading (looking at the cards representing his past) I could see this man had a connection with law and service to the Crown. From the Tarot I found this man was at peace with the work roll he had been given. He was very patriotic and there was a calmness about him. My dad told me later that Mr 'P' was well liked by many of their friends, mum added that she knew him and he was, in her words 'a lovely dancer and perfect gentleman'. Although quite famous he was the kind of man who took things in his stride and he was truly a family man first and foremost.

Apart from the Prediction shop there were only the fairground Fortune Tellers that were giving readings in the 1980's. The Fairground was closed during the winter when we were asked by an acquaintance, Leon if he might do readings, standing in for either of us, in our shop, when we needed time off for holidays or at lunch hours. Leon had been working during the Summer as the Fortune Teller on the Funfair, and was a great addition to our shop and it was a boon being able to break for lunch without worry that people would be having to wait outside.

One rainy afternoon when we were just about to close up, Leon appeared and asked if he might shelter from the heavy rain. As we sat with him for a cuppa waiting for the storm to ease off, he closed his eyes rather dramatically. He said he was getting a vision of me going into a big hotel. Leon could 'see' snowflakes falling onto my hair in this vision. He could 'see' a log fire burning in a fireplace close to the entrance of this hotel. 'It looks like The Prince of Wales hotel entrance.' he said. 'I think you are going to be the celebrity guest speaker for some big event, and it will be a big success!' he added.

Speaking only one to one with strangers in my booth was a far cry from public speaking to a large audience. It was the furthest thing from my mind at that time.

Leon's words came back to me when, during September, I was asked to host a psychic weekend to be held the first week of December, by none other than the manager of...You guessed it! The Prince of Wales hotel. In those days the 'Prince' was considered the posh place to stay and it attracted many famous people. After going to see what being hostess for the weekend would entail I found it would require me to give a talk on the Zodiac signs. Their characteristics, plus all the methods of forecasting with links to Astrology.

There would be no payment for doing the talk at 'the Prince' but I was invited to a three course meal on the Friday evening. On Saturday I would attend for afternoon tea and give a talk on Tassiology, (tea cup reading). Later I could give private readings, for a fee, to the people attending. The Sunday, after doing another short talk I could again charge a fee for reading the tea cups. Liking a challenge, I agreed.

Leon had been right in his premonition; it was snowing just as I arrived on the evening to give my talk. There was a huge fire in the hearth and the weekend was a hit with the people attending. Soon the event would become a regular feature for me at the Prince. The next 'Prince' weekend many more guests wanted readings and I was asked by the Hotel manager to invite other speakers. My shop partner, plus Leon and an Astrologer. We had dinner together with the hotel guests and later we were all able to give readings. From these events I received many letters of thanks from the guests. I received many orders for postal readings from far and wide. I'm proud to say some people attending these events in the 1980's, still keep in touch to this day. One Friday the Woman's Editor, (the one that had previously given me five stars) and another reporter from the Echo came to see me at the shop to ask if I could 'read' a palm print. Palmistry was not my favourite method of reading but I agreed to give it a go. By now many of my clients had asked me to do Psychometry (holding an object to tune into) for them as well as the Tarot or tea cup. The palm print was not ideal for 'reading' in this way but I was able to glean a few characteristics of the person from the main lines of the hand. The other information I gave would come from this 'third eye intuition' clearing my mind first, with the Psychometry method. There were no words on the sheet of paper, just the palm print. The palm was slightly smaller than my own hand and there was in imprint of a ring on his third finger.

Closing my eye's, I tried to tune in and soon got the feeling that the print was someone male and world famous. In all honesty I could not have given his name, but the first impression of the character of this man was his strong belief of patriotism to this country. It felt as if this was most important to him and he was connected to many children's charities all over the world and had, or would have two children of his own. Looking at the palm print I saw an initial '**E**' was prominent in his life and thought the person with this initial was the head of his family. Also I felt a sadness within him about a person with the initial '**M**'. The reporter jotted all this down.

The palm print also gave me the feeling this man liked delving into the mysteries of life, meaning spiritual matters. I added that he got on well with females though I knew he was married. I felt he liked female company and was not sure his wife trusted him. The article appeared in the Liverpool Echo, telling me that the palm print had been from Prince Charles on his visit to Liverpool. The article was close to accurate from what I had said, 'E' being the late Queen. 'M' being, Lord Mountbatten, (at that time having recently drowned) it was known that Charles had been devastated. I had said that the palm belonged to someone who liked spiritual matters, the mysteries of life. In the wording about this and about his wife I had been miss-quoted. However, I did place the article in my memory scrap book along with other pieces about my work.

During the remainder of the 1980's there were hundreds of interesting readings that came my way. There are so many 'life' stories of my clients, friends and family that were 'shown' to me in the pattern of the leaves and from the Astrology layout of the Tarot. The following come to mind when I contemplate the fire element. The Staff of life (Rod) are projects that are born from enthusiasm. Writing, sport, dancing, music, drama, painting are all things requiring passion to reach a goal. For me, apart from my family, all things relating to psychic or esoteric thought, including, mysteries of ancient Egypt / Early man, are the things that stir my thirst for knowledge. During the 1990's my cousin Maggie, born under Sagittarius, asked us if we wanted to go on a two-week holiday to Egypt with her, her husband Brian. (a Leo) and a work friend of theirs, David 'B' and his wife, Ann.

The six of us would be able to have two weeks B & B at a hotel very close to the Pyramids of Giza for an unbelievably low price. David and Ann 'B' had links to the manager. The other boon was the fact that David 'B' had lived in Cairo for eight years and was fluent in the spoken language.

David and Ann 'B' could not get on the same flight as my Dave, Maggie, Brian and myself so we went a day earlier. We had the name of the Hotel in order to instruct a Taxi driver from Cairo airport. We had a two hour stop in Germany on the way (making it a budget priced air fare) and touched down in Cairo at 5pm. The airport was jam packed with people, and because of a recent bombing in the City there was extra security at the arrivals exit. Maggie and I went straight to the powder room to freshen up whilst the men waited for the baggage. As we walked back, we saw Brian being physically frog marched into a glass room by two armed men in Military style uniform. We became quite worried as to the reason armed men had detained Brian. We waited for a tense half an hour, then a guard from the glass room emerged with Brian looking red and tense. We then had to haggle with the Taxi driver over the cost of the fare to the hotel. We had been told they would try to charge over the odds with us not able to speak the language. In the end we managed to fix a price of £5.00 in American dollars. We all bundled into the Taxi.

We held our nerve as we were driven through the turmoil of traffic, the likes of which we had never seen before. Four lanes of traffic crawled along for an hour on the five-mile journey. The air was still hot and the cab did not have any air conditioning. Along the side of the wide main road through Cairo we saw all manner of people. A man on a bicycle holding a seven-foot long tree. Another cyclist with two children, one on top of each other's shoulders. Here and there people would shove little children towards the open window asking for pennies. Along the route we were deafened by the sound of car horns and hooters going off every few seconds. At the Hotel the Taxi driver refused to open the boot to give us our luggage, and was asking for more money. Too hot and sweaty to put up a fight, I gave him an extra English fiver. We were just thankful to have arrived, still together and in one piece. In front of our hotel we saw the burning sands of the desert, and quite a lot on the inside too! At the sight of the Pyramids we were filled with a burst of new energy.

At the grand marble entrance of the hotel we were greeted by the young manager. He explained that there were only five members of staff and just eight guests including our party booked in for the next two weeks. Then the Hotel would be converted into a School. This seemed rather odd as the building was all marble pillars and grand stairways. It was only a stone throw from the Great Pyramid. That first evening after showers, we were so excited to be there that we walked the half mile to the nearest restaurant where we sat gazing in awe at the sight of the Sphinx and the three King's Pyramid's. We marvelled at this iconic scene as we ate hot food.

Next morning, we had to find a pharmacy as poor Mag had bites all over her feet. Blooming mosquito! To get to the pharmacy we must catch a bus, well actually it was a large van with bench seats. All manner of local trades people sat on the bus. There was a man carrying a live chicken under his arm. Another man holding on to a big Roll of carpet. We asked the driver for a pharmacy pointing to Maggie's blistered feet. Four stops on we were told to get off. A local man, speaking to the driver kindly offered to show us the way. It was something of a culture shock, but we had survived. Now we could embark on what turned out to be the holiday of a lifetime.

Dave 'B' and Ann had arranged for a Taxi service from a friendly driver they had known throughout their previous eight years in Cairo. He was Camel, and he would take us to all the places we wanted to see. He arrived each morning at 8am and stayed with us throughout the day, dropping us off at 5pm, then coming back to take us out for an evening meal at 8pm, waiting to take us home when we finished. Camel loved to chat and could speak very good English. He was thrilled to introduce us to a branch of his family who were living in a sort of tent structure on a vacant plot of land opposite our hotel. He explained that the father of this family was not a beggar, he was a caretaker, living in a makeshift structure with his wife and eight children. They would stay on this plot until a new hotel was built. He would then become a porter and be earning a wage. Until then he was willing to 'squat' for owner of the land to stop all the other homeless from squatting. The children of this family would stand in a line each morning in front of our hotel. They never begged from us, but it was obvious they were in desperate need of clothing and probably had little food each day. Maggie and I would save as much food from our breakfast to pass on to these poor children.

This giving food we did secretly so as not to offend the little Chef (a boy of thirteen) when he had proudly presented us with a 'continental' breakfast. Himself having peeled the fruit and cheese squares from their wrapper. The little family outside were glad of this, and each child gave us a beaming smile. When the holiday was over we left the family some of our clothes.

During the holiday we got to visit all the main sights and because of Dave 'B' we got to ride on Arabian horses into the desert. Riding back towards the Great Pyramid of Cheops, the moon gave us a view of it in silhouette. We were able to visit the Museum in the centre of Cairo and marvelled over the hundreds of artefacts that were on show, including the mask of the boy king, Tutankhamen. The golden mask was breath-taking and the whole holiday would prove to be a chalice of golden memories.

On a trip out to see the ancient Saqqara Pyramids we stopped at Memphis and were invited into the marble palace of the 96 years old Bedouin Chief. After buying a small object from him he gave me a bead necklace. He said the beads had been sifted from the sand when, as a small boy he was with his father as the English Archaeologist's opened a Pyramid in 1905.

All the amazing things we saw and did in Egypt are imprinted on my inner eye and I see them in all their splendour whenever I meditate. They come back to me in vivid image. On the penultimate day of our wonderful holiday Dave 'B' had to rest as he had an infection from an old mosquito bite. Ann, Maggie and Brian were also a little under the weather. Camel was waiting as usual outside at 8am. Dave and I felt fine so we decided to go to the Pyramids again and asked him to come back for us at noon.

When we had gone before there were several tourist busses and at least a hundred people wandering round but Camel said that in the hottest part of the day there would be few sight-seers around. Whilst Dave and Camel walked around the Pyramid I sat on the ground cross legged to meditate next to one of the three small Queen's Pyramids. Hands on the stone block, sitting on the sand, eyes closed I asked to see something from the time of the Queen. Almost as soon as my eyes closed I felt a tall being standing behind me. Was he guarding the Queen?

A sadness crept over me, I had the thought this presence was a Eunuch! My inner eye looked inside the Pyramid. The 'vision' surprised me, as several pieces of gold furniture were jumbled together in a corner, as if just thrown inside. There were gold seats with claw shaped arms on top of a kind of bed, plus pots and bowls. This image puzzled me until we went to the museum of Cairo the next day, the last day of the holiday. In the entrance was a large photograph, the first taken as soon as the Pyramid was opened. The photograph was almost a replica of the image I had seen in meditation. Up to that point I thought the inside of a Pyramid would be laid out neatly, furniture arranged as if in a Royal Palace.

We went to a beautiful old Mosque on a high ridge overlooking the city of Cairo. On the walls there were patterns that defy explanation. A guide pointed out to us in the cracks of the wall plaster patterns looking like maps of the world. One pattern sitting close to a 'map' of England was an image of our late Queen. This can be seen by anyone. It looked remarkably like the image on our stamps and coin. It crossed my mind that this was like some of my tea cup patterns. Does the magic of the universe somehow record these images in the fabric of a building? Is this phenomenon visible because this is a spiritual place, I wondered? Later on visiting places of natural rock I would make out more of these 'random' images. During a holiday in Tenerife I could make out many faces in the rock formations of the mountains. These looked like faces of the nine Guanche tribal leaders of the islands.

The beauty of the ancient Pyramids, the Sphinx and grand building of the Mosque took our breath away but there was a sight we saw that filled us with horror. It was called 'The City of the Dead' and was just visible from the wall of the Mosque through the cloud of smog that covers the flat plane below.

Camel took us to a corner of the City of the Dead where three different religious buildings were situated close to the place reputed to be the place where Moses was found in the bulrushes. Another place below a ruin was shown us, reputed to be the place of hiding when Mary and Joseph had to flee from Herod with the baby Jesus. At this same corner we saw young children scouring through a massive heap of garbage looking for any scrap of food or rubbish that could be used in some way.

These children were sent out on carts each morning as refuse collectors for the whole City. Their life expectancy at that time was around nine years. The City was a place of such glaringly polar opposites that it truly made us humble. The homes of these children and their families were the Victorian tombs (Mausoleums) built mainly by British aristocracy out of marble. Most sprawling Cities have these polarities of vast riches and abject poverty, but none so glaringly obvious to us at that time as Cairo. There is a feeling of great awe on looking at the magnificence against the degradation. Even a massive win on the Lottery could not solve this. It is where spirituality is at cross purposes with Political machinations. In my utopian ideals a perfect world is one of sharing and equality for all. All we can do is help support a charity that has this ideal notion at heart.

Back down to Earth at home it was time to resume our working days. I had a lady from the Spiritualist Church booked in for a reading. This lady, a Medium, had been to see me before and always gave me a spirit message when I finished her reading. She said... 'You have been to Egypt, the land of your past lives. You did a ritual whilst there and this has **drawn to you the spirit of a great big man**, more than six feet tall. A **Eunuch** who was guarding a Queen. He tells me he will be with you as you are writing. He will help you if you are wearing the **necklace** you were given from the **sands**.' This lady had no prior knowledge about all this.

I had not even told Dave that I had felt the presence of a Eunuch whilst meditating near the Pyramid. Nor had I told anyone that I had started to write a book. We had only been home a couple of days, so even friends had no knowledge of my bringing a necklace home or my experience. This message strengthened my belief in spirit, and all this from a woman that had once suffered a vile experience at the hands of the notorious Cray Twin gang.

From one recommendation at the Spiritualist Church I had a postal reading on order from an elderly lady living in Wigan. From the reading I gleaned that she would soon be moving despite being the grand age of 90 years. This lady, Megan, became a close friend and was happy attending the charity meditation group I had conducted at my home. Megan had a wonderful amount of energy that was visible to me in her aura. She had become a healer as she worked together with a gentleman owner of a Café.

Megan and her friend had visited a healing sanctuary in the South of England and had in years gone by been very much involved with the great healing work of Harry Edwards. Harry Edwards was known to me from a friend whom received healing from him a number of years earlier. This friend became a healer herself, giving that power out I believe, (channelling) that which she had earlier received.

Megan and her gentleman friend had been to America together with a gave a spiritual group to a seminar on the healing principal of 'laying on of hands'. This is where the healer 'channels' the energy from God down through the top 'head' chakra through to the hands where the hands give out this energy to the affected part of the person before them. After Megan moved she kindly gave me some tape recordings of speeches given by Harry Edwards. When the voice of Harry comes out of the speaker it has an amazing quality and listening to it has the most calming effect on the body.

Megan spent Christmas with us at 223 the year after the passing of my mother. She delighted the family with her enthusiasm in playing games with us on the We! She lived into her late 90's and though had endured a few sad losses in her life she never lost her inner child. Megan was a true inspiration to us with her inner joy. From her I learned that joy in the world around us gives us resilience and helps us combat pain.

The suit of Batons / Rods as well as Swords in the Tarot represent courage and leadership linking to the fire and air elements. The Baton and the Swords for use in battle will probably be the first thought on interpretation but we could also think of the Hermit with his staff (baton) of knowledge and Angel Michael holding the sword of truth. The Sword can indicate the need sometimes to rid ourselves of an inner cloud of past hurt. The Baton / Rod is the determination to push through. Forgiveness is often difficult when someone has pained us in their words or actions. Holding on to anger, bitterness or desire for revenge will in the long run only bring ourselves misery. None of us will reach old age without having been crossed in some way, myself included. Hating is a poison seed that we cannot allow to flourish, for our own good and for the good of others.

All too often we see those in positions of power bending the truth to further their own ends or line their own pocket, forgetting the moral codes that most ordinary people try to live by. Ego can often get in the way of the individual doing and saying what would be right for others. There are of course many examples of individuals reaching power and using it for the good of others. Dolly Parton is a person I much admire, not just for her talent, but for all the good she has quietly gone about doing for her community and wider. Reading about her life recently it was obvious to me that she enjoys the rewards her fame has given her. She has managed though to keep her ego in check whilst allowing her warm, sunny, giving personality to shine through. To her people she has been an Earth Angel.

In my life I have been lucky to have had many Earth Angels as my friends and though I now miss those that have departed the material world they have left behind a smile whenever I think of them, because of the love that they exuded. Not all of us have the power to change the lives of others in a big way but we all have the power to give someone love. Even a little smile can warm someone's day!

Many times in readings there have been signs of some kind, causing upset to the person I am reading for. Argument, Divorce, separations of distance and loss of money or treasured possessions from theft or mishap. Sad to say that some of these things cannot always be avoided. We may not want to argue but some other person could be shouting the odds and goading us. Then all we can do is try to find that inner calm and wait for the person to run out of steam. Someone very close to me has taught me this though the lesson may have to be ongoing.

In many readings the Baton would advocate determination to fix things that had caused problems, whereas a Sword might indicate the need for letting go! Disagreement can be settled by compromise. Both Baton and Sword link to strength in some way. Strength to cut ties! Strength to rise above animosity!

For any person going through a bitter divorce strength will be hard to find. We can see some couples managing to stay civil with each other. When children are involved the worse thing to do is to use them as a bargaining tool.

Not having been through this myself I can only say that in reading for others it is often the case that one parent has to be the bigger person. In the long term my hope is that this parent may reap solace by way of respect from their children when grown.

When there is a rift in a family the cause can often be seen by the cards that are drawn in a reading of the Tarot. Sibling rivalry, critical remarks from parent, in-law, brother or sister can be a trigger. Jealousy is often at the root of these problems. It can be hard to offer an olive branch because we don't want to take the blame. A rift can sometimes be healed by those doing the bending, leading by example.

Things leading to departure, when a son or daughter flies the nest is another cloud that can hurt the parent. All the more if the offspring goes to live abroad. This pain can feel like devastation, especially if the parent is single or there is no other child. This event can feel like a bereavement. The only thing the parent can do is focus on their own life and do as much as possible to keep the home fires burning with regular phone chats and a warm welcome, if and when there is a visit from their loved one.

In many ways we are all like 'ships that pass in the night' as we travel our way through life. We all make mistakes. Mistakes lead to regrets because we are human. Some people are entwined within a Karmic circle that keeps them together for life. Others only come together for a short period of time, then fate takes them in separate directions. The pattern of life is sometimes hard for us mere mortals to understand.

A reading that has many Batons / Rods will link to an aspect of skill, determination, love of method or planning to go forward, make progress. Work issues and communications will often be relevant. A person putting themselves forward for a challenge in business or for a new job can be indicated by the Baton. Remember the Baton is carried by many of our Major Arcana cards as a sign of their leadership.

One reading where the Rod or Baton was not just a symbol of ambition, but also a symbol of 'the Magicians Magic wand', was from a gentleman that worked in television.

This man had started his journey into entertainment as a Magician. He had been on tour with moderate success from his magic tricks (shown in the Tarot as the Magician card together with the Ace of Rods / Batons) but not had enough earnings to make a reasonable living. He had then found work as a freelance 'Runner' working for a TV. production of a Magic show. From the Tarot I saw he had ambition to do other work as a presenter and had an idea for a musical quiz show. He was a Leo character type himself. The Baton had represented the magic wand of his earlier work and his driving ambition!

Often the Baton tells the enquirer to be strong after a loss of possessions or money through theft or fraud, to be determined not to give up their goal. Having had dishonesty perpetrated against me on three occasions I do not profess to being always careful to listen to my own intuition. On three issues I shut out that inner warning bell.

The first time was because I was a trusting child and could not conceive that another child would be devious. The second time I was put in an awkward position by an acquaintance who vouched for a third person. That person took several of my Rune sets to sell in their gift shop, agreed on a sale or return basis. The returns did not come back, nor did the money. In the end the acquaintance that 'brokered' the deal managed to retrieve half the number of Rune sets, but no recompense for those sold. My own fault for not heading a voice in my ear telling me to get the money up front. The third 'theft' was one of copyright on a piece of writing that was 'lost' when a friend trying to help me, gave my work to a third party with links to television.

Later when the format I used was shown on prime time television, I asked the company for proof of copyright. No proof was ever shown but they professed it to be their own work saying that it was a case of serendipity! I do believe in serendipity. Having pondered on the matter of life after death and prophesy for most of my life I feel that we can all tap into the same creative force. Two inventions will be produced at the same moment in time. In the case of my copyright it seems unlikely as the organisation that produced the work had been shown my copy some time before! Perhaps these things are all part of our learning curve. Nothing for it but to let it go!

You might imagine my frustration when I saw my work almost word for word on the T.V. screen but more at myself for chickening out when the issue was about to go to court. It was too daunting to stand up in court to speak against two celebrities. If only I had found my inner baton of fire! None of us can turn the clock back and it is always best to count our blessings and not the cost.

August 9th 2018 was our golden wedding anniversary. For weeks I had enjoyed the planning and yet I could not shake of a feeling that something negative was hanging over me. All went well for our big event and we had a wonderful day with our family and friends. Matt and 'Rhyming with Orange' the band he is in gave us some great music from the 1960s and a few of their own tunes to dance to.

A when out to lunch with a close friend, Raela few weeks later, I mentioned that I had this feeling that a dark aspect was looming towards us all quite soon. It was something that I felt would have a negative effect on the whole world. Overhearing our conversation, the gentleman owner of the café, Mark, said that he had also been experiencing the same fears. We asked other friends that we knew had had psychic instincts on past world events, and found that several people had felt this 'cloud'. All I could do was pray to my Angel that whatever was looming would not cause too much harm.

Remembering the premonitions, I and a couple of close friends had felt just before the Tsunami in 04, I wished that I could somehow warn the world, but what could I say? What was this cloud going to be anyway? It turned out to be the horrid pandemic and lockdown experience. I placed this in this chapter on Rods / Batons as it was like a kind of fire that scorched the world and because of lock down, it left a lot of issues in its wake that are still reverberating around the world to this day.

Before we leave the suit of Batons / Rods we must be reminded of the warmth of the fire signs by the way those born under them show a love of interaction within a group. The Leo personalities are all what we may term 'people, people' and this warmth can lead a social gathering or community. His / her appearance is often striking in smart clothes with red or long hair, or beard.

*Sagittarius often exude a calm warmth but one that is often controlled into a direct force of energy, leading by example. This is often apparent in their mode of smart dress as they always plan how to present themselves to others.

*Aries, the Ram or sometimes, the Lamb, can teach us that there are times to push forward (ram the message home). Then times we must not rush in where Angels fear to tread. In cuddly 'sheep mode' the Aries is a warm friend. In 'Ram mode' he or she is better kept on side.

The one common aspect of the fire signs is that they can all hold the 'Baton' for a cause, especially if that cause fires them with enthusiasm. Valliant and charismatic in their presence as they lead the way. For all these fire sign personalities, and when interpreting a Rod / Baton card we might give the advice... Balance work with play so as not to burn yourself out.

Most other signs are happy to bask in the circle of warmth of an Aries, Leo, or Sagittarius for much of the time. Now and again, water signs may try to dampen down the enthusiasm of a 'fire' personality on some issues, however the signs of Cancer and Scorpios will often cling to the project put forward by a fire person. Air signs can often be seen to spur on the project of a fire personality, fanning the flames. Earth signs often admire and can be inspired by those born under fire, as their own inner fire is at times restrained through their cautious side.

Reader... Strategy, strength of purpose and loyalty are some of the good traits we might take from those born under a fire sign. Show your talents, be of good work ethic and plan your strategy.

25/ Tarot lesson, The Suit of Rods/ Batons...The Fire Element.

Representing the Zodiac signs, Aries, Leo and Sagittarius.
For interpretation... Matters linking to Effort, Drive, Ambition, Enterprise and Determination.
Song...'Working 9 to 5'...Singer version...Dolly Parton.

The suit of Rods or Batons on many Tarot designs have the imagery that will remind us of heat. It is the Sun aspect, or the stick, a branch that burns, the torch, to light our path. Also the heat of our inner self. The vim or vigour of the mind or body. We must first think of flame, the fire that drives things forward. Those born under a fire sign are often the people who drive the workforce, the business or the enterprise. We could say they have the 'clout' when it comes to planning. They light the way! The fire element has been as important to mankind as the wheel has in his development. It is natural then that many of those born under fire signs should be at the heart of organisations as the driving force behind plans. We might say they are leaders if we keep in mind the lion, as the king of the jungle!

Fire signs go in for the kill only when hunger drives him. Not striking from greed, their nature leads them only to tear a lesser being to shreds if they *are weak. As a leader they use persuasion to encourage others to follow ideals. Firm but fair as a boss, they insist on following plans, often to the letter. This aspect will apply to most of those born under a fire sign, not just Leo.*

We see a Baton / Rod carried by the characters, on many of the Major cards in the Tarot as a sign of their importance. Often held up to the sky in connection to the divine, the God energy. The following is a brief description of those represented by 'Rods / Batons'.
*Majestic Leo will lead the other zodiac signs through the jungle of life with their powerful energy. He or she make an impression as his personality can dazzle the other signs. He loves order and structured plans.

*Aries, the lusty Ram with his strong horns can push others, or can be a lovable bovine happy to chew the cud. Horned signs may sometimes 'lock horns' together.

*Sagittarius with his bow and arrow can strike forward into battle (in work or play) firmly gaining ground. Part horse, he leads in loyalty to his cause. This remarkable being can surely show the other signs how to impress.
Reader...These descriptions help to understand the fire element, not just in zodiac personalities, but within us all, to tap into our own fire at certain times.

Chapter 26

1980s – 2000 onward

As the 'Yuppie' era began, the trends of the moment could be seen everywhere. The Ra-Ra skirts, leg warmers, layered hair do's and shell suits abounded. The colours of the Summer were acid green and lemon when we had our second foreign holiday to Majorca. The children were excited, plus Dave and I needed the rest and time together as work had been so demanding for us both. The week we were due to go a sudden realisation came to me. On return my life needed a change of routine.

During the period I worked from the shop I met many lovely people and enjoyed good income that the long hours brought. Now the time had come for me to move back to working from home. I wanted to devote a little more of myself to the children and working at home would give me the best of both worlds. My work partner was happy to get in another 'seer' and agreed to pay me the amount I had put into starting the shop but it would be some time before payment would come through.

Facing the same problem I had before starting the shop... Need of office space that was private and separate from the house. The answer was a caravan. This proved to be a place of great harmony for myself and for my many visitors. The office in the garden looking out at the greenery and yet cosy and welcoming in the winter.

Many readings could touch on rather emotional topics. Now that I had made my little caravan cosy with a coffee maker and heater, many regular enquirers told me that the vibrations they felt here were comforting. Meanwhile in the House my children seemed to have tuned into the spirit world. As well as the black cat I had seen and the ghost of Mr Hoy, there was a mischievous presence making themselves felt. Both the children saw the bowl of our own live cat, Snowy, roll out of the kitchen and continue rolling for several yards onto the landing. This happened a few times but I was present one morning. The bowl rolled out of the empty kitchen and came to a stop at the door of the sitting room. Most of the 'spirit' activity was on the landing and in the main bedroom.

Friends and relations always commented on the wonderful welcoming feel of the house. We all came to think of our 'ghosts' as part of the family. There was never any feeling of menace or harm from them.

One day my mum and I sat sipping tea in their sitting room at 4pm. Dad was due home from work at 4.30pm. Through the bay window, we saw the top of a car pull into the drive. We clearly saw dad pass the window and walk slowly towards the drive to the back. Mum said she would get him a cup. After a few moments she came back into the room and said she could not see him from the kitchen. We waited a while and when dad did not come in mum asked me to look in the back garden. 'Tell him we have a brew ready'. He was not round the back of the house, nor in the garage and not in the garden. Mum remarked that it was funny he wasn't there. He would have to walk past the kitchen window to get to the back door. We looked out the front window and were surprised that dad's car was not in the drive. At 4.30pm dad came home at his usual time. Mum asked him why he had gone back out earlier. We were astounded when he said he had not been home at 4pm. We had clearly seen him, or his 'spirit' body, or it was his living ghost?

Whenever I think now of 223, that old Victorian house, I 'see' the 'ghosts' of all the many people that lived and died there over the past hundred years. It is amazing that there were only three families in total from the period 1896 to the time we left in 2010 to move to a bungalow. The house was so happy that I'm sure the past inhabitants had loved it as much as we did.

Our family enjoyed many wonderful celebrations there and our four generations lived happily together. Our time at 223 was mostly joyful. The house felt sad for a while when gran passed away in 1994. All seven of us had worked to make the house a home so it was no wonder the house dwellers of the past liked to pop in now and again.

During 1990 my dad had been to see a specialist as he was getting a little out of breath. On his first visit to hospital he was diagnosed with mild emphysema. Whilst he was out at his next routine appointment mum and I were sitting with gran when mum asked me to have a peep into her cup as there were some tea leaves at the bottom.

In the pattern of the leaves in mum's cup I could see a cloud. A problem cloud, starting (I thought) that day as the cloud had the number 7 next to it. That day was 7th December. I told her not to worry as the cloud would blow over by my birthday on 7th January as at the tail end of the cloud pattern there was another 7 next to a cup for celebration.

Mum went to greet dad as he came home from hospital. Gran and I were still chatting when mum came back a while later looking pale and worried. 'You are wrong about the cloud blowing over by January 7th,' mum said. When we asked her what was the matter she said that she now knew what the cloud was and that it could not possibly blow over. 'Well, I am sure it will' I replied as I peered again at the tea leaves. She went out of the room shaking her head. For the next few days, gran and I kept asking mum what was wrong as we could see she was worried about something. She refused to tell us anything and said she had promised because dad had sworn her to secrecy. Christmas came and though we could see mum was still worried we could not get out of her what was the cause. She and dad looked down in the dumps but were both putting on a brave face whenever the children were around. We were sure that we could cheer them up with the festivities. On Christmas day the two of them seemed brighter and we all had a pleasant day. Mum still looked as if the weight of the world were on her shoulders at New Year.

On my birthday, the 7th January I had gone down to our communal room to open cards and gifts. Dad was at a routine hospital appointment. On his return, mum looked on edge as she rushed from the room to greet him. She had a big smile on her face as she came back. 'You were right, the dark cloud in my cup has lifted!' She said with a sigh of sheer relief. When I asked what the cloud had been, she told us that dads information had gotten mixed up with another John Smith. Dad had been given only three months to live at his last hospital visit. Though he had got a health problem he would go on to live another sixteen years.

My caravan became my little haven to focus on any postal work that came in. By this time these were mainly from people that had come for readings in the past few years, then moved away. Postal readings took me a little longer as to accompany the tape I had a chart to draw up. The person receiving the tape recording could follow the chart as they listened to my interpretations. The person sends a photograph so that I am able to include a Psychometry reading. In my quieter setting it was now possible for me to pick up a few things from holding their photograph to my head. These 'flashes are like mini snapshots of a place or a gathering of people, perhaps a face. I try then to describe what I 'see' without any embellishment. Those visiting the caravan might also choose other methods I enjoyed reading, such as the Crystal ball or Runes. The caravan was my office throughout the 1980's and much of 1990's.

My cup of life was certainly full by my 40th birthday and I felt privileged to have done readings for many lovely people. Gran found it amusing that so many came for readings. She would recall her sister Nelly (Ellen) enjoying reading tea cups for the family and customers in the café where she had worked long ago, the first vegetarian café in Manchester.

Gran loved Edwina, mum and I to sit and chat with her for an hour before her bedtime at 8pm. She would regale us with events from her early life in Edwardian Liverpool where she was born, then go on to recount life in Manchester from 1910 up to the end of the second world war.

Gran was the seventh child of her family, born to a Roman Catholic Irish mother, nee Mary Ellen Muldoon, and a father from Wales, William Morris. William hated the Pope. He had lived in a Dr Bernardo's Orphanage up to the age of nine, then ran away to sea as a cabin boy. From her stories it would seem William had become quite hard from all his early experiences. Mary Ellen had come to Liverpool from Ireland with her grandmother at the age of six. She gave birth to ten children but suffered the loss of a daughter to blood poisoning from a tin, and her son Fred who went down on Lord Kitchener's ship. Two other sons were maimed in the first world war, then husband, William, also in the war, drowned too. This made us quite sad but gran followed with stories to have us rolling with laughter.

During the early 90's we lost Dave's lovely mum, Lucy. Several years before Lucy asked me to read the Tarot cards when I was attending a charity event at the Nursing home where she worked. The cards for the immediate future were positive but there was a negative sign in the cards that day and I just hoped that whatever the problem was it would not be too bad. This, plus the reading from mum's cup about the health scare for dad made me shy away from giving in depth readings for family members. This I suppose is the down side of looking at the patterns of the future. There will be clouds but there is a rainbow of wonder once the sun breaks through.

Gran went into a nursing home after a bout of pneumonia in 1990. Mum, Edwina and I would visit her most afternoons for the next four years. I noticed that the aura around gran was still bright before she was taken to hospital. On our last afternoon with her she still had colour in her aura. Later, after she had passed away her aura colours had gone. From this I felt that her soul energy had now left her physical body. Gran was gone but she and her stories are forever etched in my memory.

At gran's funeral we met up with relations from far and wide. She was the last of her siblings to depart this life, but there was a comfort in the knowledge she had helped so many of them to achieve goals in life by her generosity. Gran had worked hard, earned a good wage all her working life and loved to give, as much as she loved life and people. She had left enough money to pay for her funeral and wake but nothing in any bank. She had lived life to the full and enjoyed using her skill of needlework. One of her favourite sayings was…'Life is for the living.' In the 1980's and 1990's, despite losses our family had lots to celebrate. Our dear John and his wife Kathleen had been blessed with four darling little daughters, reminding me of one of my favourite books, 'Little Women'.

All the family would have a get-together on birthdays and at Christmas. Dave's dad, Roy would always join us for a couple of days at Christmas now that he was alone. Our house at 223 was always full of people, laughter and the smell of mums wonderful cooking. Kathleen's mum and dad would visit and her dad, Jim would recite his amazingly funny poems. He had one for every occasion. My uncle Frank, his wife Freda and Cath, their daughter, often came to visit gran and have a meal with us all. Dad loved to play his keyboard and we would dance or sing along. On lots of these events we would take photographs and on a few snapshots there would be the shadow of an extra guest. A sceptic might look at them and say it was just a shadow of the curtain, or the light reflecting from the mirror, but we family members knew there was more to it!

One year wanting to have a more of an adventure holiday Dave and I decided to go on what we called a Grail trail! The children loved stories of Castles and Knights of old so we would go in search of the Cup and Arthurian Legends. Our own investigation of the Holy Grail! Along with this was my own personal spiritual quest.

We booked a caravan near the small 'Olde Worlde' town of Shepton Mallet for our first week. If you watched the TV detective drama, Midsummer Murders, you will get an idea of the vibe. This location was ideal as we could visit Glastonbury Tor, follow the River Cam, from where it was just a tiny stream up towards Cambridge. We could go to the hill mound, Cadbury Castle, visit Wookey Hole cave, plus Stonehenge and Aylesbury Circle. If Arthur ever did exist, the place to feel his spirit would be near the River Cam, surely derived from Camelot.

We had a fantastic week romping round the hill fort. From the top looking back towards the Tor, we could clearly see the path of the old Roman Road in a straight line. This is said to be a Ley line. There are many such lines in the geography of Britain. Some are relics of Roman Britain but some are thought to be much older. Where these lines cross it is said the ground holds some kind of magnetic vibration. These are thought by many to be where the veil from our world is thinner and can be more easily crossed. There are lots of stories of strange phenomena around these sites. We walked, we listened and explored. We all wanted to believe that Cadbury mound was the true site of Camelot Castle. The legend around this site says King Arthur and his Knights of the round table are sleeping under this mound until Britain needs them.

Visiting Glastonbury Tor on a glorious day, we walked up to the top and stood under the arch. Wanting to get the 'feel' of what magic is in these ancient walls I closed my eyes to tune in by making my mind a blank. Behind my eye there appeared several flying objects going over the Tor. They looked like some kind of space craft flying in formation. This image was not what I had expected to see. If anything I had expected to see Monks or Roman soldiers. It was a puzzle and I would love to know if any other people visiting the Tor had 'seen' similar objects.In the afternoon we stopped at the Holy Well in the Well Gardens close to the ruins of the Abbey where lies the remains of a great Knight and his Lady. The grave is thought by many to contain the bones of King Arthur and Queen Guinevere. If this wasn't King Arthurs resting place, then it was still a place of mystery, connecting us with people from many hundreds of years ago.

When we went to the font of the Holy Well there was a feeling of stillness and a kind of hush came upon me as I tried to link into the past. Dave, knowing I wanted to feel the connection of the Well history, took the children round the rest of the garden.

Now I had time on my own close to the Well spring. There was a deep feeling within me that some kind of Earth magic was here. The day was sunny and clear and not even a cloud in the sky. It felt for a moment that time had stood still as I connected to the energy of the Well. The legend here is that the flow of water has never dried up even in times of great drought. The people of the town always had water. This magic is thought to be from a holy link to Christ. It is said that Joseph, uncle of Jesus, came by ship to our shores with the cup that was used at the last supper. He buried it in the ground at this exact spot. A Well then sprang forth and sparkles to this day. Before we left the Well we took photographs as we had before, at the top of the Tor and in the ruins of the Abbey.

The second week of our holiday we visited several lesser known Castles. One charming little village was where we found one, Nunney Castle. Not on our map, we had not known it was even on our route. Looking for a place to have lunch, we just came across it. Our adventure took us to Tintagle Castle. This is said to be the birthplace of Uther, father of Arthur. We then went down to the tip of Cornwall. We had booked to stay near the beach at St Ives. All the places we went to, we took photographs. On our way home we came again within a few miles of Glastonbury Tor. We rounded a bend in the road and there it was in the distance as if saying farewell to us as we journeyed home. We stopped to take one last photograph. At home after the photographs were developed we looked back at our fantastic adventure. To our amazement three photos looked as if they were taken on a misty day. On all the others, clear blue sky, not the sign of a mist. The first of the three photographs was taken on top of the Tor. The second was me sitting at the side of the Well. The third was at our last view of the Tor on the journey home. These were the spots where I had tried to 'tune in' to the past with meditation. We felt we had captured the legendary 'Mist of Avalon' in just the 'special' places. The other snaps had no sign of any mist.

Reader... Do you see the cup as half full or half empty? Let your heart be full of joy of life, let your cup of love be always full from the joy of nature. Make the most of all the world has given us by way of countryside, also of the many particles of knowledge that the great writers and thinkers have given to us in the form of books, music and art. Life is such a rich tapestry for us to explore.

26/ Tarot lesson, The Suit of Cups... The Water Element

Representing zodiac signs... Cancer... Scorpio... Pisces
For interpretation... Matters relating to the flow of... feelings, emotions, fear, love, sentiment, sexuality, rhythm, soul, fluidity and liquid.
Song... 'Rolling on the River'...Singer version... Tina Turner.

The Cup of the Tarot is traditionally viewed as the Chalice, the cup of life. If we think of the cup as a holder of something, then we can 'see' it as our own body. The vestal containing our soul and spirit as well as our blood, bone and sinew. Our outer shell! As such, it is vital to us if we want quality of life whilst on our material journey in this world. Look after the body because it is your own special container. It carries your thoughts and emotions and higher self. Be kind to your body. Sooth it when it hurts, rest it when it gets tired, clean it to be refreshed. Bathe and drink whenever you can and enjoy the water as a gift from the Gods. As a symbol the cup appeals to the romance within our soul, and as such has been the star of many legends included in many fairy stories as well as being viewed as the Chalice of the last supper, linking it to the blood of Christ. The Tarot Cup is also emotions we have inside, the cup of love.

One of the oldest story of our Britain is the legendary King Arthur with his search for the Holy Grail. We know not if his search was the actual cup used by Jesus and his disciples at the last supper, or just symbolic of the Chalice of holy goodness. We might look at the Cup of the Tarot as our inspiration to lead a path to glory, the winners award, (Trophy). Or the cup as the horn of plenty, the cornucopia (elixir of life). Or the refreshing cup of tea or wine at the end of a hard working day. Whichever way we might view the image of the 'Cup', we know it is a container. Our own container (body) must have its earthly needs of food and drink but we know that if we over indulge our appetite or thirst we will harm our vestal of life, the body.

In looking at the Tarot Cup as the container of our feelings we can see that emotional fulfilment may come from love of family, love of friend, love of partner, love of nature or love of life. These things can refresh our soul but the soul can be poisoned by hate. Hate can be the deadly virus that comes from wanting bad things to happen for others. This is often through jealousy, prejudice, greed or desire for revenge. If reversed, then the cup (upturned) indicates some emotional draining.

The Water signs of the zodiac are often sensitive to the flow of life. They are the people who may take in the care of society, the giving of solace. The people who absorb. Their role on Earth often is to help others. These zodiac personalities must beware of letting others drain them.
The following is a brief description of the 'water' personalities.
*Cancer, the wonderful creature, depicted by the crab. At home in and out of water. His home on his back gives us our first clue to this zodiac personality. Home loving and creative he or she can side step an awkward situation as deftly as a dancer. His or her negative trait might be to grab on too tightly to opinions, undaunted by any opponent. Though liking privacy, if they love you they might let you into their secrets, or show you their collection.

*Scorpio personality, a little like the crab in so far as he has his secrets but unlike the crab he will rarely divulge them unless he is in love. He or she loves with great emotion and is said to be the most ardent, sexy lover on

the planet. Like the crab, the scorpion is adaptable but will not be coerced into anything.

*Pisces character, though just as emotional, is quite unlike the other water signs in as far as he or she does not want to be the fish out of water (their element) by trying new paths. Our fishes are depicted swimming in opposite directions hinting at their inner vulnerability. The Pisces character can find it hard to make decisions. They often settle for being the small fish in the big pond, not wanting to take on the Sharks.

These traits will largely depend on his or her rising sign. One thing certain, they are very sensitive and like to swim only with like-minded others. Our water signs may seem deep, look tough, or cool on the surface but often hide a big heart.

Reader... Do you project the love you have within you? Yes! Then you radiate, and as you radiate you gather good connections. The sensitivity of the water element can be found in all of us but do we always let it flow?

Chapter 27

1990's Onward

One lady, Mrs 'D', herself a Medium from the Spiritualist Church in Liverpool came to see me accompanied by her husband. After a Tarot spread in my newly discovered Astrology layout this lady asked me to look into the 'Crystal ball'. There were several patterns that appeared but the one thing that turned out to be important was a series of numbers. Seven numbers were visible to me with the last one shown in a circle. Not knowing what the numbers meant she asked her husband to jot them down. After the reading this lady admitted that she had wanted to 'test' me out after her friend had been to see me. She said she was pleased with her reading and would pass on my name to her friends and enquirers.

A few days later Mrs 'D' rang to say that she and I had missed out on a large fortune. The numbers turned out to be the winning Lottery numbers on the very first date of the Lottery draw. Oh well! Perhaps we were both meant to go on with our unusual work. She laughed as she said it served her right for testing me. Of course I have often tried to repeat Crystal gazing in the hope of a win, but have been hampered by the negative thoughts at the back of my mind. To 'see' clearly into the future I now know that the mind has to be still, a blank if you like, so not wishing or questioning. That is why I could, and have a few times been able to foretell of a win for others but not pick out numbers when trying to do so for myself. Also maybe I would not have the desire to go on giving readings if I were to have a large amount of money. Money does, we know, change people!

There were a few times when my psychic bell rang to tell me to enter a competition. You can win this! The words that came into my mind. Five times I have won prizes in competitions. Each time a voice told me to enter. These were not all monetary gains but nice all the same! The first was a 'Find a slogan' for a butter making company. I won a butter dish and vouchers for butter. The second win was when I saw a 'Design a Hat for Ascot' competition. On the last possible day before posting that I managed to come up with a design. I won a wonderful hat designed by none other than Mrs Shilling plus £200.00 to buy an outfit to wear if you were chosen as the main winner. The prize was a day at the races in a Limo and £1000.00 to spend. The reporter that came to photograph me in my hat later told me that I just missed out on the main prize. I had put on the entry form that I was a professional Psychic consultant. The six judges said my occupation was too glamorous!!! They deemed it necessary to give first prize to a 'normal' housewife. Oh well, never mind! I was happy for the lady who won. She could show off her hat, (a cat sat lapping up milk) and I could wear mine (a bowl of fruit with cream flowing onto it from the tin of cream) at a Charity event. The promoters of the hat competition were a cream company and Chat magazine.

Another time when I saw a competition to win a Hamper and £200.00 to spend in a large store I felt I should enter. For this I had to write a poem. My poem won a hamper and a gift voucher for my daughter. My last win was two tickets to see a play being put on by a professional theatre company in Southport where we met the cast of the show at a reception supper. Not in the habit of entering competitions it was a nice surprise to be a winner though I had, had an inkling that I was going to be lucky on these occasions.

Each time I have been in need of finances work has come in to me to be able to earn what I needed. Each time I won anything it was by thinking of an idea. In life this is great, as all we need is enough to eat and keep a roof over our heads. The Angels have given me much that I am grateful of. I do believe that a lucky charm or a RUNE can attract things to us, because when we hold it and think that it will work from the power we feel in antiquity, we ourselves give it power, and so it does! A RUNE spell could attract luck to someone. It is possible for a 'spell' to work because or if we have the right mind set. Also we only get what the fates wants us to receive. My thinking, is we get little joys but only great riches if it helps our soul progress towards higher enlightenment. What is for us will not pass us by!

The Coin / Pentacle of the Tarot in divination is mostly about controlled effort. As an Earth sign myself, I can look within and see the traits of the sign. Always needing roots, but at the same time reaching for the sky, striving to a goal. The Capricorn persona, (the goat), my quest to reach for the sky is my quest to understand my true God. Not just the God that was taught me in Sunday school. The goat within me, needs to be so sure footed as to not miss a detail, a clue, in life or learning that may help me reach this enlightenment. Early in life my knowledge was limited by my 'dyslexia'. For many years it felt as if I were inferior to others in respect of academic knowledge and philosophical thought. As my love of reading increased, my fear to be shown as ignorant was eclipsed by my great thirst for answers to everything. Ask and ye shall receive!

When a bad event grips our life we humans often ask WHY! Why should this come about. The evil that can touch a good person is often caused through the mind set of someone else. A new born child is not capable of evil but we know that some individuals do go on to harm others. These people are not right thinking and do not have any foresight as to the consequences of their actions. Do we then blame God? Why would God let this happen? we might ask. The answer is that we all have individual free will, saying or doing whatever we choose. Our choices often have a knock on effect to others.

When we suffer a loss of someone close to us through death, no matter what the age of that person, we can feel quite numb, blank, uncomprehending. Often when this is the loss of a parent we feel directionless and depressed. The parent has been the one constant throughout our lives. This was how I felt with the loss of my father. Looking after him in the latter stages of his illness was like being in a trance. It felt unreal. He was very brave and never gave up fighting until the last. He passed away in December, eleven months later than the specialist predicted. My priority then had to be my mother as her grief was inconsolable. Despite her sadness she insisted we get out the Christmas tree. 'Dad would have wanted you to.' she said. My heart wasn't in it that year but Dave's dad Roy would join us, and other family members would visit. Eventually I got out the small Christmas tree and decorations. Looking at the red glass orbs on the tree I felt a bit guilty. It all felt a little disrespectful. Wishing, mentally asking dad if it was okay with him, I fell to sleep on Christmas eve.

On Christmas morning, to my surprise, there on the landing was a large butterfly, a big red one. The butterfly fluttered around the house for three days. We could not set it outside as the frost was deep and it would not have survived. After three days we did not see the butterfly again. I had read that in China, the butterfly is thought to be the soul of the dead ascending to heaven. This presence, that year felt like a message from dad. Red was okay by him! We thought no more about the butterfly, but the next Christmas when it appeared again on the landing, and yet again, for a third Christmas, it was of great comfort to me. Another wonderful sign that confirmed spirit was with me came on our next holiday. We went to Seven Wells and there were seven wild horses that came up quite close to me on a walk to the beach, again my lucky seven.

Over Christmas, I had put aside the six or seven postal readings that had been sent to me. I could not put off my work much longer as people sending for readings would be wondering what had happened to the payment, and where the readings were. So one morning during February I got up at around 6am to start my replies to some of them. By this time mum had vacated the room she had shared with dad. She had come up into our spare bedroom. Not wanting their old room to be left as a shrine, she asked me to make it into my office whilst the cold weather persisted.

There was no noise at this early hour, and the world slept as I was preparing charts prior to making the recordings. Something made me stop and look up. Thinking of dad as I lifted my head from being hunched over my work, there came a massive blast of air. An unnatural gust of wind. The gust was so strong that it blew my long hair across my face. The gust of air came from the partly closed door and swished across the room towards the window, where it moved the curtains; the sash window was closed at the time. A sudden sureness came into my mind. Dad had said his goodbye to me! After all he was always a free spirit, loving the sea and travelling. It was comforting to me that he was able to be as free as the wind now. We would never stop mourning him but we were glad his pain was over.

For most of my life I had prayed not to see the spirits of those departed but after their passing, I would welcome another conversation with my dad and my mother. Sometimes I hear my name called in the early hours of the mourning and it is okay, just my dad's voice. Dad has appeared to me on a couple of occasions since his passing but only as if superimposed upon the face of my beloved Dave. Though too modest to admit it Dave has a strong deeply spiritual vibrational energy, and I think that without knowing, he sometimes 'channels' the spirit of my dad.

From my own experiences with spirit communication and from the many similar accounts, others have told me, I am now sure that death is not the end of our existence. It is my belief that we are composed of an essence, kind of particles of the energy (God Energy) that is omnipresent and was the creator of the universe. Think of it as a massive concentrated cloud of magical God mist at the centre of the universe. This God energy has spread out to be within all living things and all places for all times. Within each of us, I believe, there are the same 'God energy' particles. They are contained inside our earthly shell, our body. When the Bible says we are made in God's image, I believe that image is not the body, the image is an essence of God within us all.

Seeing Auras all my life makes me think that the light visible around all life, is made from these particles. The aura light shows the essence of this powerful God energy we have within. We contain it in different measures. We can draw in more of this God energy at times. We can give out some of this God energy to others if wanting to heal or comfort. We are made up of it, are part of it and can use it throughout our lives. When we pass away this God energy leaves our body, the material world and goes through to join the other souls that are going back to our source. To our creator, the light, the centre, the hub of the God energy.

At its centre these God particles are more densely massed together. Our souls will desire to be part of this main light, it's hub, this joy, this love. If we are unwilling to relinquish the material world after the death of our bodies, our souls may linger around in this our earthly dimension for a while. From some communication with those in spirit it seems clear to me that the more entrenched in the material world, its riches, problems and objects we are, then we may linger, still inhabiting our home or place of work.

You will remember from earlier in my story, when through meditation I felt a great euphoria floating with and part of other souls in a wonderful sea of souls. My inner knowing tells me that this was an out of body view; just on the peripheral edge of this God energy. Not yet deceased, I could only glimpse this state of being from the outer aspect of what is ethereal and glorious at its centre.

There are some things we are given by fate… Our looks, our genetics and the parents we are born to. None of us choose these things consciously, and that is why it is nonsensical to have any prejudice about a person's appearance. Sadly, prejudice exists because there are those who will see differences rather than realising that we are all made up of blood, bone and skin. We are all the same under the skin and we are all linked, if not by direct bloodline then because we all belong to the tree of life, **(humanity)**.

When large scale disasters occur I am often asked…'Did you see this coming? In answer to this I can only say that yes I do in a way 'see' them coming. Could I help avert these things…No! It would appear that I cannot interfere with aspects of fate. An example of a strong precognition I experienced was during my father's illness. I had a growing feeling of doom. Was some world disaster about to occur or was the stress of our family situation getting on top of me? At the start of December 2004, I spoke of this to a friend of mine. She has good psychic instincts. Yes! My friend had the same fear as myself. Then another friend, a Spiritualist Medium told me she had a voice in her ear recently telling her that many people far away would be in peril and she must pray for them. There was an unknown threat, the warning of which was instinctive to some, but what?

After dad passed away I still had the inner voice, telling me there was another upset yet to come. The strange thing was that after the news of the big Tsunami of December 26th the inner 'voice' was replaced with a calm sadness. It may be a fanciful notion because of my grief, but I thought my dad, through his passing had been called to the other dimension to help those drowning. He had seen many drown during his wartime, serving in the Merchant Navy.

Another instance of a pre-warning but one that proved powerless to stop... The date was Sep 10th 2001. My daughter's boyfriend arrived at the house before she returned from work. He told us about a surprise he planned for the following evening. He asked if Dave had any objections to the two becoming engaged. Happy for them both, of course Dave said, 'None whatsoever'. A meal at her favourite restaurant was booked, a bouquet of flowers ordered if we would agree. He asked us to keep it a surprise. Later I got out my Tarot, asking my guide if the next day would be happy for Edwina. The cards I drew were, The Lovers, The Falling Tower and 2 of Cups. Puzzling! We knew Edwina was likely to say yes. The Lovers = choice. The Tower = unexpected upset, a downfall or trauma! What could go wrong? The 2 of Cups suggested the two would be united and celebrate together despite the negative middle card.

The devastation seen by us all the next day, on our television screens when the Twin Towers of New York were falling was so shocking that we were aghast. It was hard to take in! Most people could not believe their own eyes at first. We now see so much false disaster on film and T.V. we might be forgiven if our first thoughts were that these pictures could not be true. Surely they were the product of some movie stunt and the broadcaster would tell us that this was a clip from the latest Hollywood block buster. But NO! it was real. We watched in horror as people jumped or from the buildings. The 'Tower' card had shown me, literally what we saw on television.

When Edwina came home from work she was in tears about the news of the Towers. Her boyfriend had sent a massive bouquet of flowers, delivered first thing that morning. After the news of the Towers, he had phoned to say he did not know if to carry out his planned evening with her. Wiping her tears Edwina said she did not want to go out on a date that evening after all those people had lost their lives. She did not of course know about the planned surprise. 'You should get ready and go, you will be one little positive in this horrid negative heart breaking day' I told her. 'It will not stop you being sad and tearful but you can comfort each other.' I added. The '2 of Cups' had shown the little positive, lovers, raising a glass to each other. Good news that day would not counteract the evil done but were a small statement of joy. A glimmer of goodness that we hope one day will overpower the evil in this world. The Tarot had been true in the answer to my question! How this is possible I cannot say.

The brotherhood / sisterhood of human kind. The Coin or Pentacle being spherical reminds us of the circle of life, the unity we can have and should value. Because I was brought up with teaching of the Christian faith I am reminded of the wisdom spoken by Jesus when he said 'I am the son of God and you are my brothers and sisters'. In other words, we are all of one family. The Human race! In the aftermath of many disasters we hear of people that had tried to warn the authorities. There have been documented cases where messages of warning have averted deaths. There are more premonition warnings that have been ignored, perhaps we humans prefer to acknowledge only what is proven by presently known science. If we want a scientific explanation for everything we do not allow for the magic to come through. Once upon a time, a voice coming from a little box would have been thought of as some kind of trick. Science has not yet found all the answers to what powers the mind can be capable of.

In 2017 after falling, tripping over a toy car I had a medical problem. During the night I was taken dizzy and sickly. Lucky for me there was no permanent damage to my balance. Through tests at the hospital it was discovered that I had a larger than normal pineal gland. For the next two years the specialist advised a test to be done every three months. This was to see if the gland grew bigger. I was told that if it did then I may have a cyst or a cancer. If it remained the same size, then it would indicate I had been born with this 'larger than normal' gland and need not worry. After two years the good news was that my bean size gland was the same at my birth.

The question is, has my larger than normal gland given me some of these unusual psychic experiences, or did it enable me to tune into what some may not 'see'? Many people may have this same peculiarity from birth and does that help their intuition? In researching this matter on the internet, we can find information that suggests the pineal gland is the **third eye**, the seat of the soul. It would be most interesting to know how many people with a larger gland have the 'gift' of intuition, vivid dreams and premonitions. In my opinion all humans have the power to develop more psychic awareness. After all, we all have this gland!

May be this penial gland is our natural radar, and a scientific explanation for some of the so far, unexplained powers of the mind. Having a brain peculiarity, does not however explain how the future can be truly predicted by a pattern of leaves or by the picture on a card. For me, seeing these patterns and then these things coming to be, had proved Gods existence.

Reader... Have you had an event in your life that made you believe in life after death, or experienced psychic flashes of premonition or other unexpected phenomena? Perhaps you had this gift or have developed your power or may want to do so. Read the wisdom of the bible and all philosophy, explore and be open to the magic held within the rocks of the earth and within all ancient objects such as the RUNES and also within yourself. Welcome enlightenment!
EPILOG

An explanation for premonition was given me recently by a 'thinker'. The possibility that premonitions happen because of time slips. This would account for seeing a ghost. We may be looking at some kind of prism in time. At the points on the Earth where there are ley lines, perhaps there could be time warps. If these enable us to see futuristic flying machines we may think these crafts are aliens visiting us now, when in fact they are things yet to be invented. Flown by people from the future. Do we believe there are visitors from another planet? Do we believe in Angels?

Do we believe in little people, Fairies? There are a great many stories of strange beings. Can we dismiss all we are told of the supernatural, or should we keep an open mind? One thing we know about the brain is that much of it is not used in normal daily activities. Could our brain be where thoughts link to our soul, does the brain carry our antenna, our phone line to God?

A question I have often been asked is, do you believe that animals have a soul body. All I can say on this matter is that I do see auras around animals. Twice in my life the spirit of a deceased pet has visited me. I believe all living creatures have some of the 'God energy' within them. Because animals are not living such complicated lives as humans, they can, more easily tune into their instincts from their brain antenna.

The way for us to connect to the psychic part of us, this antenna, is to blank out the 'white noise' and the material world by meditation. As children we meditate naturally, often looking as if in a dream. Animals may also have this ability. As adults, the ability to zone out, to daydream is often lost. We need to recapture this by giving ourselves thinking time. Switching off from phones and electronic devices. Listen to sounds of nature.

If you do not have a time of prayer or meditation before sleep then give yourself a moment to listen to the night and sounds within yourself. If you have the chance to go camping to sleep close to the Earth take time to hear and feel the vibrations of nature as this is as close to God as we may get whilst in our earthly incarnation.

There are those who think the symbol of the Pentagram to be evil. Mainly because of popular Horror films and earlier, because of 'witch hunts' by the medieval Church and Royal authorities. On the Moroccan Tarot the pattern inside the Coin shape looks like a Tudor Rose, giving me an impression of the Rosicrucian movement made popular from that era.

My Egyptian Tarot deck shows various symbols such as the Anc, in the centre of the Pentacle / Coin / Disc. A five pointed star, shown inside the circle on this suit of many Tarot designs, has unfortunately, ignorantly, been associated with people dancing round an open fire naked, smearing themselves with blood. No doubt there are people who do this kind of thing, but most modern 'Witches' are just trying to tune into the power of light. The 'God energy' to bring harmony to the world. Let us cast off these old outdated ideas, and fears of the unknown, and open our minds to all the possibilities that lie within us.

The great spiritual buildings that have been built in the name of various religions over the centuries are a testament to the faith of those that created them. There is no doubt that these temples and churches were designed to the glory of God, as were the writings of these various faiths but though these works of art and philosophy are magnificent creations; they in themselves are not God.

The concept of God is personal to each of us as we are all different from each other. My God, the 'God Energy' I speak about is abstract, omnipotent, interdimensional, both male and female, and can be found within you. From all I have learned in this material life I would say...

Be warmed by laughter and the brightness of each new day. Breath in the fresh 'God energy' from above. Feel goodness of life and love throughout your being. Let it enhance your mind and let it flow from you in words or deeds. Read, think and learn with an open mind. This will enrich your soul.

The human condition is one of duality, this is reflected in all characters and all philosophy, as illustrated in each of the Tarot Major Arcana cards. We choose to be good or bad! For your own soul, be good, be kind, be true. Remember that we are all in this world together, 'no man is an Island'. Give out love as much as you can and it will be returned to you in some magical way. Love and respect your partner, family, friend and workmate. Love the natural world with its animals and greenery. Share good fortune that comes your way. Conquer your prejudices. Fear not what is to become of you or your loved ones after departing this world. The soul is eternal. Be mindful of joyful moments. This is what striving for enlightenment means to me.

26/ Tarot lesson, Suit of Coins / PENTACLES.

The Earth Element Representing zodiac signs... Taurus... Virgo... Capricorn. For interpretation... Matters relating to Calculation, Grounding, Growth, Foods / fruits of the Earth, Ecology, Geography, Geology and Finance. Also our planet Earth.
Song...'Only You'...singer...version...Roy Orbinson.

The circle shape of the Coins / Pentacles in the Tarot is symbolic of the whole, the Globe. Our planet, almost a circular object. The timekeeper of the Zodiac as our concept of time is measured in the year it takes for the Earth to orbit the Sun and the day it takes for the rotation of the Earth. Our Earth with its gravity keeps us all together. The message therefore from the Earth element is to unite, mix with all other elements. Inside Earth is fire. It has water on its surface, air surrounding it and so like a tree the Earth signs can interact with all the other signs, zodiac personalities. That does not always translate to perfect harmony between them and other signs. We know the Earth can erupt and spit fire in volcanic eruption. The Earth as a planet for us to live on, needs air. Thus those born under Air signs are often needed by the Earth signs. The Water signs can quench the parched Earth and so can replenish / refresh the Earth signs. Water does however eat away at the land if things get out of balance. The Earth

element lesson is to live in harmony with all other elements (zodiac personalities) as we are all one part of the whole.

Below is a brief look at the Earth sign personalities.

*Taurus personalities like their animal sign, the Bull can push on without rest when they are working. The Bull pulls the grindstone round! Dependable work ethic but if you goad him, beware! Taurus often take on tasks to alleviate a load for others. Perseverance is their example to others.

*The Virgo is both maid and mother figure of the cosmos. Mother Earth, caring duties for family, openly friendly; Virgo subjects often work in hospitality, child care or nursing. Generous, sometimes naïve in giving, Virgos love to share whatever bounty is at their disposal.

*The Capricorn person, like the goat, likes to climb to the top of a mountain. Like the Earth, his element, our goat looks calm on the surface but can be a torrent of fire beneath. This may translate, to the Capricorn person being passionate but reserved in showing it. The goat is a survivor; he will not take a step without testing the ground first. Sometimes too aware of pitfalls.

Reader... The lesson from the Earth sign Goat, Maid and Bull characters is, to be not afraid of adventure, just test the ground first. Also, live in harmony with all mankind

Dear reader... Live in your own wonderful light and use your gift, your talent for the joy it brings you. And lastly, in the words of someone that always made me laugh...May your God go with you!

Reader... Here are the remaining RUNES that have not been included / explained at the end of previous chapters. The symbols I have presented are those depicted on my own two sets of Nordic RUNES. You will note that other 'seers' may give different interpretation of each symbol and there are variations in the drawings of the symbols just as we all have our own style of handwriting.

This is the RUNE Uruz

Uruz is said to depict the wild Ox and to bring strength My interpretation is the archway to new horizons.

This is the RUNE Othila

Othila is thought to link to partings, separating paths and of acquisiton / inheritance. This Rune makes me think of the symbol of the fish and so of nourishment from the Christian 'fish' a feeding of the spiritual body.

This is the RUNE Mannaz

Mannaz is thought to indicate the self, and of interaction with divinity. Water and flow is mentioned in many traditional interpretations.

This is the RUNE Eihwaz

Eihwaz is thought to represent defence and its symbol is said to be the Yew tree.

This is the RUNE Kano

Kano is thought to represent the torch or flame and thus interprets often as bringer of clarity.

This is the RUNE Wunjo

Wunjo is thought to be the symbol of the fruit branch and bringer of joy, blessings and renewal of energy.

This is the RUNE Fehu

Fehu is thought to be the symbol of possessions. The symbol to me makes me think of arms upstretched towards the heavens... In thanks or to ask for fulfilment.

It is my hope that these last seven RUNE symbols will bring you luck and fulfilment along your path of life. The number seven being linked to intuition and secrets the Rune alphabet being a mystery of the ancient peoples I think it is fitting our Rune lesson is completed with the seven.

For the Earth

God has granted us a choice,
With one accord we must find voice.
If each to each pass message on,
All countries, creeds can act as one.

Take notice all the 'powers that be',
This world, our world, we must set free.
Bring up our children, all to care,
Give out kindness, learn to share.

Each mother's child is born of light,
Let each one learn true path of right.
Banish bloodshed, clear streets from crime.
Please listen to this simple rhyme.
Love is the key to save the Earth,
All people, creatures, plants, have worth.
We cannot let the evils grow,
Seeds of love are ours to sew.

A legacy to our future kin,
Must be a clean Earth with less sin.
From these duties let none stray,
Let light and goodness show the way

Reader… Look out for my next book

'My Soothsayer'
Life guidance towards happy love relationships by the wisdom of the Tarot, Astrology and Runes.

Also, **'A Soothsayers Celtic Heritage'**
A book about dreams, time travel, astral projection and the power of the mind to link into our forefathers, or even our past lives, through meditation.

Find me on: - mysoothsayer.com
Also on Facebook: - facebook.com/mysoothsayer

Comments from some of my 'test' readers…

Lynn says…
Once I started reading Soothsayer, I wanted to carry on reading. You have a nice relaxed way of writing. I can imagine you telling the story. You write as you speak which makes it easy to read and gives your writing a human touch. I'll definitely be buying the book as soon as it is out.

Dorothy says…
After reading the first six chapters of your book, The Soothsayer, I could not wait to read more.

Sylvia says…
I'm loving this story, when can you give me part two?

Muriel says…
Thank you for sending us the voice recording of part one from your book The Soothsayer. We found it most absorbing. I especially loved the memories of the 1950's. Pam loves that each chapter starts with the Tarot, she finds it so interesting.

My recommended books for the would be Soothsayer...

Everybody's Book of Fate and Fortune
by Edward Lyndoe. (1935. Odhams Press Ltd)

Complete Book of the Occult and Fortune Telling.
Compiled by M. C. Poinsot. (Tudor Publishing.)

The Book of RUNES
by Ralph Blum. (10th Anniversary Edition)

A Catechism of Palmestry
by Ida Ellis (second edition...George Redway 1900)

Rune Images
by upklyak on Freepik.com